Pr
The Story About the Story series:

"There is no better path to the heart of a great writer's expression than keen intuition born of deep regard, and no one more likely to have both than a fellow writer. This collection of master reader-writers appraising their admirations is not in the least predictable. Turn the pages: surprise, surprise, surprise!"

—SVEN BIRKERTS, author of *Reading Life: Books for the Ages* and *The Gutenberg Elegies: The Fate of Reading in an Electronic Age*

"The problem with this book: too many irresistible things."

—JAMES SALTER, author of *A Sport and a Pastime*

"All great criticism begins with love. After all, we read books not from obligation but for pleasure, for mental excitement, for what A. E. Housman called the tingle at the back of the neck. In *The Story About the Story* there are no merely literary essays: instead J. C. Hallman has gathered love letters, exuberant appreciations, confessions of envy and admiration. In these pages some of our finest writers stand up and testify to the power of literature to shake and shape our very souls."

—MICHAEL DIRDA, Pulitzer Prize-winning critic and author of *Bound to Please*

"Hallman's collection of reader-focused criticism focuses on the spirited, positive defense (or outright celebration) of authors and works; broad in scope and full of personal, passionate writing, this volume makes a fine reader for contemporary critics and other literati."

—*Publishers Weekly*

"Hallman has given the literary world an insightful book about the concept of 'creative criticism' penned in clever and often humorous prose by a variety of talented authors . . . The essays are truly a joy to read."

—MEREDITH GREENE, *San Francisco Book Review*

"Quite plainly, we were taken aback by how precisely the author had laid out our own aspirations for criticism in this magazine. The piece, in our humble opinion, points toward an educated, unpretentious form of literary critique that serves both literature and the everyday reader. When people want to know what we're looking for in this magazine, we'll point them to Hallman's essay and those he has collected in the book it prefaces."

—The Editors of *The Quarterly Conversation*

"This kind of writing about writing has actually always been around, you just had to know where to look for it. For anyone looking today, it seems silly to do anything other than start here."

—JUSTIN TAYLOR, *The Faster Times*

"*The Story About the Story* is an intelligent celebration of the nexus where good fiction and nonfiction meet."   —*PopMatters*

The Story

About the Story II
Great Writers Explore Great Literature

Edited by J. C. Hallman

Tin House Books
Portland, Oregon & Brooklyn, New York

Tin House Books
2617 NW Thurman St.
Portland, OR 97210.

Published by Tin House Books, Portland, Oregon, Brooklyn, New York

Distributed to the trade by Publishers Group West, 1700 Fourth St., Berkeley, CA 94710, www.pgw.com

First U.S. edition 2013
Cover design by Giuseppe Lipari and Jakob Vala
Interior design by Diane Chonette and Janet Parker
Printed in the USA
www.tinhouse.com

Table of Contents

Introduction

Ecstatically:
How to Write about Reading

by J. C. Hallman

It may be that the experience of teaching writing and literature offers up an even better explanation for the state of books in the world than the teaching of creative writing. By the time someone has taken a creative writing class (and decided to take it at least a little bit seriously) they've sort of already made it over the *hump*, and you don't have to worry about whether that person is ever going to give stories or poems a chance—they already have. The teaching of writing and literature, however—by which I mean entry-level composition courses, entry-level English courses, the kinds of classes often handed off to MFA students—is more like the front lines of the war: you see students fresh out of high school, and when it comes to the state of books in the world, the typical teacher of this kind of course is probably more like a chicken sexer than anything else. Sure, you give them grades at the end of the semester, but probably by day three or four students have lifted their literary leg, as it were, and a good teacher will have mentally separated those who will get it from those who won't and dropped them in the appropriate bucket: won't get it, won't get it, won't get it, *might* get it, won't get it, won't get it, gets it, won't get it, won't get it, and so on.

Of course the problem is that all of these won't-get-its are people who are supposed to be buying books eventually—or at least they would in a better world than ours. It's common these days to scoff at any vision like this: any vision that sees literature as anything other than an activity for a select elite. Much better, apparently, is a kind of horrid variation on the perpetual shock that was accidentally delivered to the not-apocryphal dog that forgot how to learn to escape its punishment. Modern literature is just like that—modern literature *relishes* its learned hopelessness, revels in a kind of group depression in exactly the same way it celebrates the clinical tax so often levied on its practitioners, wears its angst like a studded fetish collar connected by short lead to some mysterious and demanding master. The result is even worse than what's become of opera—at least there are people who can't sing a lick who still go to the opera.

I, for one, don't think writers should just sit around and admire one another's ennui. There *is* something to be done, there *is* a solution. The solution has to do with how we write about literature—the *craft* of criticism.

To back up a bit: What explains the vast over-representation of won't-get-its in the lit sexer's bucket? Can it really be that they're all just fucking morons? Okay, a lot of them *are* fucking morons. But *some* of them aren't. Some of them—let's allow that it's a significant enough number to explain the difference between our world, say, and a Russia whose poets became folk heroes, or a France that made Barthes a bestseller—are *not* fucking morons. So what happened to those people in our world?

High school. High school *happened* to those people. Specifically, high school *English* happened to those people. What happened to those people was the standard five-paragraph essay, a woefully misguided attempt to introduce students to literature via the sippy cup version of the great grail of modern literary criticism, that brand of literary response that borrows its style, form, and methodology from science. In other words, we *introduce* the idea of literature to people—to children—with an inexplicable contradiction: Write about art as though you are delivering the results of a years-long laboratory study about very, very sad dogs. Write about art as though it's a legal brief. This practice is why you might have a cringe reaction to that phrase, "literary criticism," a tiny yet full-body seizure, the kind of sympathetic spasm you might experience on witnessing a loved one have their fingers broken.

Surely it's the advent of science that triggered this, or perhaps it's the smoothing out of the wrinkles in the system of the modern academy. I'm cynical about this—it's all about dollars and tenure. But whatever happened launched a process of accretion, a slow-motion vault from striving toward art to striving toward what exactly I'm not even sure. The result is a whole field of writing with a few central features: a thesis/argument style of saying what one thinks; the elimination of the self—the "I"—in whatever one says; and the demotion of author from authorship to channeler of tangential importance. I'll address each of these only briefly. The thesis/argument approach borrowed from science strikes me as foolish because the scientific method actually demands that one attempt to *disprove* a theory, and when was the last time you heard of a literary critic attempting to disprove his or her own theory? The elimination of the self, the I, might be appropriate if one is articulating a complicated idea that can be measured against an absolute—a legal argument, say, to be measured against written law— but striving after objectivity that is impossible in any case can be only frivolous when it comes to the literary endeavor, which is subjective in every case. And the "death of the author," as it's sometimes put, is not only a tragic misreading of Barthes, it's also a veil that disguises the auto-apotheosis of the critic.

To sum up: What you wind up with is two sides. On the one side you have writers like those collected in *The Story About the Story* and *The Story About the Story II*: writers who think that writing about literature ought to be art itself, ought to have all of the power and sensuousness of a great piece of literature, ought to be a little bit sexy maybe, or at least feel *alive*. And on the other side you've got a bunch of people who actually spend a whole lot *more* time writing about literature than writers do—because of course writers are primarily occupied with the writing of the literature that is to be written about—and *those* people, with various turns of logic that only Orwell or a sophist could admire, have firmly established that A) they *can't* write about the author because he or she is not the text, he or she is "dead"; and B) they can't include anything at all about themselves because they are just as irrelevant as the author. In other words, the two things that are absolutely *core* to the idea of criticism for writers are absolutely *verboten* to literary critics.

Writing about literature comes in a variety of forms—the book review, the literary essay, the scholarly treatment—but these divisions strike me as a kind of literary apartheid, an artificial segregation of forms. In short, there is *no good reason* why there should be *any* writing about reading—be it five-paragraph essays, or dutiful dissertations, or book reviews—that does not strive to be its own art. There is no idea in the study of literature that is so sophisticated or functional that its case would not be made *more* persuasive were it to be delivered through an actively passionate sensibility.

So how do you do this? How, exactly, do you explore a book while projecting a passionate sensibility? Updike's answer came in response to *Pale Fire*: "Nabokov writes prose the only way it should be written, that is, ecstatically." All I'm comfortable saying is this: celebrate the self, emphasize the subjective. The essays in *The Story About the Story* and *The Story About the Story II* each offer their own answers. Variety is the whole *point*. If criticism should aspire to the condition of art, then it should be just that daunting to begin, just that torturous to execute, and just that rewarding to have produced. I don't think a drive toward art or an ability to produce it is limited to a select few, and if we can offer even a sippy cup version of a *real* reading-and-writing process to those who might otherwise find themselves poured into the wrong bucket, then we will have stemmed a leak, opened a new spigot, and left the world with better plumbing.

Criticism

Henry James

If literary criticism may be said to flourish among us at all, it certainly flourishes immensely, for it flows through the periodical press like a river that has burst its dikes. The quantity of it is prodigious, and it is a commodity of which, however the demand may be estimated, the supply will be sure to be in any supposable extremity the last thing to fail us. What strikes the observer above all, in such an affluence, is the unexpected proportion the discourse uttered bears to the objects discoursed of—the paucity of examples, of illustrations and productions, and the deluge of doctrine suspended in the void; the profusion of talk and the contraction of experiment, of what one may call literary conduct. This, indeed, ceases to be an anomaly as soon as we look at the conditions of contemporary journalism. Then we see that these conditions have engendered the practice of "reviewing"—a practice that in general has nothing in common with the art of criticism. Periodical literature is a huge, open mouth which has to be fed—a vessel of immense capacity which has to be filled. It is like a regular train which starts at an advertised hour, but which is free to start only if every seat be occupied. The seats are many, the train is ponderously long, and hence the manufacture of dummies for the seasons when there are not passengers enough. A stuffed manikin is thrust into the empty seat, where it makes a creditable figure till the end of the journey. It looks sufficiently like a passenger, and you know it is not one only when you perceive that it neither says anything nor gets out. The guard attends to it when the train is shunted, blows the cinders from its wooden face and gives a different crook to its elbow, so that it may serve for another run. In this way, in a well-conducted periodical, the blocks of *remplissage* are the dummies of criticism—the recurrent, regulated breakers in the tide of talk. They have a reason for being, and the situation is simpler when we perceive it. It helps to explain the disproportion I just men-tioned, as well, in many a case, as the quality of the particular discourse. It helps us to understand that the "organs of public opinion" must be no less copious than punctual, that publicity must maintain its high stan-dard, that ladies and gentlemen may turn an honest penny by the free expenditure of ink. It gives us a glimpse of the high figure presumably reached by all the honest pennies accumulated in the cause, and throws us quite into a glow over the march of civilization and the way we have organized our conveniences. From this point of view it might indeed go far towards making us enthusiastic about our age. What is more calcu-lated to inspire us with a just complacency than the sight of a new and flourishing industry, a fine economy of production? The great business of reviewing has, in its roaring routine, many of the signs of bloom-ing health, many of the features which beguile one into rendering an involuntary homage to successful enterprise.

Yet it is not to be denied that certain captious persons are to be met who are not carried away by the spectacle, who look at it much askance, who see but dimly whither it tends, and who find no aid to vision even in the great light (about itself, its spirit, and its purposes, among other things) that it might have been expected to diffuse. "Is there any such great light at all?" we may imagine the most restless of the sceptics to inquire, "and isn't the effect rather one of a certain kind of preten-tious and unprofitable gloom?" The vulgarity, the crudity, the stupidity which this cherished combination of the off-hand review and of our wonderful system of publicity have put into circulation on so vast a scale may be represented, in such a mood, as an unprecedented invention for darkening counsel. The bewildered spirit may ask itself, without speedy answer, What is the function in the life of man of such a periodicity of platitude and irrelevance? Such a spirit will wonder how the life of man survives it, and, above all, what is much more important, how literature resists it; whether, indeed, literature does resist it and is not speedily going down beneath it. The signs of this catastrophe will not in the case we suppose be found too subtle to be pointed out——the failure of distinction, the failure of style, the failure of knowledge, the failure of thought. The case is therefore one for recognizing with dismay that we are paying a tremendous price for the diffusion of penmanship and opportunity; that the multiplication of endowments for chatter may be as fatal as an infectious disease; that literature lives essentially, in the sacred depths of its being, upon example, upon perfection wrought; that, like other sensitive organisms, it is highly susceptible of demoralization, and that nothing is better calculated than irresponsible pedagogy to make it close its ears and lips. To be puerile and untutored about it is to deprive it of air and light, and the consequence of its keeping bad company is that it loses all heart. We may, of course, continue to talk about it long after it has bored itself to death, and there is every appearance that this is mainly the way in which our descendants will hear of it. They will, however, acquiesce in its extinction.

This, I am aware, is a dismal conviction, and I do not pretend to state the case gayly. The most I can say is that there are times and places in which it strikes one as less desperate than at others. One of the places is Paris, and one of the times is some comfortable occasion of being there. The custom of rough-and-ready reviewing is, among the French, much less rooted than with us, and the dignity of criticism is, to my perception, in consequence much higher. The art is felt to be one of the most difficult, the most delicate, the most occasional; and the material on which it is exercised is subject to selection, to restriction. That is, whether or no the French are always right as to what they do notice, they strike me as infallible as to what they don't. They publish hundreds of books which are never noticed at all, and yet they are much neater book-makers than we. It is recognized that such volumes have nothing to say to the critical sense, that they do not belong to literature, and that the possession of the critical sense is exactly what makes it impossible to read them and dreary to discuss them——places them, as a part of critical experience, out of the question. The critical sense, in France, *ne se dérange pas*, as the phrase is, for so little. No one would deny, on the other hand, that when it does set itself in motion it goes further than with us. It handles the subject in general with finer finger-tips. The bluntness of ours, as tactile implements addressed to an exquisite process, is still sometimes surprising, even after frequent exhibition. We blunder in and out of the affair as if it were a railway station—the easiest and most public of the arts. It is in reality the most complicated and the most particular. The critical sense is so far from frequent that it is absolutely rare, and the possession of the cluster of qualities that minister to it is one of the highest distinctions. It is a gift inestimably precious and beautiful; therefore, so far from thinking that it passes overmuch from hand to hand, one knows that one has only to stand by the counter an hour to see that business is done with baser coin. We have too many small school-masters; yet not only do I not question in literature the high utility of criticism, but I should be tempted to say that the part it plays may be the supremely beneficent one when it proceeds from deep sources, from the efficient combination of experience and perception. In this light one sees the critic as the real helper of the artist, a torch-bearing outrider, the interpreter, the brother. The more the tune is noted and the direction observed the more we shall enjoy the convenience of a critical literature. When one thinks of the outfit required for free work in this spirit, one is ready to pay almost any homage to the intelligence that has put it on; and when one considers the noble figure completely equipped—armed *cap-à-pie* in curiosity and sympathy—one falls in love with the apparition. It certainly represents the knight who has knelt through his long vigil and who has the piety of his office. For there is something sacrificial in his function, inasmuch as he offers himself as a general touchstone. To lend himself, to project himself and steep himself, to feel and feel till he understands, and to understand so well that he can say, to have perception at the pitch of passion and expression as embracing as the air, to be infinitely curious and incorrigibly patient, and yet plastic and inflammable and determinable, stooping to conquer and serving to direct—these are fine chances for an active mind, chances to add the idea of independent beauty to the conception of success. Just in proportion as he is sentient and restless, just in proportion as he reacts and reciprocates and penetrates, is the critic a valuable instrument; for in literature assuredly criticism *is* the critic, just as art is the artist; it being assuredly the artist who invented art and the critic who invented criticism, and not the other way round.

And it is with the kinds of criticism exactly as it is with the kinds of art—the best kind, the only kind worth speaking of, is the kind that springs from the liveliest experience. There are a hundred labels and tickets, in all this matter, that have been pasted on from the outside and appear to exist for the convenience of passers-by; but the critic who lives *in* the house, ranging through its innumerable chambers, knows nothing about the bills on the front. He only knows that the more impressions he has the more he is able to record, and that the more he is saturated, poor fellow, the more he can give out. His life, at this rate, is heroic, for it is immensely vicarious. He has to understand for others, to answer for them; he is always under arms. He knows that the whole honor of the matter, for him, besides the success in his own eyes, depends upon his being indefatigably supple, and that is a formidable order. Let me not speak, however, as if his work were a conscious grind, for the sense of effort is easily lost in the enthusiasm of curiosity. Any vocation has its hours of intensity that is so closely connected with life. That of the critic, in literature, is connected doubly, for he deals with life at second-hand as well as at first; that is, he deals with the experience of others, which he resolves into his own, and not of those invented and selected others with whom the novelist makes comfortable terms, but with the uncompromising swarm of authors, the clamorous children of history. He has to make them as vivid and as free as the novelist makes *his* puppets, and yet he has, as the phrase is, to take them as they come. We must be easy with him if the picture, even when the aim has really been to penetrate, is sometimes confused, for there are baffling and there are thankless subjects; and we make everything up to him by the peculiar purity of our esteem when the portrait is really, like the happy portraits of the other art, a text preserved by translation.

The Story

About the Story II

Great Writers Explore Great Literature

The First Novel

WENDY LESSER

I am certainly not the only person to have reread *Don Quixote*. It was done, most famously, by the fictional Pierre Menard, the Borges character who immersed himself so deeply, so thoroughly, and so intensively in Cervantes' masterpiece that he was able, at long last, to write a few chapters of it on his own—not from memory, but by having become its author anew. It was also done by the very real William Dean Howells, who wrote in a 1919 issue of *Harper's Magazine*, five months before his death, that "within my eighty-second year I have read *Don Quixote* with as much zest as in my twelfth year." Twelve seems young for a first reading, but Pierre Menard, too, started early: "When I was ten or twelve years old, I read it . . ." So it should not be surprising that I, when I first read *Don Quixote*, was eleven.

Still, it does surprise me. What did I imagine I was doing? Howells's "zest" would indicate that this primordial novel was once viewed as a childishly thrilling adventure book, like *Kidnapped*, say, or *Kim*. Is that what I thought I was getting? More likely I amalgamated it with T. H. White's *The Once and Future King*, that modern retelling of the King Arthur tales, which I read at about the same age. Knights of the Round Table, Knight of the Mournful Countenance—who knew the difference? How was I to know that the Cervantes book was an anti-chivalric epic, a parody of traditional knighthood adventures, when it sounded to my ears so much like them?

But that simplifies both my own response and Cervantes' intentions. He meant the novel to be taken on at least two levels—as the straight-forwardly amusing antics of a hopelessly incompetent knight, and as a wittily self-referential critique of chivalric literature—and I took it on both those levels. What's more, Cervantes' critique was a defense as well: he meant us to laugh at Don Quixote's folly, but also to despise those prim figures who wished to "cure" the Don by burning his books. I understood that. I also understood that Sancho Panza was both sensible and silly, that Don Quixote's sanity was as sad as his madness, and that the relationship between me and these two figures was far more complicated than the usual one that unites readers and fictional characters. When you are just starting out, it is easy to break or ignore the rules, because you often don't know what they are. Cervantes, inventing the novel from scratch, accomplished all sorts of things that later writers were too cautiously professional to try; and I, reading one of my earliest grownup books, was too young and inexperienced to be worried by the violations of form. In that sense, we were ideally matched.

It's hard to picture a seventh-grader lugging around the standard two-volume hardcover edition of Samuel Putnam's 1949 translation, but I'm pretty sure that's the one I read. I must have lugged it one book at a time, as I did this time through, opening and closing and storing and unearthing each five-hundred-page volume until both jackets became ragged with wear. But I doubt that the copy I read then even *had* a dust jacket; in fact, I can almost picture the dark, dull color of the cloth cover and feel its closely woven texture in my hands. I don't know whether the book came from my mother's shelves at home or from the school library. I do know I read some of it during classroom hours, because I can still conjure up the sense of a windowless wall near my right shoulder, student desks stretching in rows before me and to my left, and the big volume propped open in front of me as I came to the end of the last chapter. Was it a free reading period, or was I hiding in the back of the classroom so I could surreptitiously finish the book? No matter; what I remember are the tears that stung my eyes when Sancho Panza stood by his master's bedside and pleaded with him not to die, but to go back out into the fields with him ("Who knows but behind some bush we may come upon the lady Dulcinea, as disenchanted as you could wish"). And I remember how the tears brimmed over when Don Quixote answered, "In last year's nests there are no birds this year. I was mad and now I am sane; I was Don Quixote de la Mancha, and now I am, as I have said, Alonso Quijano the Good." I knew, even at eleven, that something important was being lost here—no, was being bidden farewell to. I was parting from *Don Quixote*, the book, as Alonso Quijano was parting from Don Quixote, his other, crazier, but somehow more engaging and lovable self, and the separation was not an easy one—as I discovered again this time through, when the same tears (though how *can* they be the same?) stung my eyes at forty-eight.

Emotionally, then, the book was all there for me the first time, and it came back to me, emotionally, in the same register. But if I had, as a child, the capacity to respond to *Don Quixote*'s humor and pathos—let us not say fully, since no reading can ever be complete, but at any rate adequately—I lacked something that would have allowed me to take a more accurate measure of its author's achievement. I lacked, at that point, a literary education.

Even a child can see that *Don Quixote* is a book about reading. For one thing, reading—the wrong sort of reading, or too much reading, or possibly just reading in general—is seen as the cause of the knight's affliction. But one new lesson I now draw from Cervantes' novel is that you can never do too much reading if your aim is to appreciate Cervantes' novel. With this rereading, it became apparent to me that *Don Quixote* contains or alludes to many literary works it could not have known about—works that were written between 1615 and now. This did not occur to me when I was eleven for the simple reason that I had not then read any of these other books. Nor did I necessarily think of *Don Quixote* when I read them for the first time. But things which caught my fancy on their own—the asylum theatricals in Middleton and Rowley's *The Changeling* or Peter Weiss's *Marat/Sade*, the meandering journey and mutually reinforced superstitions of the two characters in *Huckleberry Finn*, the eccentric idealism of the central figure in *The Idiot*, the way the second half of *The Executioner's Song* comments on the characters' reactions to the first half—all seem prefigured, now that I have read it again, by Cervantes' great work. Sometimes the influence is a direct one (I know for sure that Dostoyevsky was thinking of Don Quixote when he created Prince Myshkin) and sometimes it is not (I know with equal certainty that Norman Mailer had not read *Don Quixote* when he wrote *The Executioner's Song*). But that distinction matters surprisingly little, since "influence" seems a puny force compared to the one exerted by *Don Quixote*. The novel displays such an astonishing ability to anticipate its own future that one is almost tempted to give Cervantes credit for *everything* written after him.

To read *Don Quixote* as an adult is to have the rereading experience in its most potent, seminal form. I imagine that this is true even if you did not read the book as a child, because, by the time you are a grownup, you will be familiar with all the main characters and many of their adventures. Don Quixote, Sancho Panza, Dulcinea del Toboso, Rocinante, Saragossa, the Cave of Montesinos, windmills, blanket-tossings, a flying wooden horse . . . are these specific memories from my first reading, or snippets of the general culture, handed down to all of us through visual art, drama, music, and other works of literature? Like any direct encounter with an originary myth, going back to the book itself induces chills of uncanniness. When the aspiring knight-errant announces that he will henceforth be Don Quixote, his beloved will be known as Dulcinea, and his horse will be called Rocinante—when he comes up with the names in front of your very eyes—you feel almost as if you are present at Adam's naming of the animals. It is hard to believe there was ever a world that did not contain these figures, and it is equally hard to believe they are the inventions of a single writer, a mere mortal. Miguel de Cervantes may have created Don Quixote and Sancho Panza, but they got away from him immediately. And everything about *Don Quixote*—from the way the story comes to us through layers of narrators to the way Volume Two is essentially a commentary on, a rereading of, Volume One—suggests that Cervantes *knew* his characters would escape him in this way.

It is this knowingness, combined with an unusually warm, informal kind of intimacy, that makes the book so remarkable. I have heard *Don Quixote* called both premodern and postmodern, but neither label feels right. Premodernism implies a distance from us, a lack of sophistication, a quaint kind of ignorance, whereas Cervantes is *right there*, whispering in our ear, seemingly cognizant of everything that has happened to his book from the time it left his hands four hundred years ago until it came to rest in ours. And postmodernism always entails a certain level of strain—an embarrassed self-consciousness, an effort to blatantly entertain or just as blatantly alienate, a nostalgic longing for the real even as the patently fake is seen as the only acceptable result of an artistic undertaking. Nothing could be further from the delicate tone of *Don Quixote.*

I cannot begin to do justice to the complicated strategies whereby Cervantes surveys the relationship between the real and the imaginary, truth and pretense, history and fiction, or whatever you want to call these "opposing" categories which he wisely refuses to set in opposition to each other. His novel does not suggest that there is no real difference, finally, between truth and fiction; that would be the pusillanimous way out, and Cervantes has no desire to take it. On the contrary, the whole point of the deluded knight's crazy adventures hinges on the difference. But making the distinctions is never simple. Who does more harm to Sancho Panza: the fake knight who promises him a real island to govern if he comes along as knight's squire, or the real duke and duchess who temporarily give him a fake island to govern, mainly for their own amusement? Is it crazier to sing the virtues of a lady love one can never obtain, as the troubadour poets traditionally do, or to sigh for a beloved made up wholesale, as Don Quixote does with Dulcinea? Which is the greater lie: to dress up as a knight because one deludedly believes in the reality of chivalry, or to dress up as a knight because, as a neighborly gesture, one wants to fool Don Quixote into quietly returning to his home? Is a dream a lie? (This is the thrust of the Cave of Montesinos incident, to which both Sancho and the Don frequently recur.) Does a false statement given in response to other people's manipulations or deceptions carry the same moral weight as an outright lie? (Sancho Panza often finds himself in this situation.) What is the difference between a lie and a work of fiction? Do fictional works have real effects in the world? If not, why should we care about them? And if so, how dangerous are they, and what are the costs of attempting to censor them?

One of the lovely things about the Putnam edition is that it includes all the front matter which, in the Spain of Philip III, had to be attached to any published book: the certificates of price and errata, the licenses and "approbations" of various clerical and secular censors, and finally the royal privilege to publish, issued by the king himself. In the case of *Don Quixote*, these sound so much like narrative artifacts—like the layers of storytelling at the front of a Conrad novel, for instance, or like Cervantes' own invention of the Moorish narrator Cid Hamete Benengeli—that they make "Miguel de Cervantes Saavedra" seem like one of his own fictional characters, even as they testify to the historical conditions under which he was allowed to make a living as a writer. And because all the testimonials are unremittingly high-minded, attributing only the purest and most conventional motives to Cervantes' work, we begin to wonder just who is fooling whom.

Take the "approbation" by Maestro Joseph de Valdivielso, which appears at the beginning of Volume Two and praises Cervantes for "mingling jest with earnest, the pleasing with the profitable, and the moral with the facetious, dissimulating under the bait of wit the hook of reprehension. All this in pursuance of his professed aim, which is that of driving out the books of chivalry, from whose contagious and baleful influence he has done much to cleanse these realms through the employment of his fine and cunning wit." Is he *serious*? The minute you ask yourself this, you begin to focus on words like "dissimulating" and "cunning." Nothing, of course, did less toward "driving out the books of chivalry" than the publication of Volume One of *Don Quixote*; if we are to believe Volume Two, the first book ignited a new rage for chivalric reading in fashionable and unfashionable circles alike. But then, the maestro seems to realize that this is only Cervantes' "professed" aim, not his real one. Or does he? The censor's position is as indeterminate as the author's own, or as that of the village curate from La Mancha, who says of certain poetic works that he finds while sorting through Don Quixote's library: "These do not deserve to be burned like the others, for they are not harmful like the books of chivalry; they are works of imagination, such as may be read without detriment."

Among the many reasons *Don Quixote* has not dated is the fact that we are still having this discussion. Having written a book about murders and executions, argued fiercely for years about the inviolability of the First Amendment, and raised a teenage son who is allowed to sample pretty much whatever he wants on the cultural front, I am more than ever aware of how common the curate's concerns are. The questions are all the same as they were in Cervantes' time: Does the representation of violence in art beget violence in real life? Even if that connection can be demonstrated, is censorship the right response? How is the censor to distinguish between "harmful" works and commendable "works of imagination" which are no less violent—like certain passages from the Bible, Greek drama, Shakespeare's plays, or, for that matter, *Don Quixote*?

"Well," Maestro de Valdivielso might say, "but the violence in *Don Quixote* is slapstick violence, comic violence." I'm not sure what he gains if I grant this. It's true that *Don Quixote* is often funny in exactly the way a Marx Brothers movie is funny. The battle between Don Quixote and the Knight of the Mirrors (who says he has read Volume One of *The Ingenious Gentleman, Don Quixote de la Mancha,* and therefore wishes to prove himself a superior knight by vanquishing that novel's hero) plays out very much like the mirror pantomime between Groucho and Harpo in *Duck Soup.* And many of the conversations between Sancho and the Don—particularly those about mispronounced words, the relation of language to meaning, and the proper use of proverbs and sayings—could have been scripted as dialogue for Chico and Groucho. But there is a darker strain in Cervantes' slapstick as well, more like the melancholy comedy of Buster Keaton or Charlie Chaplin. There are permanent losses entailed in the pursuit of chivalric ideals—not just the four or five teeth that Don Quixote loses ("and a tooth is more to be prized than a diamond") but also the injuries he inflicts on others. "I do not know what you mean by righting wrongs, seeing that you found me quite all right and left me very wrong indeed, with a broken leg which will not be right again as long as I live," says one of his victims. And there are deaths, as well, produced by a too vigorous pursuit of the knightly code—notably in the tale of the unfortunate Claudia, who stabs her faithless fiancé through the heart, only to learn too late that he was faithful after all.

As Volume Two draws toward its close, the tone of the work becomes noticeably darker. The story of Claudia is bracketed by two incidents that, while they occupy the background, nonetheless color the whole atmosphere. In the first, Sancho Panza is standing in the woods when he feels something brushing his shoulder; he turns to look, and finds that he is surrounded by hanged men—legally strung-up criminals—whose bodies have been left dangling from the trees. And then later, when the knight and his squire reach Barcelona, they are invited to witness the operation of a ship's galleys: like "magic," the ship moves as the result of the rowers' backs being flayed. "What have these poor wretches done that they should be whipped like that," wonders Sancho, "and how comes it that this one man who goes along whistling there dares to punish so many of them? I declare, this is Hell or at the very least purgatory." Both violent incidents, the hanging and the flaying, are completely unconnected to Don Quixote's delusions. They cannot be blamed on books of chivalry. On the contrary, they are routine, accepted aspects of daily life. Still, Cervantes is able to feel and convey their shockingness.

These are not just my modern prejudices being aired here. It would be presumptuous to assume that this was the case, to believe that our ethical sensibilities had somehow advanced since 1615—as if moral insight were like medical practice, superseding all the old techniques. Morally speaking, Don Quixote lived in the age of iron, and so do we; there never has been a golden age of good behavior and probably never will be, which is why we dream about it through books like *Don Quixote*. ("'Sancho, my friend,' he said, 'you may know that I was born, by Heaven's will, in this our age of iron, to revive what is known as the Golden Age.'") When modern artists re-create Cervantes' myth, it is often for the purpose of commenting on this recurrent fact of our fallen nature—as J. M. Coetzee does, for instance, in his novel *Age of Iron*, where the role of the deluded knight is taken by a dying South African white woman, her squire is a homeless black man, and her ancient car, "like Rocinante," can barely climb a hill. As this old woman rails and rages against the effects of apartheid, she becomes more and more cut off from everything that had previously been her life. Is she the one who is crazy, or does the fault lie with her world? The answer to such questions, in the most truthful works of fiction, is never as simple as R. D. Laing would have liked it to be.

That sort of thought would never have struck me in 1963, when I was eleven. It's not just that I hadn't read R. D. Laing then. (Hardly anybody had; his heyday was a few years later.) More to the point, I hadn't given much thought, one way or the other, to the idea of crazy people. I never saw any, and the ones I heard about were all locked away in huge state asylums or otherwise kept out of sight.

Now, of course, everything is different. I suppose the changes can be traced back to the 1960s and 1970s, when it was decided that warehousing was not helpful to the insane, and large numbers of mental patients were released from the asylums. This was initially a good thing, in that the patients were supposed to go instead to halfway houses or other smaller, more familial places. But at about the same time the plug was pulled on public money for mental health care, so all the halfway houses got shut down too, and there was nowhere for the released patients to go. They ended up on the streets, and now, a generation later, those who have survived are still there.

If I saw a raggedly dressed, dirty-faced, nonsense-jabbering lunatic even once during my entire Palo Alto childhood, I have managed to obliterate the memory. My son sees such people every week of his life. Granted, we live in the city nicknamed Berserkeley, on a street favored by the meandering homeless. Still, my son's experience is not a rare one for a modern urban child. He knows all the local knights-errant by sight, and he can set his watch by the one who passes our house every afternoon pulling his two garbage-filled shopping carts.

I am not suggesting that all these ragged fellows are Don Quixote in modern dress. But the analogy does give one pause. And, on the whole, I would say that my daily experiences with Berkeley crazy people give me some sense of what might be going through the minds of the characters who encounter Don Quixote. Their two most common responses—anger and fascination—are both familiar to me.

To the extent that we, as readers, find Don Quixote's madness amusing or even interesting, we are sharing the sensibility of the people in the novel who, like the otherwise kindly and civilized duke and duchess, entertain themselves at his expense. If the second volume of *Don Quixote* is more enjoyable and entertaining than the first, it is also chillier in this respect: we, personally, are being gotten at, and the satire is cutting closer to the bone. The people who encounter the crazy knight in Volume One are simply annoyed at his craziness and its effects on them (his failure to pay for his lodgings, his destruction of other people's property, the physical injuries he inflicts, and so on). In their annoyance they are often brutal. Hence the frequency of beatings in Volume One, to the point where the plot becomes repetitive and the outcome of every encounter is one more lost tooth or bruised limb or facial cut for either Don Quixote or Sancho Panza.

In Volume Two, the response is much more sophisticated. The people, especially the aristocratic people, who meet Don Quixote in the second book have all, like us, read the first. They have been vastly entertained by the reports of his eccentric behavior, and they are happy to invite him into their homes so they can see more of it. Volume Two is much more comfortable for the knight and his squire; they sleep in soft beds, eat well, and get treated as visiting dignitaries. There is far less brutality than in Volume One, but in its stead is a kind of smiling cruelty that bears some relation to sympathetic understanding. (I'm thinking here of the distinction Bernard Williams draws when he says that "cruelty needs to share the sensibility of the sympathetic, while brutality needs not to.") Much of Volume Two is like an amateur play, a party charade, a series of scenes set up by the participants in order to fool the only two actors who are not in on the joke. Only Don Quixote and Sancho Panza think it is all real: the punishments, the trials, the rewards, the flattery. *We* know ("we" including the other players in the novel as well as the readers of the novel) that it is all a setup.

Over and over Cervantes tells us how much "enjoyment" or "amusement" or "pleasure" these high-born hosts derive from the antics of the foolish knight—antics which they themselves set in motion with their clever schemes, their accurate predictions of his responses. Apparently the desire to be amused by crazy eccentrics is widespread, infecting not just the aforementioned ducal pair but also one Don Antonio and his wife, "a beautiful lady of high station and endowed with wit and gaiety" who "had invited some of her women friends to come and show honor to her house guest and enjoy his unheard-of variety of madness." And it is widespread not only in the novel but in the culture at large. This is the period, after all, during which performances by institutionalized lunatics or village simpletons were deemed acceptable entertainment for aristocratic gatherings, or so one is led to believe by plays like *The Changeling* and *A Midsummer Night's Dream*.

But the fact that the practice existed in life does not make its inclusion in art merely conventional or morally invisible. The use of the performing madmen in *The Changeling* is meant to make us queasy, and so is the friendly, jolly exploitation of the knight and his squire in Volume Two of *Don Quixote*. To make sure we get the point, Cervantes inserts a crucial comment by his Moorish narrator: "Here, Cid Hamete remarks, it is his personal opinion that the jesters were as crazy as their victims, and that the duke and duchess were not two fingers' breadth removed from being fools when they went to so much trouble to make sport of the foolish." So we have had our wrists slapped after all. But the process doesn't stop there; Cervantes never lets you rest on your moment of moral self-awareness. It's not enough to say "How cruel of them to laugh at the insane," or even "How cruel of *me* to laugh at the insane." For at the very point when he expresses, with obvious approval, Cid Hamete's position, Cervantes also wants to move you along to a questioning of that position. Yes, the duke and the duchess are fools . . . but is being foolish the worst thing in the world? Can we live and enjoy our lives *without* ever being foolish? And isn't a great deal lost to us (including the appreciation of novels like this one) if we try to stamp out such foolishness?

Twenty-five pages before Cid Hamete's aside, we get a different perspective in a remark made by Don Antonio, the knight's other benevolent exploiter. Don Quixote, who has been staying with Don Antonio, has just lost a battle to the "Knight of the White Moon"—actually his La Manchan neighbor, the bachelor Sansón Carrasco, disguised in full chivalric regalia. It is all part of a humanitarian ploy to get the deluded Don to return home, which is the penalty that the victorious knight has exacted from the vanquished one. But Don Antonio was not in on *this* charade, and he is dismayed when he learns about it: "'My dear sir,' exclaimed Don Antonio, 'may God forgive you for the wrong you have done the world by seeking to deprive it of its most charming madman! Do you not see that the benefit accomplished by restoring Don Quixote to his senses can never equal the pleasure which others derive from his vagaries?'" This is selfishness incarnate. It's also pretty much the way we feel about the matter, or at least the way *I* feel. Perhaps for different reasons, but with much the same warmth as Antonio's, I find myself always in opposition to the "cure" camp. Whenever the curate, the barber, the housekeeper, the niece, and Sansón Carrasco come onstage, I know we are destined to hear more trite homilies about the evils of chivalric books. Like Don Antonio, I tend to be in favor of leaving Don Quixote as he is, and I'm pretty sure Cervantes encourages me to feel that way. Or rather, he encourages me at the same time as he points out the moral risks I'm taking: nothing is ever absolutely settled in *Don Quixote*, one way or the other, and even the novel's own pleasure is not unmitigatedly approved of.

But pleasure there is, in enormous doses. One of the terrific things about this book is that you can still feel, down the distance of four centuries, Cervantes' delight in this new toy he's discovered, the novelistic form. It can create characters out of nothingness and bring them to life! It can skip around geographically in the twinkling of an eye, without any pause for scene changes! It can report on private matters that took place between its characters when no one else was present! The illiterate Sancho Panza, when he learns at the beginning of Volume Two about the existence of Volume One, instantly realizes how amazing this literary form is: "He told me the story of your Grace has already been put in a book called *The Ingenious Gentleman, Don Quixote de la Mancha*. And he says they mention me in it, under my own name, Sancho Panza, and the lady Dulcinea del Toboso as well, along with things that happened to us when we were alone together. I had to cross myself, for I could not help wondering how the one who wrote all those things down could have come to know about them." Don Quixote's reaction is somewhat different. Since he has believed all along that his knightly quest is being thwarted by evil enchanters, he has no trouble incorporating this new form of magic, novel writing, into his worldview: "'I can assure you, Sancho,' said Don Quixote, 'that the author of our history must be some wise enchanter; for nothing they choose to write about is hidden from those who practice the art.'"

For us, the enchantments of the novel have become so routine as to be practically unnoticeable. As the psychoanalyst Adam Phillips said when reviewing a recent novel, "It is, after all, an effect of style to make this living in someone else's mind seem so natural, given that it is something we never, in actuality, do." *Don Quixote*'s style is the opposite sort: the novel spends little if any time inside its characters' minds, and it frequently reminds us what a very *un*natural thing we are doing when we get to know fictional characters. Distinctions that seemed clear to Cervantes have become murkier for us, and, in part because he did a lot to muddy those waters himself, it's very difficult for us to recover his freshness of perspective. As Borges (speaking through Pierre Menard) observes, "To compose the *Quixote* at the beginning of the seventeenth century was a reasonable undertaking, necessary and perhaps even unavoidable; at the beginning of the twentieth, it is almost impossible. It is not in vain that three hundred years have gone by, filled with exceedingly complex events. Among them, to mention only one, is the *Quixote* itself."

At the age of eleven, I was oblivious to much of what was innovative and unusual about *Don Quixote*. For all I knew, that was how they wrote books in those days ("those days" encompassing, in my mind, both the medieval period of chivalric literature and Cervantes' much later time—they had been collapsed, for me, into an undifferentiated past). I had read few if any nineteenth-century novels, so I had no firm expectations about novelistic form or plot construction or character revelation. I knew *Don Quixote* was a long book, and it felt like one, but what I didn't realize is that it felt even longer because of its nearly plotless, one-thing-after-another structure. Cervantes may have discovered the novel, but he had yet to discover suspense (though we begin to see the first glimmerings of it, in the form of more sustained plot development, in Volume Two). His newly minted form, if it borrowed anything from theater, took more from the vaudeville-like routines of *commedia* than from the Golden Age drama of his Spanish near-contemporaries. The desire to be entertained from one moment to the next, rather than the desire to reach an endpoint, is the readerly appetite he feeds. Not that he always feeds it with equal success: *Don Quixote* has its *longueurs*, especially in the first volume. When I was young, I skipped most of the poems that are sprinkled throughout the text; this time, after a brief struggle with my responsible-critic conscience, I did the same. The first time I read the book, it took so long to get through the initial volume that I had forgotten most of the minor characters and incidents by the time I reached its end, and the same was true this time.

Yet even here Cervantes anticipates me. If I was occasionally bored, it was apparently as nothing next to the feelings of Cid Hamete Benengeli, who (Cervantes tells us) had "a kind of grudge . . . against himself for having undertaken a story so dry and limited in scope as this one of Don Quixote." In the first volume the narrator attempted to rectify this problem by introducing a few irrelevant but diverting travelers' tales, but later he decided this had been a mistake, since "many readers, carried away by the interest attaching to the knight's exploits, would be inclined to pass over these novelettes hastily or with boredom, thereby failing to note the fine craftsmanship they exhibited." The self-criticism veiled as self-praise is incomparable, but what makes it quintessential Cervantes is the way it takes into account *our* feelings as well as the puppet author's.

If Cervantes rarely peeks into his characters' skulls, he frequently peers into ours, and the effect, especially in the second volume, is thrillingly intimate. Before we can have a fully formulated thought about his book, he has it for us, but he does it in such a witty, engaging, flattering way that we almost feel we have anticipated *ourselves*. Above all, Cervantes makes us aware that we are reading a printed object, and then he makes that awareness part of the book's plot. This produces an eerie sensation, in that the smaller universe, that of the novel, seems to have swallowed whole the larger universe in which we dwell.

When Sancho Panza first learns from Sansón Carrasco, for instance, about the existence of the printed and disseminated Volume One, they have a detailed conversation about the logical errors embedded in the text. This is a bit as if Dickens, Jane Austen, and Arthur Conan Doyle were to come back to life and begin debating with John Sutherland about his numerous challenges to their authorial consistency. But even more surprising is the way the discussion concludes. Sansón, after hearing Sancho's lengthy but finally unsatisfying explanation for the disappearance and reappearance of his stolen donkey, refuses to be placated.

"That is not where the error lies," replied Sansón, "but rather in the fact that before the ass turns up again the author has Sancho riding on it."

"I don't know what answer to give you," said Sancho, "except that the one who wrote the story must have made a mistake, or else it must be due to carelessness on the part of the printer."

And thus do the errors, whether authorial or typographical, get made a part of the permanent record. *Don Quixote* is so capacious that it can swallow even its own mistakes.

The effect of such strategies is to bring us to "the point of vertigo," as Borges says in his intriguing little essay "Partial Magic in the *Quixote*." That vertiginous feeling will come up again: it is, I am convinced, the representative sensation of rereading at its most powerful, the feeling we get when two worlds (the child's and the adult's, the fantastic and the mundane, the life lived through books and the rest of life) are superimposed on each other. But here I want to focus on what Borges makes of that discovery. I believe it is one of the few places where he goes wrong—he who otherwise understood *Don Quixote* so well that rereading "Pierre Menard, Author of the *Quixote*" has almost become a necessary adjunct to rereading Cervantes' novel (so that Menard has, in a way, been granted his wish).

At the end of "Partial Magic," Borges asks:

> Why does it disturb us that Don Quixote be a reader of the *Quixote* and Hamlet a spectator of *Hamlet*? I believe I have found the reason: these inversions suggest that if the characters of a fictional work can be readers or spectators, we, its readers and spectators, can be fictitious. In 1833, Carlyle observed that the history of the universe is an infinite sacred book that all men write and read and try to understand, and in which they are also written.

This is a grand theory, but it strikes me as false—logically false, in its if-then assumption, and also false to the feeling that *Don Quixote* produces. For me, the novel's effect is one of enlargement, not reduction. My own sense of vertigo stems from the fact that the characters have stepped outside their realm into mine, and not the other way around. Through some inscrutable mechanism, they have become more real without my having to become less so. In any case, it's hard for me to understand how I would go about considering myself fictitious—but then, I have neither the desire nor the ability to see myself as a character in the mind of God. I don't think Cervantes asks us to adopt the God-as-author model, or even the God-as-history-as-author model. What he does instead is to suggest that the reality we share with Don Quixote—this ongoing reality of ours, this limited life, which can nonetheless contain at least one novel so much larger than itself—is more than enough of a wonder.

I could not love *Don Quixote* more than I did at eleven, but I can admire it more now. As a child I took its virtues for granted. Now I am amazed by the extent to which it anticipates so much, not only about its own fate as a book, but about novels and novel writing in general. In a much more informed and visceral way than when I was eleven, I comprehend how much time separates me from Cervantes, and that makes me all the more impressed by how cunningly he has closed the gap. His voice speaks directly to us, whatever our moment in history: to William Dean Howells in 1849 and 1919, to Jorge Luis Borges (or Pierre Menard) from 1909 onward, to me in 1963 and again in 2000. For this reason, perhaps, the process of rereading *Don Quixote* feels less like a transformation than is the case with other books; the difference between the initial youthful reader and the eventual older one seems comparatively small. And that is a relief, in a way. It works to counter the sense of romantic retrospection, of elegiac time-travel, that otherwise colors a book about rereading. After all, how seriously can one take the passage of a mere thirty-seven years, when Cervantes leaps over four hundred as if they were nothing?

Worldliness and Regret: *The Charterhouse of Parma*

PHILLIP LOPATE

Stendhal first came into my life through the impassioned offices of Dr. Floyd Zuli. Improbable as it may sound to a younger generation, this professor with dark-rimmed glasses, a crew-cut, and a zeal for world literature had mesmerized our household and thousands like it into getting up at 6:30 AM and turning on the television set to catch his lectures on the novel, in a program called *Sunrise Semester*. Many took the TV course for college credit, but my folks did it for enlightenment. When I think about my parents, lowly textile clerks with no more than high school diplomas, setting the alarm early to hear a lecture on Balzac or Dickens and trying to keep up with the reading, I could weep. Weep, too, for the quaint assumption that the cream of culture should be offered to everyone, and that the people were hungry for it.

In any case, Floyd Zuli (what a name! suggestive of a Hungarian charlatan) kicked off his course with an interesting choice, Stendhal's *The Red and the Black*. We had never heard of this classic; its writer was not a "given," like Dostoyevsky or Kafka, in our Brooklyn working-class autodidact ghetto. I was immediately drawn to the mystical sound of STENDHAL, an author with one name, like a magician (or a charlatan, likewise). Of course Zuli made it clear that his real moniker was the more prosaic Henri Beyle, but Beyle's invention of a new identity for himself appealed to me. I, slogging through the indignities of high school, had some self-invention in mind as well.

At college, we read a few chapters of *Le Rouge et le Noir* in French for our language requirement class; while it seemed witty and absorbing, I decided to defer the pleasure of reading the whole novel on my own as long as possible, maybe keeping it for a kind of dessert. Also, by this time I had picked up the snobbish prejudice that the very popularity of *The Red and the Black* made it a little common, whereas *The Charterhouse of Parma* seemed to exude the aroma of a delicacy, literary caviar. So I took up my education in Stendhal with his last great novel. It was assigned for our senior colloquium seminar, come to think of it; I had no choice in the matter.

Colloquium was a semi-big deal at Columbia; you had to get in, and supposedly only the most brilliant students, with the highest grades and best academic minds, made the cut. In practice this meant that I was thrown in with a bunch of dull, overachieving pre-medical students seeking to become well-rounded, and only a few of my Humanities soul-mates. To this disappointment was added my unspoken shame, because most of the seniors were entering their second year in the seminar, while I had been rejected the year previous for junior colloquium. I didn't help my cause in that first interview by dismissing the playwright Jean Giraudoux as a lightweight, only to discover later while idly going through the Butler Library card catalogue that one of the professors interviewing me had done his doctoral dissertation on Giraudoux! In those days I was perennially provoking Columbia's (to my insecure eyes) genteel faculty with my working-class defensiveness, sometimes intentionally, sometimes not. An intentional provocation, surely, occurred in the first semester of senior colloquium, when instead of writing an analysis of *Rameau's Nephew*, I did a cheeky dialogue in imitation of Diderot about the colloquium itself, satirizing everyone in class, including the two professors, F. W. Dupee, a lion in the English Department, and Richard Kuhns, a younger, tweedier man from Philosophy, who co-taught the class. They were not amused, and demanded a substitute paper, which I never handed in. Dupee forgave me: he was a dear man, sympathetic to revolt, and a fine critic with a subtle prose style; how I could have twitted him so maliciously I'll never know. My next paper would be on *The Charterhouse of Parma*, and this time I resolved to play by the rules.

The Charterhouse of Parma has been characterized as "a miracle of gusto, brio, élan, verve, panache" by its most recent translator, Richard Howard—all of which is true, but it remains a rarefied pleasure. I took to the book immediately and avidly. Why this rather recherché novel should have so delighted me at twenty requires some background. I'd already been in thrall to a group of writers who specialized in paradox and anal-ysis—Nietzsche, who loved Stendhal, saying, "The man was a human question-mark. . . . Objection, evasion, joyous distrust, and love of irony are signs of health, everything absolute belongs to pathology"; Gide, who declared *The Charterhouse of Parma* his favorite French novel; and Dostoyevsky, my mentor, with his penchant for acerbic insight—and they had prepared me for Stendhal, who fit right into this lineage. I also loved the tradition of the comic novel: Fielding's tongue-in-cheek addresses to the reader in *Tom Jones*, Sterne's digressions within digressions in *Tristram Shandy*, Diderot's sabotage of normal plot flow in *Jacques the Fatalist*, Svevo's rationalizing narrator in *Confessions of Zeno*, Machado de Assis's sardonic, pithy style in *Epitaph of a Small Winner*. What tick-led me most, I think, was voice—the sound of outrageous candor cutting to the point, combined with a touch of irony insinuating that it could never be that simple.

In Stendhal, I found the exemplar of a spasmodic, abrupt voice whose very impatience signaled vitality. Where another writer might take paragraphs to prepare an insight, Stendhal would polish the busi-ness off with a terse epigram, such as: "Courtiers, who have nothing to examine in their souls, notice everything." His mind was so generously well-stocked he could afford to throw away one-liners. His paragraphs lacked topic sentences: rather, they were all topic sentence, one atop another. He dispensed with transition sentences whenever it suited him—a prose predecessor of the jump-cut I so loved in French New Wave directors like Godard and Truffaut. "Let us skip ten years of hap-piness . . ." was a typical brazen shortcut by Stendhal. To leave out the plodding intermediate steps, you need to possess sophistication about the deep structures of narrative, supreme confidence in your own expe-rience of life, and an almost unimaginable faith in the intelligence of your readers. Stendhal wrote with freedom unconstrained by popular criticism; he wrote, he said, for "the happy few" (the oft-quoted final words of *Charterhouse*) and for an audience a hundred years hence who would truly appreciate him. I was that audience, I liked to think.

I was especially smitten with the early battle scenes, wherein Fabrizio, our Italian hero, voluntarily enlists in the French army. Barely seventeen years old at this point in the story, he runs away from home with a head full of romantic notions and an allegiance to his idol Napoleon. It soon becomes clear that he has no idea what either war or life is about. As he darts from one place to another, following dubious escorts, dodging bullets, getting his horse stolen from him, trying to discover whether he has actually participated in a battle, and encountering all the cowardly behavior of an army in hasty retreat (this is Waterloo, remember), Stendhal observes with comic detachment that Fabrizio did not grasp in the least what was happening. Ah, to understand what is happening to you—the pattern underneath ephemeral events!

If I had to summarize in one word what I cherished about *The Charterhouse of Parma*, that word would be "worldliness." At twenty I had a romance, almost a mystique about worldliness. Not for me the adolescent pulings of *A Catcher in the Rye*: if the price of entering adulthood was the forfeiture of innocence and whatever residues of childhood wonderment I still possessed, I could not pay that price quickly enough. Disenchantment was my goal. So when *Charterhouse*'s Count Mosca, that worldly diplomat, advises his adored, Gina, the Duchess of Sanseverina, to marry an elderly man who can give her wealth in return for her title, we may be bothered that this nobleman appears to be pimping his heart's desire, but we appreciate his overall grasp of circumstances. In the same pragmatic manner, Mosca advises his handsome young rival Fabrizio, whom he rather likes, to enter the priesthood with an eye to becoming bishop: a strange choice for a libidinous young man, we might think, one requiring years of patient execution, but which makes sense in the context of nineteenth-century ambition (either the red of military life or the black of the clergy). He also advises Fabrizio to take a mistress from a conservative family, and to read in public cafes only the stupidest Ultra newspapers. We are none of us romantic heroes living in isolation; we are social animals, being watched by our potential friends and enemies. Mosca is a realist: what bothers him is not that he has been cuckolded by his wife, but that she has embarrassed him by sleeping with a political enemy.

To be worldly is to accept the consequences of knowing that men and women are not angels, that they have appetites they will seek to satisfy as well as justify, and that vice and self-destructiveness play their inevitable parts. Choderlos de Laclos, the author of *Les Liaisons Dangereuses*, another favorite worldly novel of mine at the time (and still), certainly went further in depicting depravity as the common rule: the strategies of seduction that Valmont and the Marquise de Merteuil suggest to each other in that novel turn sex into a chess game to ward off boredom. Stendhal was more interested in demonstrating the political machinations of court life, the techniques of winning by appealing to the courted party's vanity or petty spite. But in both cases it was reason aligned with recognition of appetite that intrigued me. I found the same combination in the Marquis de Sade, whom I also gobbled up at twenty. Youth, largely powerless, is often fascinated with satanic forces, and I now see what a cliché I was. But the Gothic never appealed to me, because as much as I sought evidence of evil, I was listening for, indeed craving, the sound of reasoned analysis, of calm French logic, even when it took a grotesquely hypertrophied form, as in de Sade.

The Charterhouse of Parma and *Les Liaisons Dangereuses* were both books that swept through my family, much discussed by me, my brother Lenny, and my sister Betty Ann (the youngest, Joan, was still playing with dolls). Betty Ann, who was a year younger than I, dark, attractive, and moody, was particularly drawn to portraits of strong-minded, independent, active women; she modeled herself in adolescence on Duchess Sanseverina, Mme. de Merteuil, and Billie Holiday. For Lenny and me, the Duchess, Gina, was a sort of fantasy ideal, an older, worldly woman of passion, beauty and intelligence by whom we dreamed of being taken in hand. I found myself identifying (as did, I think, Stendhal himself) with Count Mosca, a man of icy intelligence and affectionate warmth, whose impressive overview of life is not enough to win him first place in the heart of his beloved Gina. She remains much more taken with her nephew Fabrizio, that gilded youth and heedless naïf.

Wherever he goes, women fall all over themselves to please him. ("'Speak more respectfully,' said the Countess, smiling through tears, 'of the sex which will make your fortune, for you will always displease the men—you have too much spirit for prosaic souls.'") Yet even older men, like the Bishop, are fond of him, inviting him to take over their stations at some later point. Placing himself forever in danger, he is continually being rescued by the interventions of guardian angels, most notably his adoring aunt.

I did not begrudge Fabrizio his triumphs, but in no way did I identify with him. Already at twenty, I was seeing myself as the witty secondary, who would not get the girl.[1] A few months later, when we read *Sentimental Education* for colloquium, I again identified not with the dreamy aristocratic Frederic but with his resentful lower-middle-class pal Deslauriers. Possibly so did Flaubert. I wonder if this is a professional deformation: the writer, stuck at his desk, avenges himself against his dreamboat protagonist by making him seem a little vapid, condescending to or undercutting him.

At Columbia, I watched with fascination two of my classmates, Mitch and Jon, who seemed to me golden boys by virtue of their looks and breeding. I befriended both; you might even say I had crushes on them, or at least envied them. They seemed always to be in the midst of complicated troubles, torn between several girls vying for their attention, undecided between different spiritual paths and aesthetic directions. They would come to me for suggestions, and I would, despite my envy, manage to feel superior to their quandaries and dispense advice from my perch of ironic detachment. Why I should have been certain so early that I did not have it in me to be a ladies' man is a question that nags at me. Cowardice, probably, or lack of sustained interest. I don't think it's ever entirely a matter of looks (nor was I ugly), but rather, of a certain persistence, or receptivity to the chase, which may bubble up from an incompleteness of self that requires amorous adventure to fill—that hazy incompleteness that is often more enticing to women, who see a

---

1 Technically, Count Mosca does get Gina, making her his mistress and later his wife, but it is her nephew she loves: the proof is that she lives only for a short time after the death of Fabrizio, "whom she adored."

chance to fill in the blanks, to mold improvements, than the man who projects himself as a "finished portrait" (such as I was already attempting to do.) Gina cannot love Count Mosca with all her heart because he is too cautious and too aware of each consequence, while Fabrizio has the reckless, impetuous, disregarding spirit of a sleepwalker, which she associates with capacity for passion. (She's right, it turns out, though his passion will be for Clélia, not for her.)

What did I make of Fabrizio when I first read the book? I could never retrieve those responses, were it not for the fact that I happened to keep my colloquium paper. Here it sits before me—typewritten on onion-skin, with Professor Dupee's penciled comments—a shipwrecked sailor rescued from the ark of time. "Fabrizio, the Unconscious Hero" was the title. At the risk of being laughed at for exposing my undergraduate prose, I will quote the beginning:

> The unconscious hero was a favorite character of novelists in the eighteenth and nineteenth centuries. He seemed particularly adapted to a form which was reaching fruition at the time, and which grew from the picaresque novel in many respects: the comic novel of adventure. Fielding is without question the main exponent of his form, just as *Tom Jones* and *Joseph Andrews* are the works which give it definition. However, the formula he perfected—the unconscious hero's ejection from the secure surroundings of his childhood into the larger world, his naïve attitudes when confronted with obvious examples of evil, his near-passive participation in a string of marvelous incidents which thrust him into the path of danger and grotesque characters, and finally, his arrival at a stable position—was employed in works as diverse as *Candide*, *Roderick Random*, *Gulliver's Travels*, *Justine* and *The Charterhouse of Parma*.

After more literary contextualizing, I then went on to say:

> The lack of great consciousness in a novel's protagonist seems to increase his susceptibility to coincidence. The rational, active, tragic hero in literature constructs his own destiny, and if he is

defeated by fate the implication remains that he himself laid the groundwork for his failure. The unconscious hero, however, becomes much more controlled by the laws of chance. As such he is usually more fortunate, for he can always be saved by the accidental discovery of a faithful servant like Lodovico, who will nurse him back to health, or by the coincidence of a passport inspector who happens to know Gileti, and who lets Fabrizio through in order to protect his friend. . . . A hero like Joseph Andrews, Tom Jones or Fabrizio possesses other characteristics which become closely associated with his unconsciousness: he is incredibly handsome, so much so that most people are immediately won over to him by his physical appearance; he is graceful, strong, courageous, and sufficiently proud of his honor to fight against personal attacks; he is naïve, gallant and susceptible to romantic notions; he is frequently passive. A character with these attributes is quite useful to the writer of an adventure novel, because the writer must be able to create a perpetual stream of incidents and plot twists. If the hero is handsome, then at any moment a woman may fall passionately in love with him, arouse her lover's jealousy and incite a duel, which will probably end in our hero wounding or killing his adversary and fleeing the police.

In retrospect, it seems to me I was taking a little mocking revenge against the popular, handsome boys who were my friends. Though Mitch and Jon were exceedingly intelligent, I took as my consolation prize the prejudiced view that they were unconscious Fabrizios, and I, the ever-alert Count Mosca. My dream was to become Stendhal, never his romantic hero.

The rest of the paper supported my thesis by showing the many ways the novelist employed to demonstrate and analyze Fabrizio's unconsciousness. For example, the anti-clerical Stendhal blamed Catholicism, "the instruction given him by the Jesuits of Milan. That religion *deprives one of the courage to think of unfamiliar things*, and especially forbids *personal examination*, as the most enormous of sins, a step towards Protestantism." Or he blamed his character's youth: "Fabrizio's reasoning could never succeed in penetrating farther; he went a hundred ways around the difficult without managing to surmount it. He was too young still; in his moments of leisure, his mind devoted itself with rapture to enjoying the sensations produced by the romantic circumstances with which his imagination was always ready to supply him. He was far from employing his time in studying with patience the actual details of things in order to discover their causes."

I cited Fabrizio's unconscious cruelty toward his aunt, after she had rescued him from prison: "He tortures his benefactress and savior by ignoring her completely and doting on the memory of her rival, Clélia." I went on to indict him: "His passion for Clélia ultimately leads to the death of his love, their child, the Duchess and Fabrizio himself. Yet none of this tragedy would have occurred had Clélia and Fabrizio taken a rational course of action." (This is definitely a twenty-year-old talking!) I quoted Stendhal's seeming preference for reason over imagination, which delighted me: "The presence of danger gives a touch of genius to the reasoning man, places him, so to speak, above his level: in the imaginative man it inspires romances, bold, it is true, but frequently absurd."

In the end, I gave Fabrizio his due by noting that his instincts had elevated him above the common run of man, and won him the adoration of his priceless aunt. To show that this heroism was of a peculiarly unconscious nature, I quoted Gina herself, letting her have the last word: "I love in him his courage, so simple and so perfect that, one might say, he is not aware of it himself."

⟾•⟾

In the next twenty years, I stockpiled Stendhal's books: going on vacation, when I wanted something I knew would amuse me, I would pluck a title of his from the shelf. *The Red and the Black* proved to be, like *Vanity Fair*, one of those marvelous books whose vivacity and charm far exceed anything you might expect from a classic. I now regard it as Stendhal's best. Some of his lesser novels, like the refined novella *Armance*, the rather slight *Lamiel*, and the multi-volume *Lucien Leuwen*, are interesting on every page but never come to any point (in fact *Lucien Leuwen* was probably left unfinished because Stendhal realized he was spinning his wheels). I have come to the conclusion that Stendhal may not have been a natural novelist; like Kafka, he would get deeper and deeper into a story and not know how to plot an exit. I've also read his Italian tales, such as "Vanina Vanini," which have the economy of Kleist, if not the same payoff. In these short stories he seems to be forcing himself to complete a narrative arc. Their plots did not stay with me, but the storyteller remained good company throughout.

Finally, I turned to Stendhal's literary nonfiction, and was deeply enchanted. *On Love*, his book-length meditation, is such an astonishing font of wisdom, observation, philosophy, reverie, and paradox. It excited me enough to try to imitate the master with a chapter called "Journal of Decrystallization" in my novel *Confessions of Summer*. Later, after I had gravitated to the personal essay, I gobbled down his two autobiographical texts: *The Life of Henry Brulard* and *Memoirs of an Egotist*. The "I" in these unfinished memoirs is one of Stendhal's greatest characters: irascible, enthusiastic, pedantic, defiantly Oedipal, despising his father and adoring his mother. I also read his *Roman Journal* and some of the *Life of Rossini*. By this time, he had become for me one of those writers, like Montaigne, whose sentences are incurably interesting, regardless of whether the piece they are embedded in comes together.

Recently I returned to where I started and re-read, for the third time, *The Charterhouse of Parma*.

I am getting old. This fact, which troubles me immensely, cannot help but inspire indifference in you, the reader. I completely understand your refusal to be moved by my aging. I even applaud it. And in part I feel it myself: Who cares? But I ask myself: What has all this aging accomplished? It has made me lose the ability to appreciate as keenly as I once did a literary masterpiece.

This has happened to almost all the literary enthusiasms of my youth. Kerouac and his hitchhiking epics I can no longer take seriously or read for pleasure; Dostoyevsky's hysteria seems bullying, its shrillness repels me. The Stendhal who ruminates on love, travel, and other experience continues to replenish me; but I find *Charterhouse* a bit tiresome. Not all of it, of course. I still love the battle scenes, and the great interior monologues of Count Mosca and Fabrizio in Chapter 7, and Gina flinging herself into her nephew's arms. I still love much of the analytical aphorisms. But as a whole, it feels a little precious, artificial, forced. *The Charterhouse of Parma* was dashed off, we know, in fifty-two days, at the end of 1838, and the swiftness of its composition shows, in its excessive penchant for summary, its likeness to a single whoosh of sustained exhalation, its bravura, tour-de-force qualities, and its repetitions and hasty windup.

Stendhal's recurrent brickbats, such as using the warmhearted Italians to reproach the French nation's calculation and materialism, have grown stale. Count Mosca's long Machiavellian disquisitions on the inner workings of the court are no longer as fascinating this time around. The book also feels like an uneasy commingling of two traditions: the French psychological novel (from *The Princesse de Clèves* down to *Adolfe*) and the Italian tale, with farcical elements of opera *libretti* and *commedia dell'arte*. In my youth I had accepted this mix of genres as an enrichment; this time I balked, because I was less willing to submit to the novel as a waking dream.

It could be that worldliness itself, the initial spellbinding attraction of *Charterhouse*, no longer possesses the same allure, the same meaning for me. That attribute is no longer so unattainable: I have it—or as much as I am ever going to have.

I now distrust Stendhal's brief for romantic love. His skepticism is more credible to me than his romanticism. *Charterhouse* plays as a conflict between reason and passion. Stendhal admired passion but, I think, didn't really believe in it. He needed it, though, to advance the plot, so that he wouldn't get bogged down again, as had happened with *Lucien Leuwen*, in observation without an engine to drive it. He also needed a magnetic hero, and here we come to my central complaint. Fabrizio is a bore, a cipher, unfit to hold the focus of such a complex novel. His raptures by the lake, his mooning over Clélia in prison, all these passages dragged for me.

How could I have not seen this when I was younger?

I went back and read my college paper. What impressed me was my patience with Fabrizio. Of course I was also largely unformed, largely unconscious at the time, and willing to grant him the benefit of the doubt. For all my underlying malice against this lucky pup, the younger me still accorded him the respect of a legitimate leading man. I was curious, rather than irritated, about why Stendhal chose him as his narrative vessel, and even went to the trouble of developing a literary theory around it. What has happened to me over the years that I have gotten so dismissive? Is it that, aging and balding, I no longer have even minimal patience for hearing stories about the troubles of privileged youths? Or has experience taught me that we were all golden boys, golden girls, once upon a time, and therefore the archetype has lost its envious fascination?

I was particularly taken with Fred Dupee's penciled comments on the first page: "Thorough and well reasoned essay—on a fruitful topic. I only think that you might distinguish more between F's unconsciousness and the consequences of it for this temperament; his being able to 'live happily in the moment,' as Stendhal says. Isn't it this last that makes him great, rather than unconsciousness itself?" Living happily in the moment has proved not to be my forte. I think I suspected it would not be even at twenty, and was already mounting defenses against its lack. My old professor was gently pointing to that blind spot.

Dupee himself was, I think it safe to say, bisexual, in his longings if not in practice. He had, in fact, a crush on my friend Jon, which the latter told me about. It may be that the homoerotically inclined retain more of a lifelong enchantment with the youthful Adonis figure, which would enable them to appreciate better the comedy of the superior, older Gina fainting in anguish at the indifference of the younger Fabrizio. It may be that great artists, be they Mozart or Stendhal or Shakespeare, always possess something of the hermaphrodite in their character. I am just speculating here. In any case, Stendhal believed in Italy, in happiness, in *dolce far niente*, in a way I no longer could. And to that extent, the novel could no longer work as well for me.

Nevertheless, because I knew I was wrong in my judgment, I went back and read parts of it again. With surprising pleasure. Taken a little at a time, like some poisons or homeopathic substances, *The Charterhouse of Parma* remains—delicious.

The Development of Anne Frank

JOHN BERRYMAN

> *We learn in time of pestilence that there are more things to*
> *admire than to despise.*
> > —Albert Camus, *The Plague*

When the first installment of the translated text of *The Diary of Anne Frank* appeared in the spring of 1952, in *Commentary*, I read it with amazement. The next day, when I went into town to see my analyst, I stopped in the magazine's offices—I often did, to argue with Clem Greenberg, who was a sort of senior adviser to what was at that time the best general magazine in the country in spite of, maybe because of, its special Jewish concerns—to see if proofs of the diary's continuation were available, and they were. Like millions of people later, I was bowled over with pity and horror and admiration for the astounding doomed little girl. But what I *thought* was: a sane person. A sane person, in the twentieth century. It was as long ago as 1889 when Tolstoy wound up his terrible story "The Devil" with this sentence: "And, indeed, if Evgeni Irrenev was mentally deranged, then all people are mentally deranged, but undoubtedly those are most surely mentally deranged who see in others symptoms of insanity which they fail to see in themselves." Some years later (1955), setting up a course called Humanities in the Modern World at the University of Minnesota, I assigned the diary and reread it with feelings even more

powerful than before but now highly structured. I decided that it was
the most remarkable account of *normal* human adolescent maturation
I had ever read, and that it was universally valued for reasons comparatively insignificant. I waited for someone to agree with me. An article
by Bettelheim was announced in *Politics*, appeared, and was irrelevant.
The astute Alfred Kazin and his wife, the novelist Ann Birstein, edited
Anne Frank's short fiction—ah! I thought—and missed the boat.

Here we have a book only fifteen years old, the sole considerable surviving production of a young girl who died after writing it. While decisively
rejecting the proposal—which acts as a blight in some areas of modern
criticism—that a critic should address himself only to masterworks, still I
would agree that some preliminary justification seems desirable.

It is true that the book is world famous. I am not much impressed
by this fact, which I take to be due in large part to circumstances that
have nothing to do with art. The author has been made into a spokes-
man against one of the grand crimes of our age, and for her race,
and for all its victims, and for the victims (especially children) of all
the tyrannies of this horrifying century—and we could extend this
list of circumstances irrelevant to the *critical* question. Some proportion of the book's fame, moreover, is even more irrelevant, as arising
from the widespread success of a play adapted from it, and a film.
That the book *is* by a young girl—an attractive one, as photographs
show—must count heavily in its sentimental popularity. And, finally,
the work has decided literary merit; it is vivid, witty, candid, astute,
dramatic, pathetic, terrible—one falls in love with the girl, one finds
her formidable, and she breaks one's heart. All right. It is a work infinitely superior to a similar production that has been compared to it,
The Diary of "Helena Morley," beautifully translated by Elizabeth
Bishop in 1957. Here is a favorable specimen of the Brazilian narrative: "When I get married I wonder if I'll love my husband as much
as mama loves my father? God willing. Mama lives only for him and
thinks of nothing else. When he's at home the two spend the whole
day in endless conversation. When papa's in Boa Vista during the week,
mama gets up singing wistful love songs and we can see she misses
him, and she passes the time going over his clothes, collecting the eggs,
and fattening the chickens for dinner on Saturday and Sunday. We

eat best on those days."[1] Clearly the temperature here is nothing very unusual, and no serious reader of Anne Frank, with her extraordinary range and tension, will entertain any comparison between the two writers. But I am obliged to wonder whether Anne Frank has *had* any serious readers, for I find no indication in anything written about her that anyone has taken her with real seriousness. A moment ago we passed, after all, the critical question. *One finds her formidable*: why, and how, ought to engage us. And first it is necessary to discover what she is writing about. Perhaps, to be sure, she is not truly writing about anything—you know, "thoughts of a young girl," "Jews in hiding from the Nazis," "a poignant love affair"; but such is not my opinion.

Suppose one became interested in the phenomenon called religious conversion. There are books one can read. There is one by Sante de Sanctis entitled *Religious Conversion*, there are narratives admirably collected in William James's lectures, *The Varieties of Religious Experience*, there is an acute account of the most momentous Christian conversion, Paul's, by Maurice Goguel in the second volume (*The Birth of Christianity*) of his great history of Christian origins. If one wants, however, to experience the phenomenon, so far as one can do so at second hand—a phenomenon as gradual and intensely reluctant as it is also drastic—there is so far as I know one book and one only to be read, written by an African fifteen hundred years ago. Now in Augustine's *Confessions* we are reckoning with just one of a vast number of works by an architect of Western history, and it may appear grotesque to compare to even that one, tumultuous and gigantic, the isolated recent production of a girl who can give us nothing else. A comparison of the *authors* would be grotesque. But I am thinking of the originality and ambition and indispensability of the two books *in the heart of their substances*—leaving out of account therefore book 10 of the *Confessions*, which happens to award man his deepest account of his own memory. I would call the subject of Anne Frank's diary even more mysterious and fundamental than St. Augustine's, and describe it as: the conversion of a child into a person.

---

1 Helena Morley, *The Diary of Helena Morley*, trans. Elizabeth Bishop (New York: Ecco Press, 1977), 82.

At once it may be exclaimed that we have thousands of books on this subject. I agree: autobiographies, diaries, biographies, novels. They seem to me—those that in various literatures I have come on—to bear the same sort of relation to the diary that the works *on* religious conversion bear to the first seven books of the *Confessions*. Anne Frank has made the process itself available.

Why—I asked myself with astonishment when I first encountered the diary, or the extracts that *Commentary* published—has this process not been described before? universal as it is, and universally interesting? And answers came. It is *not* universal, for most people do not grow up, in any degree that will correspond to Anne Frank's growing up; and it is *not* universally interesting, for nobody cares to recall his own, or can. It took, I believe, a special pressure forcing the child-adult conversion, and exceptional self-awareness and exceptional candor and exceptional powers of expression, to bring that strange or normal change into view. This, if I am right, is what she has done, and what we are to study.

The process of her development, then, is our subject. But it is not possible to examine this without some prior sense of two unusual sets of conditions in which it took place: its physical and psychological context, first, and second, the qualities that she took into it. Both, I hope to show, were *necessary* conditions.

For the context: it was both strange, sinister, even an "extreme situation" in Bettelheim's sense,[2] and pseudo-ordinary; and it is hard to say which aspect of the environment was more crippling and crushing. We take a quicksilver-active girl thirteen years old, pretty, popular, voluble, brilliant, and hide her, as it were, in prison; in a concealed annex upstairs at the rear of the business premises her father had commanded;

---

2 Bruno Bettelheim's well-known article, "[Individual and Mass Behavior in] Extreme Situations," [*Journal of Abnormal and Social Psychology* 38 (1943): 417–52, reprinted] in *Politics*. I am unable to make anything of his recent article in *Harper's*, weirdly titled "The [Ignored] Lesson of Anne Frank," which charges that the Franks should not have gone into hiding as a family but should have dispersed for greater safety; I really do not know what to say to this, except that a man at his desk in Chicago, many years later, ought not to make such decisions perhaps; he also complains that they were not armed. Some social scientist will next inform the Buddha of *his* mistake—in leaving court at all, in austerity, in illumination, and in teaching.

in darkness, behind blackout curtains; in slowness—any movement might be heard—such that after a time when she peeks out to see cyclists going by they seem to be flying; in closeness—not only were she and her parents and sister hopelessly on top of each other, but so were another family with them, and another stranger—savagely bickering, in whispers, of course; in fear—of Nazis, of air raids, of betrayal by any of the Dutch who knew (this, it seems, is what finally happened, but the marvelous goodness of the responsible Dutch is one of the themes of the *Diary*), of thieves (who came)—the building, even, was once sold out from under them, and the new owner simply missed the entrance to their hiding place. All this calls for heroism and it's clear that the personalities of the others except Mr. Frank withered and deteriorated under conditions barely tolerable. It took Anne Frank herself more than a year to make the sort of "adjustment" (detestable word) that would let her free for the development that is to be our subject.

But I said, "as it were, in prison." To prison one can become accustomed; it is *different,* and one has no responsibilities. Here there was a simulacrum of ordinary life: she studied, her family was about her, she was near—very near—the real world. The distortion and anxiety are best recorded in the dreadful letter of April 1,1943. Her father was still (sort of) running the company and had briefed his Dutch assistant for an important conference; the assistant fell ill and there wasn't time to explain "fully" to his replacement; the responsible executive, in hiding, "was trembling with anxiety as to how the talks would go." Someone suggested that if he lay with his face on the floor he might hear. So he did, at 10:30 a.m., with the other daughter, Margot, until 2:30, when half-paralyzed he gave up. The daughters took over, understanding scarcely a word. I have seldom, even in modern literature, read a more painful scene. It takes Anne Frank, a concise writer, thirteen sentences to describe.

Let's distinguish, without resorting to the psychologists, temperament from character. The former would be the disposition with which one arrives in the world, the latter what has happened to that disposition in terms of environment, challenge, failure, and success, by the time of maturity—a period individually fixed between, somewhere between, fifteen and seventy-five, say. Dictionaries will not help us; try *Webster's Dictionary of Synonyms* if you doubt it. Americans like dictionaries, and they are also hopeless environmentalists (although they do not let it trouble their science, as Communists do). I ought therefore perhaps to make it plain that children do differ. The small son of another friend was taking a walk, hand in hand, with his father, when they came to an uneven piece of sidewalk and his father heard him say to himself, "Now, Peter, take it easy, Peter, that's all right, Peter," and they went down the other end of the slightly tilted block. My own son, a friend of both, is in between, Dionysiac with the first, Apollonian with Peter. I think we ought to form some opinion of the *temperament* of Anne Frank before entering on her ordeal and thereafter trying to construct a picture of her character.

The materials are abundant, the diary lies open. She was vivacious but intensely serious, devoted but playful. It may later on be a question for us as to whether this conjunction *but* is the right conjunction, in her thought. She was imaginative but practical, passionate but ironic and cold-eyed. Most of the qualities that I am naming need no illustration for a reader of the diary; perhaps "cold-eyed" may have an exemplar: "Pim, who was sitting on a chair in a beam of sunlight that shone through the window, kept being pushed from one side to the other. In addition, I think his rheumatism was bothering him, because he sat rather hunched up with a miserable look on his face. . . . He looked exactly like some shriveled-up old man from an old people's home" [December 10,1942]. So much for an image of the man—her adored father—whom she loves best in the world. She was self-absorbed but unselfpitying, charitable but sarcastic, industrious but dreamy, brave but sensitive. Garrulous but secretive; skeptical but eloquent. This last *but* may engage us, too. My little word *industrious*, like a refugee from a recommendation for a graduate student, finds its best instance in the letter, daunting to an American student, of April 27, 1944, where in various languages she is studying in one day matters that—if they ever came up for an American student—would take him months.

The reason this matters is that the process we are to follow displays itself in a more complicated fashion than one might have expected: in the will, in emotion, in the intellect, in libido. It is surprising what it takes to make an adult human being.

The Only Solution to the Soul Is the Senses: A Meditation on Bill Murray and Myself

DAVID SHIELDS

'm in a swoon over Bill Murray because he takes "my issues"—
gloom, rage, self-consciousness, world-weariness—and offers ways
out, solutions of sorts, all of which amount to a delicate embrace of the
real, a fragile lyricism of the unfolding moment. He thus flatters me
that under all my protective layers of irony I, too, might have depth of
feeling as well. I admire his slouching insouciance but don't possess it,
admire it precisely because I don't possess it. I realize, of course, that a
certain redemptive posture is the unique property of movies and movie
stars, but Murray's grace is manifest at least as often outside his movies
as in them. The first line of his book, *Cinderella Story: My Life in Golf*,
is "The light seems to come from everywhere."

In the last decade there have been a few exceptions—primarily
Groundhog Day and *Rushmore*—but Murray has been so good in so
many bad movies that it's as if he makes bad movies on purpose as a way
to demonstrate the truth of Denis Leary's dictum (to which I subscribe),
"Life sucks; get a fuckin' helmet." Murray's movies, in general, suck;
he's the fuckin' helmet. In a self-interview in which he asked himself
to explain why so few of his films have succeeded, he replied, mock-sol-
emnly, "I've had lots of good premises." *The Razor's Edge* being, again,
an interesting exception, Murray seems to believe that, given the horror
show of the universe, the supreme act of bad faith would be to appear in a

pretentious work of art aspiring to be beautiful, whereas my impulse has always been to try to find in art my only refuge from the storm.

Murray's metaphor for the Sisyphean struggle is: "In life, you never have to completely quit. There's some futile paddling toward some shore of relief, and that's what gets people through. Only the really lucky get a tailwind that takes them to the shore. So many get the headwind that they fight and, then, tip over and drown." Life is futile; failure is a sign of grace; Murray is fuck-up as existential fool. His loserdom is the exact opposite, though, of, say, Woody Allen's, who seems intolerably sniffly by comparison. I'm much, much more like Allen than I am like Murray, which is why I admire Murray (Jewish adoration of un-Jewish stoicism). Asked to name people he finds funny, Murray mentions Bob Hope, David Letterman, Conan O'Brien, Eddie Izzard—WASPy wise guys, goyish slackers, no whiners allowed.

In *Meatballs*, Murray is counselor at a summer camp for losers. When they're getting demolished in a basketball game against a much tonier camp, Murray instructs his charges to run around pantsing their opponents. Forget the score; fuck the rules; do fun things; give yourselves things to remember. Camp director Morty takes himself and the camp way too seriously (so many blocking figures in Murray movies are officious Jews; what's that about—Hollywood's knee-jerk self-hatred?) and so Murray leads all the other kids in always calling him "Mickey," turning him into a mouse. The great crime in any Bill Murray movie is self-seriousness, because as Murray's fellow Irishman Oscar Wilde said, "Life is too important to take seriously." Wilde also said, "The only solution to the soul is the senses," which is a key to Murray's appeal: he's in touch with his animal self and teaches the kids to be in touch with theirs. We're all meatballs; we're all just bodies. If I were a girl or gay, I'd have a searing crush on him in this movie, because just the way he carries his body seems to say *Here is fun. I'm where fun happens.* When he (crucially: unsuccessfully) courts another counselor, he does so without an ounce of earnestness. Losers are winners; they get that life is an unmitigated disaster. At one point he leads the campers in a chant, "It just doesn't matter, it just doesn't matter, it just doesn't matter." My problem is that even though I know on an intellectual level that "it just doesn't matter," on a daily level I treat everything as if it does.

Murray's shtick—anti-star Star, anti-hero Hero, ordinary-guy Icon—
is built in part upon the fact of his unglamorous appearance. In sketches
on *Saturday Night Live*, Gilda Radner would often call him "Pizza
Face," and it's obvious he's never done anything to improve his deeply
mottled skin. (Seemingly half my adolescence was spent in a dermatolo-
gist's office.) Murray's absence of vanity allows him to get to emotional
truths in a scene, as opposed to, say, T. Cruise, whom you can tell is always
only concentrating on one question: How do I look? I was cute enough
as a little kid to appear in an advertisement for a toy store; my father
took the photographs, and here I am in the family album, riding a plastic pony and brandishing a pistol with crypto-cowboy charm. Although
now I'm certainly not handsome, I don't think I've ever quite outgrown
that early narcissism. Murray's not fat, but he has a serious paunch; as
opposed to some middle-aged buffster like Harrison Ford, Murray's fifty
and looks all of it. Bless him for that: it's a gift back to us; he makes us all
feel less shitty. He posed for a *New York Times Magazine* profile wearing a drooping undershirt and with uncombed, thinning, gray hair. It's
a comparison Murray would surely loathe for its la-di-da-ness, but the
photograph reminds me of Rembrandt's late self-portraits: a famous man
who understands his own mortal ordinariness and is willing to show you
the irredeemable sadness of his eyes in which that knowledge registers.
   Murray's sadness is not other movie stars' pseudo-seriousness; he
seems genuinely forlorn—always a plus in my book. Speaking to Terry
Gross on *Fresh Air*, Murray said, "Movies don't usually show the failure
of relationships; they want to give the audience a final, happy resolu-
tion. In *Rushmore*, I play a guy who's aware that his life is not working,
but he's still holding on, hoping something will happen, and that's
what's most interesting." Gross, stunned that Murray would identify so
strongly with someone as bitter and remorseful as Herman Blume, tried
to pull Murray up off the floor by saying, "I mean, you've found work
that is meaningful for you, though, haven't you?" Murray explained
that Blume is drawn to the energetic teenager Max Fischer, who is the
founder and president of virtually every club at Rushmore Academy,
but "sometimes it makes you sadder to see someone that's really happy,
really engaged in life when you have detached." He said this as if he
knew exactly what he was talking about.

The Razor's Edge—a film which he had desperately been wanting to do for years and which he co-wrote—is his ur-story. The first part of the Maugham novel is set in Chicago, but Murray moved the first part of the film to Lake Forest, next door to Wilmette, the North Shore suburb in which he grew up. The bulk of the book and film are set in Paris, where Murray spent a year, studying French and Gurdjieff and fleeing from post-*Ghostbusters* fame.

Surrounded by cripples and sybarites, amoralists and materialists, Murray's character in *The Razor's Edge*, Larry Darrell, travels to China, Burma, and India searching for meaning, and the best he can come up with is: "You don't get it. It doesn't matter." It just doesn't matter. Such is the highest wisdom a Murray character can hope to achieve: a sort of semi-Zen detachment, which only deepens his dread (sounds familiar to me).

Angst translates easily to anger. Discussing megalomaniacal celebrities, Murray said, "Whenever I hear someone say, 'My fans,' I go right for the shotgun." In *Kingpin*, Murray plays an impossibly arrogant bowler who, in one scene, says hello to the two women sitting at the next table. The less attractive woman responds by saying, "Hi," and Murray says, "Not you [nodding to the less attractive woman]. You [nodding to the more attractive woman]." Murray can access his own cruelty—he ad-libbed these lines—but isn't defined by it. He simply doesn't radiate malevolence, as, say, James Woods used to do, but neither is he cuddlesome-cute, à la Tom Hanks; this mixture keeps me productively off balance, makes me unsure whether to embrace him or be slightly afraid of him.

He seizes the regenerative power of behaving badly, being disrespectful toward condescending assholes. In his self-interview, in which he pretended to be discoursing with Santa Claus, he said, "I was at the New York Film Critics Circle Awards one year. They called me up when somebody canceled two days before the thing, and asked me to present some awards. So I went, and one of the funniest film moments I've ever had was when they introduced the New York film critics. They all stood up; 'motley' isn't the word for that group. Everybody had some sort of vision problem, some sort of damage. I had to bury myself in my napkin. As they kept going, it just got funnier and funnier looking. By the time they were all up, it was like, 'You have been selected as the people who have been poisoned; you were the unfortunate people who were not in the control group that didn't receive the medication.'" This is a little amazing, even shocking to me; I fancy myself something of a literary troublemaker, but I can't imagine being quite this publicly dismissive toward the powers-that-be in the book world (privately, of course, I'm acid itself—what bravery). I suppose his career is less dependent than mine is upon good reviews, i.e., he's actually popular; still, he has what Hemingway said was the "most essential gift for a good writer: a built-in, shock-proof shit detector."

Hemingway's hometown of Oak Park is about twenty miles southwest of Murray's hometown of Wilmette; both men have or had a gimlet-eyed view of the disguises the world wears. It's more broadly midwestern, though, than only Hemingwayesque, I think. Dave Eggers, who grew up in Lake Forest, has it. Johnny Carson, who was raised in Nebraska, and David Letterman, who was raised in Indiana, also have it—this quality of detachment, which is a way of not getting sucked in by all the shit sent your way, of holding on to some tiny piece of yourself which is immune to publicity, of wearing indifference as a mask. I strive for the same mystery in my own persona but fail miserably, since it's so evident how much neediness trumps coolness.

Murray is, in other words, ironic. He's alert to and mortified by the distance between how things appear to be and how they are. In *Michael Jordan to the Max*, a grotesquely worshipful IMAX film-paean, Murray, as a fan in the stands, says, "It's like out of all the fifty thousand top athletes since, you know, prehistoric times—brontosaurus and pterodactyls included—he [Jordan]'s right there." This is a modest example, but it betrays Murray's impulse: to unhype the hype, to replace force-fed feeling with something less triumphal, more plausible and human and humble. In *Stripes*, Murray delivers a rousing speech to his fellow soldiers to encourage them to learn overnight what they haven't learned during all of boot camp—how to march. "We're Americans," he says, "we're all dogfaces, but we have within us something American that knows how to do this." Murray saves the speech from sentimentality by mocking the sentimentality. *I'm not really in this situation*, Murray's character seems to be thinking; *I'm not really in this movie*,

Murray seems to be thinking. That reminds us, or at least me, of our own detachment and puts us in the scene, thereby making the moment credible and, ironically, moving. Here, as in so many other Murray movies, he somehow manages to install a level or two of Plexiglas between himself and the rest of the movie. At its most dire, Murray's persona is simply anti-feeling; at its most fierce it's anti-faux-feeling. This is what gives his persona such an edge: it's unclear whether his self-mockery is saving grace or Nowhere Man melancholia. It's both, obviously, to which I can attest or hope to attest. Maybe detachment is a way to get to real feeling; maybe it's a dead end from which no feeling arises.

Murray's characteristic manner of delivering dialogue is to add invisible, ironic quotes around nearly every word he says, as if he weren't quite convinced he should go along with the program that is the script, as if he were just trying out the dialogue on himself first rather than really saying it to someone else in a movie that millions of people are going to see, as if he were still seeing how it sounds. The effect is to undermine every assertion at the moment it's asserted. As a stutterer and writer, I'm a sucker for Murray's push-pull relationship to language; it's undoubtedly one of the main sources of the deep psychic identification I've always felt toward him. In *Tootsie*, as Dustin Hoffman's roommate who's a playwright/waiter, Murray says about his work-in-progress, "I think it's going to change theatre as we know it." Murray says the line in a way that no one else could, simultaneously embodying and emptying out cliché. We're aware that he's full of shit, but we're also aware that he's aware he's full of shit. For which we adore him, because he reminds us how full of shit we are every hour of every day. He's also a welcome relief from Dustin Hoffman's earnestness.

His pet technique for underlining his self-consciousness is knocking, loudly, on the fourth wall. Serving as guest broadcaster for a Chicago Cubs baseball game, which Murray once said is the single best performance of his life, he answered the phone in the adjoining booth, stuck out his tongue at the camera, called down to the players on the field. At pro-am tournaments, Murray wears goofy outfits, jokes with the crowd, hits wacky shots—in an effort to tear a hole in the sanctimonious veil surrounding the game of golf. At a Carnegie Hall benefit concert with a Sinatra theme, Murray, backed by a full orchestra, sang "My Way";

Murray told an interviewer, "I basically rewrote the lyrics and changed them around to suit my own mood. I started getting laughs with it, and then I was off the click track. I mean, there's a full orchestra playing to its own charts, so they just keep playing, you know. And the fact I'm off the lyric and talking and doing things—it doesn't matter to them. They don't keep vamping; it's not like a piano bar. They just keep going to the end. So I said let's see if this big band is going to stay with me here, and they didn't. They just kept barreling right ahead. But I managed to catch them at the pass. I headed them off at the pass and turned it around and got out of it again." It's crucial to Murray's comedy that the orchestra is there, playing away, serious as society—the formal strait-jacket he wriggles out of.

By far my favorite joke I've heard recently goes:

Knock-knock.

Who's there?

Interrupting Cow.

Interrupt—

Moo.

Murray and I—other people, too, obviously—share an impulse to simultaneously annihilate and resuscitate received forms. I have an extraordinarily vivid memory of a very brief video clip I saw twenty years ago of a juggler who was riding a unicycle and pretending to have great difficulty controlling the knives he was juggling. He was in absolute control, of course, but I loved how much trouble he pretended to be having; I loved how afraid he pretended to be; I loved how much it was both a parody of the form and a supreme demonstration of the form. I loved it so much (an artist pretending death was going to win, but art had it under control all along, thank you very much) it brought me to tears.

Murray's acute self-consciousness is paralyzing, but also curiously freeing: it frees him up to be a rebel (just barely). In *Razor's Edge*, he's the only character who is both (just) sane and (beautifully) whimsical, which is the balance he strikes in nearly every movie, his signature mixture of hip and square. He knows better than anyone else that you don't always have to do what they tell you to do, but he also tends to realize that the way out of the slough of despond is delight in other people, making him clubbable. In *Stripes*, asked by the drill sergeant what he's doing, Murray's character says, "Marching in a straight line, sir." It's not a straight line, but what he's doing is still, finally, marching. Although Murray is utterly insubordinate toward the sergeant, he winds up earning the sergeant's admiration by leading a rescue mission at the end. Murray is a goof-off and anti-establishment, but he winds up having the right stuff. He gets it together but on his own terms, if "own terms" can be defined unambitiously.

One of the many good jokes of *Tootsie* is that Murray, playing an avant-garde playwright, is nobody's idea of an avant-garde playwright: everything in his body—his competence, his responsibility—screams acceptance of things as they are. He defies without sabotaging authority. When an interviewer asked Murray whether *Rushmore* director Wes Anderson's gentle approach toward actors was effective, Murray replied, a bit huffily, "Well, that's good manners, you know? That's tact." Murray went to Loyola Academy, a prep school, in Wilmette, and all his hell-raising is in a way the unthreateningly bad behavior of a slumming preppy. The ultimate effect of all his hijinks on the links is to deepen golf's hushed, moneyed silence (Murray's antics would seem redundant at a football game). There's the official way and then there's your own way; Murray does it his own way, he never gets co-opted, but—and this is his magic trick, this is the movies, this is what is so deeply reassuring about his persona—he still succeeds (leads the rescue mission, rids the city of ghosts). He therefore is a perfect bridge figure between, to paint in broad strokes, fifties conformity, sixties rage, seventies zaniness, eighties and nineties capitalismo; hence his appeal—he convinces us that we're still a little rebellious inside even as we're finally doing what everyone else is doing. As the child of left-wing activists, I'm frequently embarrassed by how bourgeois my yearnings are; Murray's relatively unangry versions of *épater le bourgeois* coat my conformity in glee.

This very deep contradiction in Murray is directly related to the way corrosive irony, in him, sits atop deep sentimentality. (So, too, for myself: walking out of the theatre after *Terms of Endearment*, I subjected it to a withering critique while tears were still streaking down my face.) When he was guest commentator at the Cubs game, he mocked every player on the opposing team in a parody of fan fanaticism ("That guy shouldn't even be in the major leagues, and he knows it. He's lying to himself; he really should go back into some sort of community service in his hometown"), but he refused every opportunity the cameraman handed him to score easy points off the enormously fat African-American umpire Eric Gregg, whose uniform had been lost and who just couldn't get comfortable in his borrowed clothes. Before the Cubs played their first night game at Wrigley Field, Murray visited the booth again, this time for just a few minutes, mercilessly ribbing the legendary announcer Harry Caray before suddenly declaring, "This is the most beautiful park in the world."

I feel so earthbound compared to Murray, so uncelebratory. Asked about his parodies of bad singers, Murray explained, "You have to see what the original center of the song was and how they destroyed it. It's the ruining of a good song that you want to re-create. You have to like the stuff and you have to, I guess, know that when you have the microphone you have the opportunity to touch somebody. And when you don't do it with the lyric of it, and your own excuse for technique comes in and steps on top of it, that's, I guess, what I object to when I'm mimicking something." That old story: rage is disappointed romanticism.

Disappointed romanticism, however, isn't romanticism. Murray isn't Tom Hanks; he never, or almost never, does romantic comedy. He likes himself too much, for as Murray says, "The romantic figure has to behave romantically even after acting like a total swine. It's, 'I'm so gorgeous you're going to have to go through all kinds of hell for me,' and that isn't interesting to me. Romance is very particular. There's something about romance, that if you don't have to have someone, you're more desirable." Murray has the dignity of not having to have someone, or at least not going on and on about it.

He is, in short, male, a guy's guy, still extremely boyish though he was born in 1950, broad-shouldered, six feet three, upbeat about his masculinity in a way that seems quite foreign and enviable to me. My voice is high and soft, as a way to control my stutter, but also as if in apology for my Y chromosome. His father, who died when Murray was nineteen, was a lumber salesman. One of five brothers (and nine siblings), Murray now has five sons (and no daughters) from two marriages. So much of his persona, his shtick, his appeal is that he revels in and excels at the brutal but obviously affectionate teasing that is characteristic of large families, whereas more than one person has asked me, apropos of nothing in particular, whether I'm an only child (I'm not).

Occasionally psychotic but never neurotic, Murray plays well against nervous types, as I'm trying to make him do in this essay. He's not me. He's not Woody Allen. He's not Dustin Hoffman. In *Tootsie*, in which Dustin Hoffman plays an obnoxious actor, Michael Dorsey, who pretends to be a woman in order to get a part in a soap and, by "becoming" a woman, learns to be a better man, Murray is the true north of "normal" masculinity, our ordinary-guy guide, the big galoot around whom the gender-bending bends. "I think we're getting into a weird area," he informs Hoffman when Hoffman gets preoccupied with his female alter ego's wardrobe. "Instead of trying to be Michael Dorsey the great actor or Michael Dorsey the great waiter," he advises Hoffman before ushering him into his surprise birthday party, "why don't you just try to be Michael Dorsey?" Murray's the king of hanging out. He already knows how to be himself and how to be kind, how to be male but not be a jerk, whereas Hoffman needs to learn how to do this. Hoffman, the high-strung Jew, must learn how to do what Murray already does instinctively—to like life, to like the opposite sex, to embrace his own anima. *Live, live, live*, as Strether, that priss, finally realizes in Henry James's *The Ambassadors*, and as Murray has always known, as Murray always conveys.

Murray's boyishness is, at its most beguiling, childlikeness: openness to surprise. In *Cinderella Story: My Life in Golf*, Murray writes, "The sum and substance of what I was hoping to express is this. In golf, just as in life—I hoped I could get that line in the book somewhere [Murray's relentless ironic gaze, his ear for cliché]—the best wagers are laid on oneself." In *The Man Who Knew Too Little*, Murray plays Wallace Ritchie, a dim American man who, visiting his businessman-brother in London, thinks he's attending an avant-garde "Theatre of Life" performance and unbeknownst to him is caught up in an international spy-versus-spy scheme. Murray, as Ritchie, wins the day—defeats the bad guys, gets the girl—because he just goes with the flow, is cool and relaxed, never stops believing that he's watching and participating in an unusually realistic performance. Ritchie's relaxedness is Murray's relaxedness, Ritchie's distance is Murray's: life is theatre with arbitrary rules. His bemused bafflement toward everything that happens is a handbook for Murray's acting technique and his approach to life—the absurdity of all action, but (and therefore) grooving in the moment.

When Murray was the guest commentator at the Cubs game, he somehow made anything the camera focused on—a hot-dog wrapper, an untucked shirt—seem newly resonant, of possible interest, because unlike every person to ever broadcast a baseball game, Murray talked about what was actually going on in his head, was actually seeing what was going on in front of his eyes rather than viewing it through a formulaic filter, was taking in the entire ballpark rather than just the sporting event per se. His eyes haven't gone dead yet. Life, seen through such eyes, becomes existentially vivid. Broadcasting this game, Murray seemed as interested in the physical universe as a beagle, sniffing the ballpark for new sensory input. The only solution to the soul is the senses. He's a combination of two characters from the movie *American Beauty*: the kid with the video camera who can see ribbons of beauty in a plastic bag being blown around in the wind, and the Kevin Spacey character, who processes everything through his sulphur-spewing irony machine. I'm Spacey and want to be the kid with the video camera.

It's Murray's attempt to be authentic, and underlining of his attempt to be authentic, that I admire most; all of my current aesthetic excitements derive from my boredom with the conventions of fiction and my hope that nonfiction (autobiography, confession, memoir, embarrassment, *whatever*) can perhaps produce something that is for me "truer," more "real." The tape I have of Murray broadcasting the Cubs game has live audio rather than commercial breaks between innings; Murray sounds exactly the same off air as he does on. He's incapable of doing Stentorian Announcer let alone Star Turn. I adore this about him. At one point in his life he was strongly influenced by the philosophy of Gurdjieff, whose Madame Blavatskyesque work I can't bring myself to

read but one of whose titles is *Life Is Only Real, Then, When "I Am."*
A bad translation, to be sure, but the self-conscious quote marks around
"I Am," the slight or not so slight inscrutability, the deep yearning to
apprehend and embody reality—that's Murray's program.

The royal road to the authentic for Murray is through the primitive.
People who pretend that they are truly civilized Murray finds ridiculous. In *Caddyshack*, a movie about class warfare phrased as a golf
comedy, he plays a groundskeeper who is obsessed with killing gophers.
Chevy Chase is the embodiment of the golfing fop—moneyed, charming, handsome. Murray is riddled by doubt, self-pitying, working-class
("I got a blue-collar chip on my shoulder," Murray said. "That part of
it was not hard"). Chase, for all his bonhomie, isn't in touch with the
primitive force of the universe; Murray is (he's the only one capable of
recognizing that a dark brown clump floating in the country-club swimming pool isn't a turd but a Baby Ruth bar, which he eats). The movie
teaches the young golfer-protagonist that Chase is wrong, Murray is
right. The only way for Young Golfer to grow up is by learning how to
say fuck you to the "snobatorium"—the country club's version of golf
and life.

Would that rebellion were so easy. Still, when the interviewer Charlie
Rose advised Bill Murray to take a sabbatical, because lawyers do, Murray
said, "If law firms do it, Charlie, it probably can't be right." (That "probably" is quintessential Murray—anti-establishmentarian but not utterly.)
Rose also advised him about the importance of "proportionality" in one's
life—balance between work and play. "I want to learn that one, too,"
Murray said, pretending to search for a pencil. "Let me write it down."
In *Wild Things*, Murray is the lone actor among several other middle-
aged actors in the movie who is granted the privilege of grasping the
movie's vision: human beings are beasts, life is a scam, manipulate the
other beasts in the jungle to your own advantage. It would be impossible
to cast Murray as someone who didn't understand this.

Maybe it's not much of a revelation to anyone else, but to me it always
seems to be: we're finally just physical creatures living in the physical
world. Murray knows this in the bottom of his bones. If Murray didn't
ad-lib the following lines in *Tootsie*, he should have: "I don't want a full
house at the Winter Garden Theatre. I want ninety people who just

came out of the worst rainstorm in the city's history. These are people who are alive on the planet, until they dry off. I wish I had a theatre that was only open when it rained." All of Murray's verbal play happens atop a foundation of understated physical grace. In *Space Jam*, Murray isn't Michael Jordan, but it's crucial that he isn't Wayne Knight, either. He's halfway between jock god and blubbery nerd—someone we can identify with. After kibitzing with Michael Jordan at the golfing tee, wearing madras shorts and cornball shirt and shoes, he finally whacks the hell out of the ball. So, too, at pro-am tournaments it wouldn't work if, after goofing around for twenty minutes, he couldn't finally play the game. By being both ridiculous and competent, he becomes beautifully contradictory—the unicycle-riding knife juggler who pretends to be anxiety-stricken but isn't.

I imagine that Murray would be a bit of a bully in the way a hip older brother or popular camp counselor might be—making you feel bad if you just don't want to have fun right now as Murray defines fun, not allowing you to just mope if that's what you want to do. I imagine he would be a drill sergeant on this score—toward his sons, say—because a frenetically kept-up *joie de vivre* is how he's managed to paper over his fairly real despair, and if he can, he's going to bring everyone along with him out of hell. I admire this and resent it a little; why can't we mope if we want to mope? Maybe the only solution to the soul isn't the senses; maybe it's deeper soul-searching (probably not); maybe there is no soul.

"To be, to be, sure beats the shit out of not to be," he writes at the end of *The Cinderella Story*. At the very end of *Where the Buffalo Roam*, in which Murray plays Hunter Thompson, Murray quotes Lord Buckley's epitaph: "He stomped on the terra." This is the nucleus of Murray: we're made of clay; we better cause a little ruckus while we can. He's the anti-Malvolio in our midst; he's Tigger versus the suits. Life is absurd— make it your own absurdity. Instead of wearing artiste basic-black—my dumb uniform—Murray typically wears his own weird mix of plaids and prints of different patterns and colors—a tartan vest, for instance, with a paisley tie, and a sky blue shirt. Or black pants, a brown striped shirt, and a tan vest. Nutty clothes—so out they're in, cool because he's wearing them. In *What About Bob?* Murray, as Bob Wiley, the patient of anhedonic psychiatrist Leo Marvin (Richard Dreyfuss, the un–Lee Marvin), visits the Marvins' summerhouse and succeeds in making even dishwashing, for Chrissake, fun for Marvin's family, though not for Dr. Marvin, of course. Murray and Dreyfuss reportedly came to despise each other in the making of the movie—Murray's unscripted silliness drove Dreyfuss crazy, in exactly the same way Bob drives Leo mad in the movie—and I know we're supposed to love Murray and hate Dreyfuss, and I do, I do, but I'm much closer to serious, striving Dr. Marvin than I am to antic Bob, which is, I suppose, what this essay is about: my distance from Murray, my yearning to be him, the gap between us, the way he makes life seem bearable (fun, amusing) if I could only get with his giddiness. (I can't.) In Murray's golf book, Cheryl Anderson, a golf pro, says, "I was practicing at the far end of the Grand Cypress range one morning. There wasn't another soul there, just a set of clubs in one of the stands a few yards from me. Then a figure appeared in the distance. He was on a bicycle, at the same time carrying a boom box. It was Bill. He gave me a quick nod, then walked to the clubs, set down his box, and flipped on a tape. It was an out-there rock group called Big Head Todd and the Monsters. He hit balls to the music for a while, then picked up the box, nodded goodbye, and pedaled off."

Physical grace as a container, then, for spiritual grace, if that's not putting too fine a point on it. "A lot of *Rushmore* is about the struggle to retain civility and kindness in the face of extraordinary pain," Murray said shortly after the film was released. "And I've felt a lot of that in my life." This is what Murray knows so well and what I've been trying to learn from him: life is a shit-storm; laugh (somehow and barely). In his self-interview, he tells Santa a story about making *Scrooged*: "We're shooting in this Victorian set for weeks, and [Buddy] Hackett is pissed all the time, angry that he's not the center of attention, and finally we get to the scene where we've gotta shoot him at the window, saying, 'Go get my boots,' or whatever. The set is stocked with Victorian extras and little children in Oliver kind of outfits, and the director says, 'All right, Bud, just give it whatever you want.' And Hackett goes off on a rant. Unbelievably obscene. He's talking—this is Hackett, not me— about the Virgin Mary, a limerick sort of thing, and all these children and families . . . the look of absolute horror. He's going on and on and

on, and finally he stops. It's just total horror, and the camera's still rolling. You can hear it, sort of a grinding noise. And the director says,
'Anything else, Bud?'" Murray loves the director's dignity against the
shit-storm, his refusal to be cowed or fazed.

In an article in *Film Comment*, "The Passion of Bill Murray," Greg
Solman says about Murray's performance in *Mad Dog and Glory*,
"What's remarkable about the performance is how well Murray can
now convey the intrinsic humor of his characters and situations but dif-
ferentiate them from others in his past by eliminating irony, sarcasm,
and self-reflexivity." This seems to me wrong. In the twenty-five years
Murray's been acting, he's gotten better not by ever going away for a
second from irony but by finding deeper and deeper levels of emotion
within it. At the end of *Scrooged*, Murray, the scabrous president of a
television network who recovers the Christmas spirit, walks onto the set
of the cheesy, live Christmas special he's produced, announcing: "It's
Christmas Eve. It's the one night of the year where we all act a little
nicer, we smile a little easier, we cheer a little more. For a couple of
hours out of the whole year we are the people that we always hoped
we would be. It's a miracle, it's really a sort of a miracle, because it
happens every Christmas Eve. You'll want it every day of your life, and
it can happen to you. I believe in it now. I believe it's going to happen to me now. I'm ready for it." A few moments later, when he has
trouble dragging his long lost beloved, Claire, in front of the camera,
Murray, clearly improvising, says, "This is like boning a marlin." It's
Murray's fidelity to his own mordant consciousness and the locating of
joy within that mordancy that is, to me, the miracle. This is getting a
little overadulatory, so I'll stop.

An unfortunate fact about stuttering is that it prevents you from ever
entirely losing self-consciousness when expressing such traditional and
truly important emotions as love, hate, joy, and deep pain. Always first
aware not of the naked feeling itself but of the best way to phrase the
feeling so as to avoid verbal repetition, you come to think of emotions
as belonging to other people, being the world's happy property and not
yours—not really yours except by way of disingenuous circumlocution.
Hence my iron grip on ironic distance; hence my adoration of Murray;
hence my lifelong love of novels (*The Great Gatsby*, *A Separate Peace*,

Ford Madox Ford's *The Good Soldier*, Günter Grass's *Cat and Mouse*) in which a neurasthenic narrator contemplates his more vital second self; hence this essay. My first novel is about a sportswriter's vicarious relationship with a college basketball player; my most recent book, a diary of an NBA season, is largely given over to my obsession with Gary Payton. What is it about such a relationship that speaks so strongly to me? Art calling out to Life, Un-Life wanting Life? Are these just parts of myself in eternal debate or am I really this anemic? Murray, for all his anomie, likes being in the world. Bully for him. I love standing in shadow, gazing intently at ethereal glare.

Their Eyes Were Watching God: **What Does Soulful Mean?**

ZADIE SMITH

When I was fourteen I was given *Their Eyes Were Watching God* by my mother. I was reluctant to read it. I knew what she meant by giving it to me, and I resented the inference. In the same spirit she had introduced me to *Wide Sargasso Sea* and *The Bluest Eye*, and I had not liked either of them (better to say, I had not *allowed* myself to like either of them). I preferred my own freely chosen, heterogeneous reading list. I flattered myself I ranged widely in my reading, never choosing books for genetic or sociocultural reasons. Spotting *Their Eyes Were Watching God* unopened on my bedside table, my mother persisted:

"But you'll like it."

"Why, because she's *black*?"

"No—because it's really good writing."

I had my own ideas of "good writing." It was a category that did not include aphoristic or overtly "lyrical" language, mythic imagery, accurately rendered "folk speech" or the love tribulations of women. My literary defenses were up in preparation for *Their Eyes Were Watching God*. Then I read the first page:

Ships at a distance have every man's wish on board. For some they come in with the tide. For others they sail forever on the horizon, never out of sight, never landing until the Watcher turns his eyes away in resignation, his dreams mocked to death by Time. That is the life of men.

Now, women forget all those things they don't want to remember, and remember everything they don't want to forget. The dream is the truth. Then they act and do things accordingly.

It was an aphorism, yet it had me pinned to the ground, unable to deny its strength. It capitalized *Time* (I was against the capitalization of abstract nouns), but still I found myself melancholy for these nameless men and their inevitable losses. The second part, about women, struck home. It remains as accurate a description of my mother and me as I have ever read: *Then they act and do things accordingly.* Well, all right then. I relaxed in my chair a little and laid down my pencil. I inhaled that book. Three hours later I was finished and crying a lot, for reasons that both were, and were not, to do with the tragic finale.

I lost many literary battles the day I read *Their Eyes Were Watching God.* I had to concede that occasionally aphorisms have their power. I had to give up the idea that Keats had a monopoly on the lyrical:

> She was stretched on her back beneath the pear tree soaking in the alto chant of the visiting bees, the gold of the sun and the panting breath of the breeze when the inaudible voice of it all came to her. She saw a dust-nearing bee sink into the sanctum of a bloom; the thousand sister-calyxes arch to meet the love embrace and the ecstatic shiver of the tree from root to tiniest branch creaming in every blossom and frothing with delight. So this was a marriage! She had been summoned to behold a revelation. Then Janie felt a pain remorseless sweet that left her limp and languid.[1]

I had to admit that mythic language is startling when it's good:

> Death, that strange being with the huge square toes who lived way in the West. The great one who lived in the straight house

---

1 But I still resist "limp and languid."

like a platform without sides to it, and without a roof. What need has Death for a cover, and what winds can blow against him?

My resistance to dialogue (encouraged by Nabokov, whom I idolized) struggled and then tumbled before Hurston's ear for black colloquial speech. In the mouths of unlettered people she finds the bliss of quotidian metaphor:

"If God don't think no mo' 'bout 'em than Ah do, they's a lost ball in de high grass."

Of wisdom lightly worn:

"To my thinkin' mourning oughtn't tuh last no longer'n grief."

Her conversations reveal individual personalities, accurately, swiftly, as if they had no author at all:

"Where y'all come from in sich uh big haste?" Lee Coker asked. "Middle Georgy," Starks answered briskly. "Joe Starks is mah name, from in and through Georgy."

"You and yo' daughter goin' tuh join wid us in fellowship?" the other reclining figure asked. "Mighty glad to have yuh. Hicks is the name. Guv'nor Amos Hicks from Buford, South Carolina. Free, single, disengaged."

"I god, Ah ain't nowhere near old enough to have no grown daughter. This here is mah wife."

Hicks sank back and lost interest at once.

"Where is de Mayor?" Starks persisted. "Ah wants tuh talk wid *him.*"

"Youse uh mite too previous for dat," Coker told him. "Us ain't got none yit."

Above all, I had to let go of my objection to the love tribulations of women. The story of Janie's progress through three marriages confronts the reader with the significant idea that the choice one makes between partners, between one man and another (or one woman and another) stretches beyond romance. It is, in the end, the choice between values, possibilities, futures, hopes, arguments (shared concepts that fit the world as you experience it), languages (shared words that fit the world as you believe it to be) and lives. A world you share with Logan Killicks is evidently not the same world you would share with Vergible "Tea Cake" Woods. In these two discrete worlds, you will not even think the same way; a mind trapped with Logan is freed with Tea Cake. But who, in this context, dare speak of freedoms? In practical terms, a black woman in turn-of-the-century America, a woman like Janie, or like Hurston herself, had approximately the same civil liberties as a farm animal: "De nigger woman is de mule uh de world." So goes Janie's grandmother's famous line—it hurt my pride to read it. It hurts Janie, too; she rejects the realpolitik of her grandmother, embarking on an existential revenge that is of the imagination and impossible to restrict:

> She knew that God tore down the old world every evening and built a new one by sun-up. It was wonderful to see it take form with the sun and emerge from the gray dust of its making. The familiar people and things had failed her so she hung over the gate and looked up the road towards way off.

That part of Janie that is looking for someone (or something) that "spoke for far horizon" has its proud ancestors in Elizabeth Bennet, in Dorothea Brooke, in Jane Eyre, even—in a very debased form—in Emma Bovary. Since the beginning of fiction concerning the love tribulations of women (which is to say, since the beginning of fiction), the "romantic quest" aspect of these fictions has been too often casually ridiculed: not long ago I sat down to dinner with an American woman who told me how disappointed she had been to finally read *Middlemarch* and find that it was "just this long, whiny, trawling search for a man!" Those who read *Middlemarch* in that way will find little in *Their Eyes Were Watching God* to please them. It's about a girl who takes some time to find the man she really loves. It is about the discovery of self in and through another. It implies that even the dark and terrible banality of racism can recede to a vanishing point when you understand,

and are understood by, another human being. Goddammit if it doesn't claim that love sets you free. These days "self-actualization" is the aim, and if you can't do it alone you are admitting a weakness. The potential rapture of human relationships to which Hurston gives unabashed expression, the profound "self-crushing love" that Janie feels for Tea Cake, may, I suppose, look like the dull finale of a "long, whiny, trawling search for a man." For Tea Cake and Janie, though, the choice of each other is experienced not as desperation, but as discovery, and the need felt on both sides causes them joy, not shame. That Tea Cake would not be *our* choice, that we disapprove of him often, and despair of him occasionally, only lends power to the portrait. He seems to act with freedom, and Janie to choose him freely. We have no power; we only watch. Despite the novel's fairy-tale structure (as far as husbands go, third time's the charm), it is not a novel of wish fulfillment, least of all the fulfillment of *our* wishes.[2] It is odd to diagnose weakness where lovers themselves do not feel it.

After that first reading of the novel, I wept, and not only for Tea Cake, and not simply for the perfection of the writing, nor even the real loss I felt upon leaving the world contained in its pages. It meant something more than all that to me, something I could not, or would not, articulate. Later, I took it to the dinner table, still holding on to it, as we do sometimes with books we are not quite ready to relinquish.

"So?" my mother asked.

I told her it was basically sound.

◆

At fourteen, I did Zora Neale Hurston a critical disservice. I feared my "extraliterary" feelings for her. I wanted to be an objective aesthete and not a sentimental fool. I disliked the idea of "identifying" with the fiction I read: I wanted to like Hurston because she represented "good writing," not because she represented me. In the two decades since, Zora Neale Hurston has gone from being a well-kept, well-loved secret among black women of my mother's generation to an entire literary

---

2 Again, *Middlemarch* is an interesting comparison. Readers often prefer Lydgate and are disappointed at Dorothea's choice of Ladislaw.

industry—biographies[3] and films and Oprah and African American literature departments all pay homage to her life[4] and work as avatars of black woman-ness. In the process, a different kind of critical disservice is being done to her, an overcompensation in the opposite direction. In *Their Eyes Were Watching God*, Janie is depressed by Joe Starks's determination to idolize her: he intends to put her on a lonely pedestal before the whole town and establish a symbol (the Mayor's Wife) in place of the woman she is. Something similar has been done to Hurston herself. She is like Janie, set on her porch-pedestal ("Ah done nearly languished tuh death up dere"), far from the people and things she really cared about, representing only the ideas and beliefs of her admirers, distorted by their gaze. In the space of one volume of collected essays, we find a critic arguing that the negative criticism of Hurston's work represents an "intellectual lynching" by black men, white men and white women; a critic dismissing Hurston's final work with the sentence "*Seraph on the Suwanee* is not even about black people, which is no crime, but *is* about white people who are bores, which is"; and another explaining the "one great flaw" in *Their Eyes Were Watching God*: Hurston's "curious insistence" on having her main character's tale told in the omniscient third person (instead of allowing Janie her "voice outright"). We are in a critical world of some banality here, one in which most of our nineteenth-century heroines would be judged oppressed creatures, cruelly deprived of the therapeutic first-person voice. It is also a world in which what is called the "Black Female Literary Tradition" is beyond reproach:

> Black women writers have consistently rejected the falsification of their Black female experience, thereby avoiding the negative stereotypes such falsification has often created in the white American female and Black male literary traditions. Unlike many of their Black male and white female peers, Black women writers have usually refused to dispense with whatever was clearly Black

---

3 The (very good) biography is *Wrapped in Rainbows: The Life of Zora Neale Hurston* by Valerie Boyd. Also very good is *Zora Neale Hurston: A Life in Letters*, collected and edited by Carla Kaplan.

4 *Dust Tracks on a Road* is Hurston's autobiography.

and/or female in their sensibilities in an effort to achieve the
mythical "neutral" voice of universal art.[5]

Gratifying as it would be to agree that black women writers "have
consistently rejected the falsification" of their experience, the honest
reader knows that this is simply not the case. In place of negative falsification, we have nurtured, in the past thirty years, a new fetishization.
Black female protagonists are now unerringly strong and soulful; they
are sexually voracious and unafraid; they take the unreal forms of earth
mothers, African queens, divas, spirits of history; they process grandly
through novels thick with a breed of greeting-card lyricism. They have
little of the complexity, the flaws and uncertainties, depth and beauty
of Janie Crawford and the novel she springs from. They are pressed
into service as role models to patch over our psychic wounds; they are
perfect;[6] they overcompensate. The truth is, black women writers, while
writing many wonderful things,[7] have been no more or less successful
at avoiding the falsification of human experience than any other group
of writers. It is not the Black Female Literary Tradition that makes
Hurston great. It is Hurston herself. Zora Neale Hurston—capable of
expressing human vulnerability as well as its strength, lyrical without
sentiment, romantic and yet rigorous and one of the few truly eloquent
writers of sex—is as exceptional among black women writers as Tolstoy
is among white male writers.[8]

It is, however, true that Hurston rejected the "neutral universal" for
her novels—she wrote unapologetically in the black-inflected dialect in

---

5 All the critical voices quoted above can be found in *Zora Neale Hurston's* Their
Eyes Were Watching God: *Modern Critical Interpretations*, edited by Harold Bloom.

6 Hurston, by contrast, wanted her writing to demonstrate the fact that "Negroes
are no better nor no worse, and at times as boring as everybody else."

7 Not least of which is Alice Walker's original introduction to *Their Eyes Were
Watching God*. By championing the book, she rescued Hurston from forty years
of obscurity.

8 A footnote for the writers in the audience: *Their Eyes Were Watching God* was
written in seven weeks.

which she was raised. It took bravery to do that: the result was hostility and disinterest. In 1937, black readers were embarrassed by the unlettered nature of the dialogue and white readers preferred the exoticism of her anthropological writings. Who wanted to read about the poor Negroes one saw on the corner every day? Hurston's biographers make clear that no matter what positive spin she put on it, her life was horribly difficult: she finished life working as a cleaner and died in obscurity. It is understandable that her reclaiming should be an emotive and personal journey for black readers and black critics. But still, one wants to make a neutral and solid case for her greatness, to say something more substantial than "She is my sister and I love her." As a reader, I want to claim fellowship with "good writing" without limits; to be able to say that Hurston is my sister and Baldwin is my brother, and so is Kafka my brother, and Nabokov, and Woolf my sister, and Eliot and Ozick. Like all readers, I want my limits to be drawn by my own sensibilities, not by my melanin count. These forms of criticism that make black women the privileged readers of a black woman writer go against Hurston's own grain. She saw things otherwise: "When I set my hat at a certain angle and saunter down Seventh Avenue. . . . the cosmic Zora emerges. . . . How *can* anybody deny themselves the pleasure of my company? It's beyond me!" This is exactly right. No one should deny themselves the pleasure of Zora—of whatever color or background or gender. She's too delightful not to be shared. We all deserve to savor her neologisms ("sankled," "monstropolous," "rawbony") or to read of the effects of a bad marriage, sketched with tragic accuracy:

> The years took all the fight out of Janie's face. For a while she thought it was gone from her soul. No matter what Jody did, she said nothing. She had learned how to talk some and leave some. She was a rut in the road. Plenty of life beneath the surface but it was kept beaten down by the wheels. Sometimes she stuck out into the future, imagining her life different from what it was. But mostly she lived between her hat and her heels, with her emotional disturbances like shade patterns in the woods—come and gone with the sun. She got nothing from Jody except what money could buy, and she was giving away what she didn't value.

The visual imagination on display in *Their Eyes Were Watching God* shares its clarity and iconicity with Christian storytelling—many scenes in the novel put one in mind of the bold-stroke illustrations in a children's Bible: young Janie staring at a photograph, not understanding that the black girl in the crowd is her; Joe Starks atop a dead mule's distended belly, giving a speech; Tea Cake bitten high on his cheekbone by that rabid dog. I watched the TV footage of Hurricane Katrina with a strong sense of déjà vu, thinking of Hurston's flood rather than Noah's: "Not the dead of sick and ailing with friends at the pillow and the feet . . . [but] the sodden and the bloated; the sudden dead, their eyes flung wide open in judgment. . . ."

Above all, Hurston is essential universal reading because she is neither self-conscious nor restricted. She was raised in the real Eatonville, Florida, an all-black town; this unique experience went some way to making Hurston the writer she was. She grew up a fully human being, unaware that she was meant to consider herself a minority, an other, an exotic or something depleted in rights, talents, desires and expectations. As an adult, away from Eatonville, she found the world was determined to do its best to remind her of her supposed inferiority, but Hurston was already made, and the metaphysical confidence she claimed for her life ("I am not tragically colored") is present, with equal, refreshing force, in her fiction. She liked to yell "Culllaaaah Struck!"[9] when she entered a fancy party—almost everybody was. But Hurston herself was not. "Blackness," as she understood it and wrote about it, is as natural and inevitable and complete to her as, say, "Frenchness" is to Flaubert. It is also as complicated, as full of blessings and curses. One can be no more removed from it than from one's arm, but it is no more the total measure of one's being than an arm is.

——◆—◆——

But still, after all that, there is something else to say—and the "neutral universal" of literary criticism pens me in and makes it difficult. To write critically in English is to aspire to neutrality, to the high style of, say, Lionel Trilling or Edmund Wilson. In the high style, one's

---

9 See chapter 16 for a sad portrayal of a truly color-struck lady, Mrs. Turner.

loves never seem partial or personal, or even like "loves," because white novelists are not white novelists but simply "novelists," and white characters are not white characters but simply "human," and criticism of both is not partial or personal but a matter of aesthetics. Such critics will always sound like the neutral universal, and the black women who have championed *Their Eyes Were Watching God* in the past, and the one doing so now, will seem like black women talking about a black book. When I began this piece, it felt important to distance myself from that idea. By doing so, I misrepresent a vital aspect of my response to this book, one that is entirely personal, as any response to a novel shall be. Fact is, I *am* a black woman,[10] and a slither of this book goes straight into my soul, I suspect, for that reason. And though it is, to me, a mistake to say, "Unless you are a black woman, you will never fully comprehend this novel," it is also disingenuous to claim that many black women do not respond to this book in a particularly powerful manner that would seem "extraliterary." Those aspects of *Their Eyes Were Watching God* that plumb so profoundly the ancient buildup of cultural residue that is (for convenience's sake) called "Blackness"[11] are the parts that my own "Blackness," as far as it goes, cannot help but respond to personally. At fourteen I couldn't find words (or words I liked) for the marvelous feeling of recognition that came with these characters who had my hair, my eyes, my skin, even the ancestors of the rhythm of my speech.[12] These forms of identification are so natural to white readers—(Of course Rabbit Angstrom is like me! Of course Madame Bovary is like me!)— that they believe themselves above personal identification, or at least believe that they are identifying only at the highest, existential levels (His soul is like my soul. He is human; I am human). White readers

---

10 I think this was the point my mother was trying to make.

11 As Kafka's *The Trial* plumbs that ancient buildup of cultural residue that is called "Jewishness."

12 Down on the muck, Janie and Tea Cake befriend the "Saws," workers from the Caribbean.

often believe they are colorblind.[13] I always thought I was a colorblind reader—until I read this novel, and that ultimate cliché of black life that is inscribed in the word *soulful* took on new weight and sense for me. But what does *soulful* even mean? The dictionary has it this way: "expressing or appearing to express deep and often sorrowful feeling." The culturally black meaning adds several more shades of color. First shade: *soulfulness* is sorrowful feeling transformed into something beautiful, creative and self-renewing, and—as it reaches a pitch— ecstatic. It is an alchemy of pain. In *Their Eyes Were Watching God*, when the townsfolk sing for the death of the mule, this is an example of *soulfulness*. Another shade: to be soulful is to follow and *fall in line* with a feeling, to go where it takes you and not to go against its grain.[14] When young Janie takes her lead from the blossoming tree and sits on her gatepost to kiss a passing boy, this is an example of *soulfulness*. A final shade: the word *soulful*, like its Jewish cousin, *schmaltz*,[15] has its roots in the digestive tract. "Soul food" is simple, flavorsome, hearty, unfussy, with spice. When Janie puts on her overalls and joyfully goes to work in the muck with Tea Cake, this is an example of *soulfulness*.[16]

This is a beautiful novel about soulfulness. That it should be so is a tribute to Hurston's skill. She makes "culture"—that slow and particular[17] and artificial accretion of habit and circumstance—seem

---

13 Until they read books featuring nonwhite characters. I once overheard a young white man at a book festival say to his friend, "Have you read the new Kureishi? Same old thing—loads of Indian people." To which you want to reply, "Have you read the new Franzen? Same old thing—loads of white people."

14 At its most common and banal: catching a beat, following a rhythm.

15 In the *Oxford English Dictionary*: "*Schmaltz* n. informal. excessive sentimentality, esp. in music or movies. ORIGIN 1930s: from Yiddish *schmaltz*, from German *Schmalz* 'dripping, lard.'"

16 Is there anything less soulful than attempting to define soulfulness?

17 In literary terms, we know that there is a tipping point at which the cultural particular—while becoming no less culturally particular—is accepted by readers as the neutral universal. The previously "Jewish fiction" of Philip Roth is now "fiction." We have moved from the particular complaints of Portnoy to the universal claims of Everyman.

as natural and organic and beautiful as the sunrise. She allows me to indulge in what Philip Roth once called "the romance of oneself," a literary value I dislike and yet, confronted with this beguiling book, cannot resist. She makes "black woman-ness" appear a real, tangible quality, an essence I can almost believe I share, however improbably, with millions of complex individuals across centuries and continents and languages and religions. . . .

Almost—but not quite. Better to say, when I'm reading this book, I believe it, with my whole soul. It allows me to say things I wouldn't normally. Things like *"She is my sister and I love her."*

Sonya's Last Speech, or, Double-Voicing: An Essay in Sixteen Sections

CHARLES BAXTER

1. MY CHEKHOV PROBLEM

The Fifth Forum movie theater in Ann Arbor, before it became the Ann Arbor Theater and then was closed (now it's a seedy singles' bar called "Closer" or "Closer"—I don't know which way to pronounce it), was, in its day, one of those low-tech operations that existed before the advent of multiplexes. One employee would sell tickets, another would dole out the popcorn and candy, and a third sat up in the projection booth, dozing between reels. In the early 1980s it was one of the only theaters in southeastern Michigan where you could go to see independent and foreign films. I went there often, usually by myself. I'd buy my popcorn and sit down in the back because I don't like to sit close; I get headaches. In theaters like the Fifth Forum, your shoes would often slip on the greasy floor because of random deposits of buttered popcorn, and in fact the smell of candy wrappers and grease now has the association for me of what I'd call movie-longing, the sugared buttery smell of someone else's desires coming to life on the screen.

The Fifth Forum is the only theater where I've walked out on the same movie twice. The movie in question was *My Dinner with Andre*, with Wallace Shawn and Andre Gregory. The first time I saw it, I thought it was a pretentious piece of downtown pseudo-art—a kitschy talkfest for intellectuals—and I walked out after about thirty-five minutes. I thought the script was insubstantial and found Andre Gregory insufferable. But then I read the reviews and was almost shouted at by my highbrow friend for having turned my back on this monument to the cinematic art, so I paid my admission again a week later and sat down and watched about forty minutes of it before walking out again into the late-spring Ann Arbor night.

A few years later, a movie called *Vanya on 42nd Street* came to the Fifth Forum, and I thought: *I'd better go see this, even if I don't want to.* For one thing, it had the dire combination of Wallace Shawn and Andre Gregory again, though this time with Shawn as actor and Gregory as director, in an adaptation of Anton Chekhov's *Uncle Vanya*, a play I knew pretty well. Duty sent me down there. I could imagine some academic Grand Inquisitor at a cocktail party asking me ("you're a literary type, right?") whether I had seen it and my flustered response that, no, last weekend I had gone to see *Aliens*.

The truth is that I always have had a Chekhov problem. It's serious. My Chekhov problem is that I usually go through a siege of boredom with his plays and stories before I arrive at a condition of aesthetic excitement. With me, it's either boredom or excitement, nothing in between. In a way, I am like a Chekhov character, who sits passively for three acts before getting his gun in the last act. In the stories, there is a large element of gray—even in Russian, according to Nabokov, the prose feels gray—and sometimes, in my late-twentieth-/early-twenty-first-century way, I'm just not up for the path through the monochrome to the small, perfectly placed explosions. This is my failing, and I hate these moments because they expose me to myself as the philistine that I know myself to be, especially after work, when I want to see cars explode and people shot dead for no reason, and monsters, if they're available, to cheer me up.

So anyway I sat there in the Fifth Forum, my shoes slipping on the popcorn butter on the floor and a recalcitrant spring in the seat giving my ass a poke every now and then. The movie came on, with its rehearsal framework, and I thought: *There's Larry Pine playing Dr. Astrov, he's pretty good.* And then—it had been a long day of teaching in Detroit at Wayne State—I felt myself drifting off to yawn-and-sleepy time, but through sheer willpower, and aided by my Coca-Cola, I managed to stay awake in a state of half-dozing twilight consciousness, waiting for the first speech in the play that I care about, Sonya's outburst about how plain she is. Sonya, in this production, was played by Brooke Smith, an actor (in those days we said "actress") I had never heard of.

Brooke Smith delivered the speech, and I sat bolt upright.

From then on I was in a state of nearly sick excitement, nervous sweat oozing out of me. But I also happened to know, having once studied *Uncle Vanya*, that Sonya gives the last speech in the play, a curtain speech, and for various reasons I was afraid of it. And when we finally got there, to that speech, I found myself first disabled with tears, and then very close to sobs. The movie ended and I could not leave the theater. I had to be ushered out by the pimply teenaged usher, who took a very dim view of me. "Show's over, man," he said, broom in hand. I drove back home, thinking, "What just happened?"

2. TEARS

To paraphrase Stephen Dobyns's poem "Lil' Darlin'," *I don't like tears.* And not just because I'm a man. I don't believe in tears because the feelings behind them often have force but also no content; often, if there *is* content, the content is unreliable. Tears are an unstable and unseemly aesthetic response; they are a sign of intensity but not necessarily of quality or precision. Good art is always precise. Just because a reaction is intense doesn't mean that it's true, or accurate. Tears suggest manipulation in the aesthetic materials, or a personal vulnerability to certain kinds of subject matter. A one-time friend of mine who had a mild sociopathic streak once observed to me that people cry at movies and books not because what they had seen or read was true but *because they had been exposed to something they wished were true but that they knew to be false.* That is, the untruth (*not* the truth) of something causes you to cry.

This is a good reason not to believe in tears. These considerations also deposit us in the dreaded land of Sentimentality, where we don't know where we are. More of this later.

3. WHAT SONYA SAYS—(A QUICK PARAPHRASE)

At the end of *Uncle Vanya*, Sonya has discovered that Dr. Astrov, with whom she is in love, will never love her in return. Astrov is, instead, attracted to Sonya's beautiful stepmother, Elena, who eventually rejects him. Sonya's uncle Vanya has also fallen in love with Elena, who finds Vanya ridiculous. Elena, in turn, is unhappily married to someone I will refer to simply as "the professor," a pretentious hypochondriac who has schemes to sell off the estate but who is blocked in these efforts by Vanya and Sonya, who actually own it. There are other characters. By the end of the play, Sonya has been grievously disappointed in love and in life. Vanya's disappointments are similar and equally intense. In the last act, out of love and desperation, she has been compelled to talk her beloved uncle out of suicide. Then the beautiful stepmother, the professor, and Dr. Astrov depart in their respective sleighs, leaving Sonya alone with her uncle and a couple of other minor characters.

Chekhov has a purely dramatic problem here, which is that every one of his central characters, including Astrov, has been disappointed or frustrated or abandoned. If the curtain were to close on this situation, the playwright would have a truthful but unsatisfyingly undramatic finale on his hands. It would be like trying to end a story in which all the characters have lost everything. Chekhov did write such stories. Nevertheless, he usually avoided endings of that type, where the events may seem to be true to life, but within the story, do not *feel* right. "In the Ravine" is a bit like that. Aesthetic excitement should always trump depressive feelings. So Sonya's final speech provides the play with a grand and desperate rhetorical flourish that is uplifting, or is meant to be, a big moment in which happiness and sorrow, the past and the present, are combined (Eugene O'Neill does the same thing at the end of *Long Day's Journey into Night*—and most of Shakespeare's plays end with this kind of curtain speech, as does *The Great Gatsby*).

Depending on which translation from the Russian you use, Sonya makes approximately three assertions in her curtain speech.

1. She and her uncle will go on working without reward, and then they'll die ("meekly" or "submissively" or "without complaining" depending on the translation).
2. In the afterlife she and her uncle will tell God their story, and they will look down on the world and life, now made "beautiful" and "bright," and they will reflect back on their sufferings with peace and forbearance.

3. She and her uncle will be at peace (or will "rest") and their sufferings will be transformed into a caress; for the two of them, an absence of joy in life will turn, after death, into repose. In effect, they will experience redemption. *I believe this*, Sonya insists; *I really do.*

4. CHARLIE IS SUSPICIOUS

But there is something wrong, off-key, that makes me suspicious in retrospect about this speech's content: Sonya has rarely in the play mentioned God or faith or the afterlife or religion or angels. She is, as one of my students once said, an "earthy girl." All this leaves the suspicion dawning in the mind that Sonya doesn't actually believe a word of what she's saying. There's another small detail in the speech that makes the observer skeptical: Sonya says that she believes all this, and then she repeats that phrase, in a protesting-too-much style: *yes, yes, she really believes it, she really does.* She asserts her belief several times. She insists on it. Who wouldn't be skeptical? She's formulating these claims about redemption to cheer up her uncle Vanya, and maybe to cheer up herself, and to cheer up an unwary audience sitting out there in the dark. In effect, she's double-voicing: She's saying what she would like to be true as if it *were* true, even though she probably knows it isn't. In speaking to her uncle, Sonya is really talking to herself. That's the nature of double-voicing. People talk to themselves when they are ostensibly talking to others, and they talk themselves this way out of despair all the time. These rhetorical maneuvers don't get into literature that often, or, rather, they do, and we don't bother to notice.

5. A NOTE ON THE TRANSLATIONS (FROM VALERIE LAKEN, MY FORMER STUDENT AND A FINE FICTION WRITER IN HER OWN RIGHT)

"In general Chekhov translations are not too suspect, mainly because he doesn't play with language too much, not as much as most other big Russian authors. But a couple of points that just occurred to me off the bat: his language feels a bit simpler than some translations I've seen. For example, the Ronald Hingley translation I have has the line, 'We shall hear the angels, we shall see the sky sparkling with diamonds.' Well, this feels slightly flowery to me. There is no 'sparkling' in the original (it's just 'We will see the whole sky in diamonds'). There is no shall/will difference in Russian. And there are no articles in Russian either, no 'the' or 'a/an,' so, for example, that line could also be translated as 'We will hear angels' (not 'the' angels, which to me assumes they exist). Minor matters, surely, but to me Sonya doesn't seem like a flowery girl but a more practical one. One other quick note: the last word, 'otdokhnem,' the phrase that keeps getting repeated, which in Hingley is translated as 'we shall find peace.' What he's rendering as 'to find peace' is really one Russian verb, 'otdokhnut.' It certainly does mean 'to find peace,' but interestingly it is much more commonly used to mean 'to rest, to relax, to rest up, to take a vacation.' It is the everyday go-to verb for any of those meanings, a very common (not lofty) verb. So anyway, it obviously resonates with all the work Sonya and Vanya are doing in that scene and in general."

6. ONE TRANSLATOR, LAURENCE SENELICK, IS ALSO SUSPICIOUS

"The Russian, *My otdokhnyom*, connotes 'We shall breathe easily' and is connected etymologically to words such as *dushno*, used by characters to say they are being stifled. The literal English translation, 'We shall rest,' with its harsh dental ending, fails to convey Sonya's meaning sonically or spiritually."

7. PEACE, REST. WHAT'S THE DIFFERENCE?

The reason this matters so much is that we can't really be sure what Sonya means "spiritually" or otherwise in this speech. In a way, there is no literal meaning; it's all metaphoric. She has given us no spiritual context for her remarks. She is speaking about a hypothetical condition. She's improvising a solution. And what she is offering up in this hypothesis is a quasi-Christian explanation for the logic of life's suffering. It's not heaven she's offering to her uncle, exactly; it's rest. It's ordinary: a kind of plain old catnap that goes on for eternity. Of course, sometimes sleep looks like heaven, especially if you're an insomniac, as both Vanya and Sonya are in the play (the play is full of insomniacs).

Most versions of heaven are, I am compelled to say, implausible. The story of heaven is not a story that I happen to believe, unless heaven is also here and now and within. But "rest" is not particularly implausible, and both words imply the other: Peace involves rest, most of the time, and rest is nearly always peaceful.

8. CHARLIE IS STILL SUSPICIOUS

But no matter how you parse Sonya's last speech, no matter how you translate it, there is still life beyond the grave; there is still a god who listens rather than speaks and who does not condemn; there are still angels, and diamonds; there is still a flood of mercy (or "compassion that will fill the world"). And all these artifacts of faith are appearing in the play for the first time, like props brought on from the wings by busy stagehands in the play's closing moments. Rhetoric is the deus ex machina here, and Sonya is insisting on it, insisting three times that she believes what she says. Within this desperate and fevered set of assertions, there is also, almost literally, a god and an afterlife brought on in the machine to be on the stage to save the situation, and the play, and Vanya, and maybe Sonya, too, as well as the ticket holders. But if God and the angels are the solution, then what is the problem?

The problem in the closing pages of *Uncle Vanya* is the problem the entire play has created, which is the problem of living without hope, the problem of depression and of despair that follows suffering. *Uncle Vanya* is very clearly about a particular theme, which is not true of all of Chekhov's plays. But *Uncle Vanya* is consistently about spiritual, sexual, and career disappointment: having a set of hopes and then seeing them dashed. In life such problems must be solved one way or another and put into a place where the disappointment is somehow endurable, and the threat of despair or depression does not loom ominously. The subject matter in turn creates an aesthetic problem—that is, how to present suffering so that the object that holds it (the play, the story) is aesthetically satisfying. This problem invariably leads to a second challenge, which requires an answer of some sort: How does one go on living in a condition of despair? How do you continue if you've been fatally disappointed by your life? If your life has failed, if your hopes have failed, if nothing has worked out, if you've been disappointed in everything you've tried, if you cannot imagine a future, then why go on living? Don't say, "masochism." That's no answer. In *The Myth of Sisyphus*,

Albert Camus famously observed, "There is but one truly philosophical problem, and that is suicide. Judging whether life is or is not worth living amounts to answering the fundamental question of philosophy."

How do you deal with depression and despair in a play or a story or a poem without making the play or the story or the poem depressing and aesthetically unsatisfying? Or sentimental and sententious? Is this a pseudoproblem? I don't think so.

Despair, at the close of *Uncle Vanya*, is Sonya's challenge. Aesthetic deflation—flatness—is Chekhov's. Sonya's task is to remedy a murderous melancholia, to address that question, and to solve Chekhov's problem into the bargain: Because she loves her uncle Vanya, she must cheer him up enough so that he (and she herself) can live. Chekhov must write a speech that will give the play the appearance if not the reality of uplift. Sonya is not thinking of herself, but of course she can't avoid considering her own situation as a spinster-to-be, and by speaking to Vanya, perhaps she will cheer herself up as well. How she does this should be of interest to any writer or to anyone who has wrestled with this particular beast.

What happens is that Sonya gets carried away. She knows it, Vanya knows it, but often, I think, the audience doesn't know it.

Sonya begins by telling Vanya to wait. Waiting is what one does when all the alternatives are dire, impossible, or closed off. Then, because she really can't see any earthly solution, she says something she probably doesn't believe about *the* or *an* afterlife, and because the weight of despair is finally too much for anyone to bear, there comes a moment when she herself is swept away by what she is saying and begins to believe it herself. Double-voicing occurs when *a need overcomes skepticism or even common sense*; and faith, or a comforting hypothesis, is poured in to fill that void. This is heartbreaking to witness. The speaker, who begins by improvising, starts to believe his or her own words, and then insists on that belief. In parallel situations, the salesman begins to believe his own pitch; the liar loses track of his lies. Sonya, as I've suggested, is speaking to Vanya but really she addresses herself. And after all, her situation mirrors his.

Chekhov is always asking us this question, "How does anyone live with emptiness?" His stories and plays often create a condition bordering on despair, in which happiness is located elsewhere, such as Moscow for the three sisters, or in loving Dr. Astrov for Sonya, or the preservation of the countryside for Dr. Astrov himself. And then, when no expectation finds its way into actuality, Chekhov's plays grandly, and heroically, struggle with their aftermath condition, and characters begin telling each other what they themselves need to hear. No one is better than Chekhov in depicting the conversations of people shut out from Heaven.

It is not quite right to say that double-voicing appears whenever we are trying to explain and to will a wish into existence—I mean, when we are trying to engineer wish fulfillment. Double-voicing can appear at any time when I'm trying to say something to you and you serve as my means to speak to myself publically about my condition. The content could be a wish, or it could be anything that the "I" needs to hear. I may or may not realize that I'm talking to myself; dramatically, it hardly matters.

Near the end of Paula Fox's novel *Desperate Characters*, for example, Otto says to Sophie, his wife, "I wish someone would tell me how I can live." Otto and Sophie's summer house has been vandalized, and they are standing in the middle of the wreckage in the living room. Otto thinks they should move.

"How about Halifax?" [Otto asks]
"It's only furniture..." [Sophie says]
"There isn't any place for the way I feel."
"Listen, Otto. *It was just furniture.*" [Sophie is talking to herself; she'd stay calmer if she weren't.]

There follows a dialogue that, point for point, all but doubles for the concluding moves in Chekhov's play in its strategies for coping with violence and emptiness. Paula Fox's novels, and Fyodor Dostoyevsky's, and André Malraux's (and Saul Bellow's) are interfused with such moments.

Really, you can find double-voicings everywhere. It's not hard to write them yourself if you're aware of what your characters are doing, and particularly if they themselves are unaware of it. I'm describing the land of rationalizations, and rationalizations are always, by nature, dramatic. In its meanest and cruelest form, double-voicing occurs when the bullshitter gets carried away by his own bullshit and starts to believe it. (This is not, I hasten to add, the situation with Sonya, who is not trying to profit from her uncle or to take advantage of him.) Double-voicing can be found in pristine, mint condition in many of Ernest Hemingway's stories, with his blankly stoic characters reassuring their timid inner selves by heartily and manfully reassuring others. Note the schizophrenia in this situation, a schizophrenia that I have always felt is endemic to Hemingway's fiction. In Hemingway, double-voicing comes very close to a cosmological constant. Instead of being about God or rest or the angels, the statements are about enduring in the face of things, or getting over those things. "There isn't any good in promising," Nick says, at the conclusion of "Cross-Country Snow," letting himself off the hook that marriage and his wife's pregnancy have hung him on.

The dying man, surrounded by attendants, says, "Hey. I'm all right." Who is he talking to, if not himself?

9. SENTIMENTAL? SENTIMENTAL HOW?

Thus, by a circuitous route, we are back at the problem of sentimentality; Hemingway, as some have argued, presents a form of masculinist sentimentality, while Chekhov...well, Chekhov does something else. The question of what sentimentality is, is actually a tricky one to ask, because in fact nobody really knows what sentimentality is anymore.

Nevertheless, whenever I talk to my friend, The Cold Fish, about *Uncle Vanya*, The Cold Fish always tells me that the ending is sentimental, which is why, he claims, my eyes spurt tears.

"Sentimental" was not always defined this way. In the nineteenth century every educated person knew that "sentimental" was the adjectival modifier derived from "sentiment," as in the German poet Friedrich Schiller's famous essay "On the Naïve and Sentimental in Literature" (*Über naïve und sentimentalische Dichtung*, 1795). As the composer John Adams has written, "The 'unconscious' artists are the *naïve* ones. For them art is a natural form of expression, uncompromised by self-analysis or worry over its place in the historical continuum." The sentimental artist, by contrast, being self-aware, tries to find the lost unity of the naïve; he is essentially a searcher, all too aware of his place in history.

By these definitions, every student enrolled in an M.F.A. program is a sentimental artist. I do not mean this as a literary or existentialist critique. We are all latecomers in the history of literature, and most of us agree that pure spontaneity is lost to us, and that we must learn the forms if we are to succeed at what we want to do.

In the nineteenth century, the sentiments consisted of the entire keyboard of our feelings. Every key on the keyboard sounded a different sentiment. Our task as human beings (were we to live in that era as literate citizens) would be to educate our sentiments, to learn and perhaps master our emotions by feeling our way through adolescence and young adulthood, the usual trial and error, learning to play this particular keyboard. We would learn the tonalities of our emotions and how they are played, but *not* in an effort to get rid of them. It is arguable whether our feelings can be mastered, but in the nineteenth century many people thought that they could be. *The Blue Flower* by Penelope Fitzgerald is a wonderful introduction to these ideas. Gustave Flaubert's novel *Sentimental Education*, which Robert Baldick has called "undoubtedly the most influential French novel of the nineteenth century, and to many minds the greatest," concerns the coming-of-age and learning-through-disillusion of its protagonist, Frédéric. Frédéric's education of his sentiments hasn't been maudlin and has nothing to do with maudlin displays of emotion; that connotation is missing from the word's use in that period. "Sentimental" used as a term of negative critique arose later, as a reaction to the onslaught of sensibility and the mostly inaccurate rhetoric of pure feeling. Feeling cannot analyze itself simply by using the language of feeling. But for Flaubert and for his contemporaries, even in English, "sentimental" simply referred to the keyboard, not to the rhetoric.

10. THE INEXISTENCE OF INSENTIMENTALITY

In our century, following the First World War, the word "sentimental" gradually grew to mean "manipulatively maudlin." Sentimentality was understood to be a form of extremity. In retrospect, the word was attached to certain texts, such as Charles Dickens's *The Old Curiosity Shop,* and to certain scenes, such as the death of Little Nell in that novel. Dickens's *A Christmas Carol* is a touchstone of the sentimental, with its hilariously angelic cripple, Tiny Tim, crying out, "God bless us, every one," and its extremist villain, the hideous Ebenezer Scrooge, converted in one night from mean-spirited penny-pincher to openhearted benefactor. Sentimentality, understood this way, is rhetorical, that is, always going for the tear ducts, trying to accomplish with emotion what it cannot manage any other way. It traffics in stories of innocence versus villainy and is the first cousin of melodrama. There is something fascist about sentimentality, even when it is used for populist or progressivist ends. It wants you to feel and not to think. It avoids thought by invoking emotion, and only emotion, instead. All its ideas exist simply to evoke an emotion, typically of tears, or rage. John Irving, for example, is a great admirer of the art of *A Christmas Carol*, and you can see him deploying many of its tropes at the end of *The Cider House Rules*.

So I am arguing that manipulative aesthetic effects certainly exist, but that there is something deeply mistaken about the use of the word "sentimental" in contemporary writing workshops and in contemporary criticism generally. The word should be temporarily banned. It's close to being meaningless. We don't know what we're talking about when we use this word now because it points to an extreme for which there is no other corresponding point in the spectrum. It's as if we tried to define "day" without having any word for "night." We know what "day" is because we know what "night" is. But if a work is "sentimental," then what quality stands over there as its opposite? "Unsentimental"? What is that? It's praise. But what is any aesthetic object that lacks feeling and emotion and sentiment? The game is rigged: We don't have a word for that condition. John Gardner suggested "frigid," but I have never heard anyone use that word in any context in over twenty years of workshopping fiction, and I have heard people use the word "sentimental" more often than I've had hot dinners.

11. BACK TO SONYA

Uncle Vanya cannot be considered a sentimental *play* simply because of Sonya's last speech. If anything is sentimental, it is the speech itself (or maybe Sonya is, by saying it), but the closer one looks at the speech—its habit of insisting on what is most dubious, its double-voicing, its desperate invocation to God and the angels and a belief in the afterlife—it begins to look more and more like a symptom rather than a statement. In the film version, Wallace Shawn, as Vanya, laughs twice during the speech, as if he realizes how preposterous Sonya's words are, and he shakes his head as if to indicate that—no, he doesn't believe it. Even Sonya, in this version, laughs at herself, at her own symptoms. Chekhov, after all, was a doctor, and often his characters act and speak in what I'd call a symptomatic way. It is as if Chekhov were saying, "Look. This is what people say and do when they're in despair. Don't blame me if this is what Sonya says. It's beautiful, in a way, and besides, almost everyone talks like this or thinks like this sooner or later. All I'm doing is reporting on what someone says in the depths of this particular condition. That's my task."

It isn't as if Sonya is asking for the moon and the stars. Her hopes are small. Her last words are, "We'll be at peace." This is sentimental?

12. ANOTHER THEORY OF TEARS

I don't believe what Sonya says but I want to, even if it's untrue. Like Shawn's Vanya, I laugh at her, at first, and I shake my head. And then, when I'm confronted by a hope for peace—this minimal hope, this ordinary wish, this humble carrot held out in front of me—I can't stand it, and my defenses give way.

13. SPIN-OFFS

What's also interesting about Sonya's last speech is how it seems to have resonated with poets and memoirists. It is explicitly referred to in Donald Justice's last poem, "There is a gold light in certain old paintings." This poem is the final one in his *Collected Poems*, from 2004, published by Knopf. Of its three stanzas, the first evokes the imagery of Christianity and its afterlife, the second, Greek mythology (and *its* afterlife). The third stanza remembers Sonya's last speech, though now shorn of God and therefore entirely secularized. Sonya is given the last word, and the last words of Donald Justice's entire poetic career. Justice's stanzas here have very soft cadences, and end-line word repetitions on the second and fourth lines and the two concluding lines of each stanza. Word repetitions of this sort, at least from Tennyson's "Ulysses" onward, typically convey a sense of weariness, resignation and inaction, though not, I think, of harmony.

"There is a gold light in certain old paintings"

1
There is a gold light in certain old paintings
That represents a diffusion of sunlight.
It is like happiness, when we are happy.
It comes from everywhere and from nowhere at once, this light,
    And the poor soldiers sprawled at the foot of the cross
    Share in its charity equally with the cross.

2
Orpheus hesitated beside the black river.
With so much to look forward to he looked back.
We think he sang then, but the song is lost.
At least he had seen once more the beloved back.
    I say the song went this way: *O prolong*
    Now the sorrow if that is all there is to prolong.

3
The world is very dusty, uncle. Let us work.
One day the sickness shall pass from the earth for good.
The orchard will bloom; someone will play the guitar.
Our work will be seen as strong and clean and good.
    And all that we suffered through having existed
    Shall be forgotten as though it had never existed.

We find Sonya's last speech also evoked in Peter Trachtenberg's brilliant *7 Tattoos: A Memoir in the Flesh*, from 1997, a meditation on the author's vices and self-abuses, and that ends with a coda in which Trachtenberg announces himself as a convert to Sonya's set of beliefs, of quietude and baseline minimal hopes.

14. THE MAN WITH THE BLUE GUITAR
Chekhov specifies in his stage directions that Sonya's last speech is accompanied from its halfway point onward by the music of a guitar, played by Telegin, a bit of an oaf, but a nice oaf. In the movie, this

music is omitted, as is Sonya's insistence on her own belief and her observation that her uncle is weeping.

When you are pouring your guts out, someone is almost always off in the next room, practicing the accordion or cutting coupons out of the newspaper or vacuuming up the bread crumbs under the dining-room table. Icarus falls out of the sky, and the farmer goes on plowing his fields. Someone is not paying attention, and Chekhov always notices this: how the world is ending in one room, and in the other room, people are playing cards and getting drunk or playing the guitar. I understand that Telegin's music may be a consolation, but I don't hear it that way.

In Charles Ives's great piece *The Unanswered Question*, the trumpet keeps asking the same musical question, getting more and more frenzied and desperate, and underneath the trumpet, the orchestra just goes on playing the same cycle of major chords, like the universe slowly circling around itself, ignoring its own agony.

15. WALLACE SHAWN'S SHAKE OF THE HEAD

In the movie version of Sonya's last speech, Wally Shawn, as Vanya, at a critical moment, shakes his head and laughs. He doesn't believe what Sonya is telling him, either. He doesn't believe any of it. Christianity is offering up its meager portion of comfort once again. But he listens. He can't move. Even Sonya laughs once, at the preposterousness of what she's saying.

When someone is trying to console you—"things will get better, you'll get well, the world will be interesting again, look at how much better you feel"—the temptation is always to laugh, to disbelieve. And yet you sit there, and listen.

In the stage directions, Vanya is crying. Wallace Shawn's shake of the head amounts to a similar refusal of comfort.

That shake of the head says, "No, none of this is true. You know it, and I know it."

And yet, in despair, you do not move. You stay because what you are listening to is the noise of consolation, detached from its utility. "Keep talking, J.P.," the narrator of Raymond Carver's "Where I'm Calling From" says. In his condition, he says, he'd listen to someone who was talking about how he took up playing horseshoes.

16. SONYA'S LAST SPEECH

In the film by Louis Malle, the director holds Vanya and Sonya, doubles for each other, in a two-shot, Vanya in profile and Sonya full in the face, so that we see them both onscreen at the same time. Sonya is subtly backlit so that her hair has a halo-like glow.

Now, in the early years of the twenty-first century, is there any consolation left to us for the horrors we have witnessed (even by proxy) and the various despairs, depressions, and traumas we have suffered? Is comfort possible to us, in any form at all, in an epoch of holocausts? Comfort and consolation may, indeed, have passed from our lives; it is just possible that we are, historically, beyond them. This is not a trivial matter. To reformulate an old Marxist sentence, *Tell me what you think of Sonya's last speech, and I will tell you who and what you are.*

Anna Karenina

THOMAS MANN

T oday high tide is at ten. The waters rush up the narrowing
strand, carrying foam-bubbles and jelly-fish—primitive children of an unnatural mother, who will abandon them on the sands
to death by evaporation. The waves run up, almost to the foot of my
beach-chair; sometimes I must lift away my plaid, wrapped legs as
the waters encroach and threaten to cover them. My heart responds
blithely, though also with utter respect, to these sportive little tricks
the mighty ocean plays me; my sympathy, a deep and tender, primitive,
soul-extending stirring, is far indeed from any annoyance.

No bathers yet. They await the midday warmth to wade out into
the ebbing tide, little flutters and shrieks escaping them as they begin
their pert yet fearful toying with the vast. Coast-guards in cork jackets,
lynx-eyed, tooting their horns, watch over all this amateurish frivol-
ity. My "workshop" here surpasses any I know. It is lonely; but even
were it livelier, the tumultuous surf so shuts me in, and the sides of
my admirable beach-chair, seat and cabin in one, familiar from my
youth up, are so peculiarly protective that there can be no distraction.
Beloved, incomparably soothing and suitable situation—it recurs in my
life again, and again as by a law. Beneath a sky where gently shifting
continents of cloud link the blue depths, rolls the sea, a darkening green
against the clear horizon, oncoming in seven or eight foaming white
rows of surf that reach out of sight in both directions. There is superb

activity farther out, where the advancing waves hurl themselves first and highest against the bar. The bottle-green wall gleams metallic as it mounts and halts and curls over, then shatters with a roar and an explosion of foam down, down, in ever recurrent crash, whose dull thunder forms the deep ground-bass to the higher key of the boiling and hissing waves as they break nearer in. Never does the eye tire of this sight nor the ear of this music.

A more fitting spot could not be for my purpose: which is to recall and to reflect upon the great book whose title stands at the head of my paper. And here by the sea there comes to mind inevitably an old, I might almost say an innate association of ideas: the spiritual identity of two elementary experiences, one of which is a parable of the other. I mean the ocean and the epic. The epic, with its rolling breadth, its breath of the beginnings and the roots of life, its broad and sweeping rhythm, its all-consuming monotony—how like it is to the sea, how like to it is the sea! It is the Homeric element I mean, the story going on and on, art and nature at once, naïve, magnificent, material, objective, immortally healthy, immortally realistic! All this was strong in Tolstoy, stronger than in any other modern creator of epic art; it distinguishes his genius, if not in rank, yet in essence, from the morbid manifestation, the ecstatic and highly distorted phenomenon, that was Dostoyevsky. Tolstoy himself said of his early work *Childhood* and *Boyhood*: "Without false modesty, it is something like *The Iliad*." That is the merest statement of fact; only on exterior grounds does it fit still better the giant work of his maturity, *War and Peace*. It fits everything he wrote. The pure narrative power of his work is unequalled. Every contact with it, even when he wished no longer to be an artist, when he scorned and reviled art and only employed it as a means of communicating moral lessons; every contact with it, I say, rewards the talent that knows how to receive (for there is no other) with rich streams of power and refreshment, of creative primeval lustiness and health. Seldom did art work so much like nature; its immediate, natural power is only another manifestation of nature itself; and to read him again, to be played upon by the animal keenness of this eye, the sheer power of this creative attack, the entirely clear and true greatness, unclouded by any mysticism, of this epic, is to find one's way home, safe from every danger of affectation and morbid trifling; home to originality and health, to everything within us that is fundamental and sane.

Turgenyev once said: "We have all come out from under Gogol's *Mantle*"—a fiendishly clever pun which puts in a phrase the extraordinary uniformity and unity, the thick traditionalism of Russian literature as a whole. Actually, they are all there simultaneously, its masters and geniuses, they can put out their hands to each other, their life-spans in great part overlap. Nikolai Gogol read aloud some of *Dead Souls* to the great Pushkin, and the author of *Yevgeny Onyegin* shook with laughter—and then suddenly grew sad. Lermontov was the contemporary of both. Turgenyev, as one may easily forget, for his frame, like Dostoyevsky's, Lieskov's, and Tolstoy's, belongs to the second half of the nineteenth century, came only four years later than Lermontov into the world and ten before Tolstoy, whom he adjured in a touching letter expressing his faith in humanistic art, "to go back to literature." What I mean by thick traditionalism is illustrated by an anecdote that most significantly connects Tolstoy's artistically finest work, *Anna Karenina*, with Pushkin.

One evening in the spring of 1873, Count Leo Nikolayevich entered the room of his eldest son, who was reading aloud to his old aunt Pushkin's *Stories of Byelkin*; the father took the book and read: "The guests assembled in the country house." "That's the way to begin," he said; went into his study and wrote: "In the Oblonsky house great confusion reigned." That was the original first sentence from *Anna Karenina*. The present beginning, the *aperçu* about happy and unhappy families, was introduced later. That is a marvelously pretty little anecdote. He had already begun much and brought much to triumphant conclusion. He was the fêted creator of the Russian national epos, in the form of a modern novel, the giant panorama *War and Peace*. And he was about to excel both formally and artistically this chef d'oeuvre of his thirty-five years in the work he had now in hand, which one may with an easy mind pronounce the greatest society novel of world literature. And here he was, restlessly prowling about the house, searching, searching, not knowing how to begin. Pushkin taught him, tradition taught him, Pushkin the classic master, from whose world his own was so remote, both personally and generally speaking. Pushkin rescued him, as he hesitated on the brink; showed him how one sets to, takes a firm grip, and plumps the reader *in medias res*. Unity is achieved, the continuity of that astonishing family of intellects which one calls Russian literature is preserved in this little piece of historical evidence.

Merezhkovsky points out that historically and premodernly only Pushkin among these writers really possesses charm. He inhabits a sphere by himself, a sensuously radiant, naïve, and blithely poetic one. But with Gogol there begins what Merezhkovsky calls critique: "the transition from unconscious creation to creative consciousness"; for him that means the end of poetry in the Pushkin sense, but at the same time the beginning of something new. The remark is true and perceptive. Thus did Heine speak of the age of Goethe, an aesthetic age, an epoch of art, an objective-ironic point of view. Its representative and dominant figure had been the Olympian; it died with his death. What then began was a time of taking sides, of conflicting opinions, of social consolidation, yes, of politics and, in short, of morals—a morality that branded as frivolous every purely aesthetic and universal point of view.

In Heine's comments, as in Merezhkovsky's, there is feeling for temporal change, together with feeling for its opposite, the timeless and perpetual. Schiller, in his immortal essay, reduced it to the formula of the sentimental and the naïve. What Merezhkovsky calls "critique" or "creative consciousness," what seems to him like contrast with the unconscious creation of Pushkin, as the more modern element, the future on the way, is precisely what Schiller means by the sentimental in contrast to the naïve. He too brings in the temporal, the evolutional, and—"*pro domo*," as we know—declares the sentimental, the creativeness of conscious critique, in short the moralistic, to be the newer, more modern stage of development.

There are now two things to say: first, Tolstoy's original convictions were definitely on the side of the aesthetic, of pure art, the objectively shaping, anti-moralistic principle; and second, in him took place that very cultural and historical change which Merezhkovsky speaks of, that move away from Pushkin's simplicity towards critical responsibility and morality. Within his own being it took such a radical and tragic form that he went through the severest crises and much anguish and even so could not utterly repudiate his own mighty creativeness. What he finally arrived at was a rejection and negation of art itself as an idle, voluptuous, and immoral luxury, admissible only in order to make moral teachings acceptable to men, even though dressed in the mantle of art.

But to return to the first position: we have his own unequivocal declarations to the effect that a purely artistic gift stands higher than one with social significance. In 1859, when he was thirty-one years old, he gave, as a member of the Moscow society of Friends of Russian Literature, an address in which he so sharply emphasized the advantages of the purely art element in literature over all the fashions of the day that the president of the society, Khomyakov, felt constrained to rejoin that a servant of pure art might quite easily become a social reformer even without knowing or willing it. Contemporary criticism saw in the author of *Anna Karenina* the protagonist of the art-for-art's-sake position, the representative of free creativeness apart from all tendentiousness or doctrine. Indeed, it considered this naturalism the characteristically new thing; the public must in time grow up to it, though at present they had got used, in the works of others, to the presentation of political and social ideas in the form of art. In point of fact, all this was only one side of the business. As an artist and son of his time, the nineteenth century, Tolstoy was a naturalist, and in this connection he represented—in the sense of a trend—the new. But as an intellectual he was beyond (or rather, he struggled amid torments to arrive beyond) the new, to something further still, on the other side of his, the naturalistic century. He was reaching after conceptions of art which approached much nearer to "mind" (*Geist*), to knowledge, to "critique" than to nature. The commentators of 1875, impressed by the first chapters of *Anna Karenina* as they appeared in a Russian magazine, the *Messenger*, seeking benevolently to prepare the way with the public for the naturalism of the work, did not dream that the author was in full flight towards an anti-art position, which was already hampering his work on his masterpiece and even endangering its completion.

This development was to go very far, the vehemence of its consistency shrank from nothing; neither from the anti-cultural nor even from the absurd. Before long, he was to regret in public having written *Childhood* and *Youth*, the work of his freshest youthful hours—so poor, so insincere, so literary, so sinful was this book. He was to condemn root and branch the "artist twaddle" with which the twelve volumes of his works were filled, to which "the people of our day ascribe an undeserved significance." It was the same undeserved significance that they ascribed to art itself—for instance, to Shakespeare's plays. He went so far—one must set it down with respect and a sober face, or at least with the smallest, most non-committal smile—as to put Mrs. Harriet Beecher Stowe, the author of *Uncle Tom's Cabin*, far above Shakespeare.

We must be at pains to understand this. Tolstoy's hatred for Shakespeare dated from much earlier than is usually supposed. It signified rebellion against nature, the universal, the all-affirming. It was jealousy of the morally tormented for the irony of the absolute creator, it meant the straining away from nature, naïveté, moral indifference, towards "*Geist*" in the moralistically critical sense of the word; towards moral valuations and edifying doctrine. Tolstoy hated himself in Shakespeare, hated his own vital bearish strength, which was originally like Shakespeare's, natural and creatively a-moral; though his struggles for the good, the true and right, the meaning of life, the doctrine of salvation, were after all only the same thing in another and self-denying form. The immensity of his writings sometimes resulted in a gigantic clumsiness which forces a respectful smile. And yet it is precisely the paradoxically ascetic application of a titanic helplessness arising from a primeval force that, viewed as art, gives his work that huge moral *élan*, that Atlas-like moral muscle-tensing and flexing which reminds one of the agonized figures of Michelangelo's sculpture.

I said that Tolstoy's hatred of Shakespeare belongs to an earlier period than is generally thought. But all that which later made his friends and admirers like Turgenyev weep, his denial of art and culture, his radical moralism, his highly questionable pose of prophet and confessor in his last period—all that begins much further back, it is quite wrong to imagine this process as something suddenly occurring in a crisis of conversion in later life, coincident with Tolstoy's old age. The same kind of mistake occurs in the popular opinion that Richard Wagner suddenly got religion—whereas the matter was one of a development vastly and fatally consistent and inevitable, the direction of which is clearly and unmistakably traceable in *The Flying Dutchman* and in *Tannhäuser*. The judgment of the Frenchman, Vogüé, was entirely correct when, on the news that the great Russian writer was now "as though paralysed by a sort of mystic madness," Vogüé declared that he had long ago seen it coming. The course of Tolstoy's intellectual development had been present in the seed in *Childhood* and *Boyhood* and the psychology of Levin in *Anna Karenina* had marked out the path it would take.

So much is true, that Levin is Tolstoy, the real hero of the mighty novel, which is a glorious, indestructible signpost on the woeful Way of the Cross the poet was taking; a monument of an elemental and creative bear-strength, which was first heightened and then destroyed by the inner ferment of his subtilizing conscience and his fear of God. Yes, Levin is Tolstoy—almost altogether Tolstoy, this side Tolstoy the artist. To this character Tolstoy transferred not only the important facts and dates of his own life: his experiences as a farmer, his romance and betrothal (which are completely autobiographic), the sacred, beautiful, and awe-full experiences of the birth of his first child, and the death of his brother—which forms a pendant of equal and boundless significance—not only there but in his whole inner life, his crises of conscience, his groping after the whole duty of man and the meaning of life, his painful wrestling over the good life, which so decisively estranged him from the doings of urban society; his gnawing doubts about culture itself or that which his society called culture, doubts of all this brought him close to the anchorite and nihilist type. What Levin lacks of Tolstoy is only just that he is not a great artist besides. But to estimate *Anna Karenina* not only artistically but also humanly, the reader must saturate himself with the thesis that Constantin Levin himself wrote the novel. Instead of being the man with the pointer, indicating the incomparable beauty of the painting as a whole, I shall do better to speak of the conditions of difficulty and stress under which the work came to birth.

That is the right word: it came to birth; but there did not lack much for it not be born. A work of this kind, so all of one piece and that piece so absorbing, so complete in the large and in the small, makes us suppose that its creator gave himself utterly to it with entire and devoted heart and, like one driven to self-expression, committed it, so to speak, in one gush to paper. That is a misapprehension; although, even so, the origin of *Anna Karenina* does in fact lie in the happiest, most harmonious period of Tolstoy's life. The years in which he worked on it belong to the first decade and a half of his marriage with the woman whose literary image is Kitty Shtcherbatsky and who later suffered so much from her Lievotshka—until at last just before his death the old man broke away and ran. It is she who, in addition to her constant pregnancies, and her abundant activities as mistress of the farm, as mother and housewife, copies *War and Peace* seven times with her own hand— that first colossal intellectual harvest of the period that brought the doubting, brooding man relative peace in the patriarchal animalism of marriage and family life in the country. It was the period at which the poor Countess looked so yearningly back when Leochen had become "the prophet of Yasnaya Polyana" and succeeded under self-torture, and even so up to the end never quite succeeded, in brooding to death all his sensual and instinctive passions: family, nation, state, church, club, and chase, at bottom the whole life of the body, but most particularly art, which for him quite essentially meant sensuality and the body's life.

Well, those fifteen years were a good, happy time, though from a later, higher point of view, good only in a low and animal sense. *War and Peace* had made Tolstoy the "great writer of Russia," and as such he went to work to write a new historical and national epos. He had in mind a novel about Peter the Great and his times. And for months he carried on conscientious and comprehensive studies for it in the libraries and archives of Moscow. "Lievotshka reads and reads," it says in the Countess's letters. Did he read too much? Did he take in too much, did he spoil his appetite? Oddly enough, it turned out that the Czar reformer, the imperial compeller of civilization, was at bottom an unsympathetic figure to Tolstoy. To hold the position he had achieved as the national epic-writer, he had wanted to repeat his performance in *War and Peace*. It would not come off; the material unexpectedly resisted him. After endless preparatory labour he flung the whole thing away, sacrificed his whole investment of time and study, and turned to something quite different: the passion and stumbling of *Anna Karenina*, the modern novel of St. Petersburg and Moscow high society.

The first onset, by dint of Pushkin's help, was fresh and blithe. But before long Tolstoy got stuck, though the reader in his untrammeled enjoyment would never guess it. For weeks and months the work only dragged on or did not go at all. What was the trouble? Household cares, children's illnesses, fluctuations in his own health—oh, no, these were all nothing compared with a piece of work like *Anna Karenina*—or they ought to be. What is really disturbing is doubt of the importance and personal urgency of what we are doing. Might we not do better to learn Greek, to get some fundamental knowledge of the New Testament? Then the schools for the children of peasants we have founded. Should they not claim more of our time and thought? Is not the whole of belles-lettres folly? And is it not our duty or even much more consistent with our deepest need to bury ourselves in theological and philosophical studies in order to find at last the meaning of life? That contact with the mystery of death which he had had when his older brother died had made a strong impression on Tolstoy's own vitality, powerful to the point of mysticism, which demanded spiritual wrestling, not in a literary way but in something confessional on the pattern of Saint Augustine and Rousseau. Such a book, sincere as far as human power could make it, weighed on his mind and gave him increasing distaste for writing novels. Actually, he would never have finished *Anna Karenina* if it had not begun appearing in the *Rusky Vyestnik* (*Russian Messenger*) of Katkov. The fact made him responsible to the publisher and the reading public. In January 1875 and the following three months successive numbers of the novel appeared in the magazine. Then they left off, because the author had no more to deliver. The first months of the next year produced a few fragments, then seven months' pause. Then in December one more number. What we find simply enchanting, what we cannot imagine as originating in anything except a state of prolonged inspiration—Tolstoy groaned over. "My tiresome, horrible *Anna Karenina*," he wrote from Samara, where he was drinking mares' milk. *Sic!* Literally. "At last," he wrote in March 1876, "I was driven to finish my novel, of which I am sick to death." Of course in the process the enthusiasm and eagerness came back by fits and starts. But it was just at such times that the writing was prone to go more slowly—owing to fastidious artistry that caused endless filing and remodelling and improving out of a stylistic perfectionism which still shows through the most inadequate translation. This amazing saint took his art the more seriously the less he believed in it.

The publication dragged on, with constant interruptions, as far as the eighth book. Then it stopped, for now the thing had become political and the national epic-writer of Russia had in the latest number expressed himself so heretically about Slavophilism, the current enthusiasm for the Bulgarian, Serbian, Bosnian brothers in their fight for freedom against the Turks, the much ado over the volunteers and the patriotic nonsense uttered by Russian society, that Katkov dared not print it. He demanded cuts and changes, which the author in high dudgeon refused to make. Tolstoy had the final numbers printed separately with a note on the disagreement.

What I have boldly called the greatest society novel in all literature is an anti-society novel. The Bible text: "Vengeance is mine, I will repay, saith the Lord," stands at its head. The moral momentum of the work was certainly the desire to lash society for the cold, cruel rebuff inflicted by it on a woman who goes astray through passion but is fundamentally proud and high-minded, instead of leaving to God the punishment for her sins. Indeed, society might well do just that, for after all it is society and its irrevocable laws that God too avails Himself of to exact the payment. It shows the fatal and inevitable character of Anna's doom that it proceeds inscrutably, step by step, up to the frightful end out of her affront to the moral law. So there is a certain contradiction in the author's original moral motive, in the complaint he lodges against society. One asks oneself in what way would God punish if society did not behave as it does? Custom and morality, how far are they distinguishable, how far are they—in effect—one and the same, how far do they coincide in the heart of the socially circumscribed human being? The question hovers unanswered over the whole novel. But such a work is not compelled to answer questions. Its task is to bring them out, to enrich the emotions, to give them the highest and most painful degree of questionableness. Thus it will have performed its task, and in this case the story-teller's love for his creature leaves no doubt at all, no matter how much suffering he painfully and relentlessly visits on her.

Tolstoy loves Anna very much, one feels that. The book bears her name; it could bear no other. But its hero is not Anna's lover, the strong, decent, chivalrous, and somewhat limited officer of the Guards, Count

Vronsky. Nor is it Alexander Alexandrovich, Anna's husband, with whatever profound skill Tolstoy has modeled this incomparable, at once repellent and superior, comic and touching cuckold. No, the hero is another person altogether, who has as good as nothing to do with Anna's lot, and whose introduction in a way twists the theme of the novel and almost pushes its first motive into second place. It is Constantin Levin, the introspective man, the author's image—he, no other, with his brooding and scrutinizing, with the peculiar force and obstinate resistance of his critical conscience, that makes the great society novel into an anti-society novel.

What an extraordinary fellow he is, this surrogate of the author! What in the French *pièce à thèse* is called the *raisonneur*—Levin is that in Tolstoy's society world. Yet how un-French! To amount to something as a critic of society, one must, I suppose, be in society oneself; but precisely that he is not in the least, this tortured, radically remote *raisonneur,* despite his native right to move in the highest circles. Strong and shy, defiant and dubious, with an intelligence of great anti-logical, natural, even helpless abundance, Levin is at bottom convinced that decency, uprightness, seriousness, and sincerity are possible only in singleness, in dumb isolation, each for himself; and that all social life turns him into a chatterer, a liar, and a fool. Observe him in the salons of Moscow, or on cultural occasions when he has to make conversation, play a social part, express "views." Such a coming together of people seems to him banal, he sees himself a blushing fool, a prattler, a parrot. This Rousseauian quite sincerely considers all urban civilization, with the intellectual and cultural goings-on bound up in it, a sink of iniquity. Only life in the country is worthy of a man—though not the country life that the city man in sentimental relaxation finds "charming." Levin's learned brother, for instance, even boasts in a way that he enjoyed such an unintellectual occupation as fishing. No, what Levin means is the real, serious life on the land, where you have to work hard, where the human being dwells truly and perforce at the heart of that nature whose "beauty" the guest from civilization sentimentally admires from outside.

Levin's morality and conscientiousness are strongly physical, having reference to the body and bound up with it. "I need physical exercise," he says to himself, "otherwise my character suffers." He resolves to help the peasants with the mowing and it gives him the highest moral and physical pleasure (a splendid and Tolstoyan chapter). His scorn of the "intellectual" or, better, his disbelief in it, estranging him as a product of civilization, involving him in contradictions, is radical. It leads him, when he has to come right down to it, into paradoxes, into opinions hard to express among civilized beings. Take for instance popular education—or, worse still, any education at all. Levin's position towards it is the same as his position towards nature: "The same people whom you say you love."—"I never said that," thought Constantin Levin. —"Why should I bother my head about schools where I shall never send my own children and where the peasants will never send theirs either? And on top of that, I am not even convinced that it is necessary to send them!"—"You can make better use of a peasant and laborer who can read and write than of one who cannot."—"No, ask anybody you like," countered Constantin Levin decisively; "a worker with some schooling is distinctly worse."—"Do you admit that education is a blessing for the people?"—"Yes, that I admit," responded Levin thoughtlessly, and saw at once that what he had said was not really just what he thought.— Very bad! A difficult, dangerous case! He recognizes the blessings of "education," because what he "really" thinks about it, in the nineteenth century, cannot be put into words and for that reason may even be unthinkable.

Of course he moves in the thought-channels of his century, and they in a certain way are scientific. He "observes humanity, not as something standing outside of zoological law but as something dependent on its environment, and he proceeds from this dependence in order to discover the laws lying at the base of its development." So at least the scholar understands him; and it is no other than Taine to whom he there makes acknowledgment, good, great, nineteenth-century. But there is something in him that either goes back behind the scientific spirit of his epoch or goes on beyond it, something desperately bold, inadmissible, impossible in conversation. He lies on his back and looks up at the high and cloudless sky. "Do I not know that that is infinite space and not a round vault? But however I screw up my eyes and strain my sight I cannot see it not round and not bounded; and in spite of my knowledge about infinite space I am incontestably right when I see a solid blue dome, and more right than when I strain my eyes to see beyond it. . . . Can this be faith?"

But whether faith or the new realism, it is no longer the scientific spirit of the nineteenth century. In a sort of way it recalls Goethe. And Levin-Tolstoy's skeptical, realistic, rebellious attitude towards patriotism, towards the Slavic brethren and the war volunteers, does the same. He declines to share in the enthusiasm, he is solitary in the midst of it, precisely as Goethe was at the time of the Freiheitskrieg— although in both cases something new, the democratic, joined the national movement and for the first time the popular will conditioned the conduct of the government. That too is nineteenth-century; and Levin, or Lievotshka, as the poor Countess called him, could simply not do with the truths of his time. He called them comfortless. He is a step further on; I cannot help calling it a very dangerous step, which, if not safeguarded by the profoundest love of truth and human sympathy, can quite easily lead to black reaction and barbarism. Today, it takes no forlorn, single-handed courage to throw overboard the scientific discipline of the nineteenth century and surrender to the "mythus," the "faith"—in other words, to a paltry and culture-destroying vulgarity. Masses of people do it today; but it is not a step forward, it is a hundred miles backwards. Such a step will be in a forward direction only when it is taken for humanity's sake, only if another step follows it straightway, moving from the new realism of the solid blue vault to the neither old nor new but humanly eternal idealism of truth, freedom, and knowledge. Today there are some desperately stupid ideas about reaction in the air.

A digression—but a necessary one. Levin, then, cannot do with the ideals of his epoch, he cannot live with them. What I call his physical morality and conscientiousness is shaken to the depths by the experience of the physically transcendent and transparent mysteries of birth and death; and all that the times teach him about organisms and their destruction, about the indestructibility of matter and the laws of conservation of energy, about evolution, and so forth, all that looks to him not only like utter ignorance of the whole problem of the meaning of life but also like a kind of thinking that makes it impossible for him to get the knowledge he needs. That in infinite time, infinite space, infinite matter, and organism, a cell frees itself; that it persists for a while and then bursts and that this bubble is he himself, Levin; that seems to him like the malicious mockery of some demon. It cannot indeed be refuted; it must be overcome some other way, that one may not be driven to shoot oneself.

What to his profounder necessities looks like a mortal lie and a kind of thinking which is no sort of instrument for the apprehension of truth——that actually is the naturalistic materialism of the nineteenth century, whose inspiration is honest love of truth, despite the comfortless pessimism that is its necessary aura. The honesty must be preserved; but a little illumination is required in order to do justice to life and its deeper concerns. So there is real humor in the fact that in *Anna Karenina* a simple little peasant shows the brooding man the way out of his despair. This little peasant teaches him, or recalls to his mind, something he has always known: true, he says, living for our physical well-being and in order to fill our bellies is natural and inborn and laid upon us all. But even so, it is not righteous or even important. What we have to do is to live for the "truth," "for our souls," "as God wills," for "the Good." How wonderful that this necessity is laid upon us just as naturally inborn and imposed as the need to fill our bellies! Wonderful indeed; for the sure conviction common to all men that it is shameful to live only for the belly, and that one must rather live for God, for the true and the good, has nothing to do with reason, but quite the contrary. It is reason that makes us care for the body and in its interest to exploit our neighbors all we can. Knowledge of the good, asserts Levin, does not lie in the realm of reason; the good stands outside the scientific chain of cause and effect. The good is a miracle, because it is contrary to reason and yet everyone understands it.

There is something outside of and beyond the melancholy science of the nineteenth century, which resigned all attempt to give meaning to life. There is a spiritual factor, a spiritual need. And Levin is enchanted and soothed by this absurdly simple statement of the human being's supra-reasonable obligation to be good. In his joy he forgets that also that melancholy materialistic naturalistic science of the nineteenth century had, after all, as motive power, human striving for the good. He

forgot that it was stern and bitter love of truth that made it deny meaning to life. It too, denying God, lived for God. That, too, is possible, and
Levin forgets it. Art he does not need even to forget; he knows, it seems,
nothing about it, obviously thinking of it only as the society prattle of
the "cultured" about painting, the Luccas, Wagner, and so on. Here is
the difference between him and Leo Tolstoy. Tolstoy knew art; he had
suffered frightfully from and for it, achieved mightier things in it than
the rest of us can hope to achieve. Perhaps it was just the violence of his
artist personality that made him fail to see that knowledge of the good
is just the opposite of a reason to deny art. Art is the most beautiful,
austerest, blithest, most sacred symbol of all supra-reasonable human
striving for good above and beyond reason, for truth and fullness. The
breath of the rolling sea of epic would not so expand our lungs with
living air if it did not bring with it the astringent quickening spice of
the spiritual and the divine.

The Last of the Breed: Homage to Louis L'Amour

JANE TOMPKINS

I was volunteering temporarily as a file clerk at the Share Our Selves center for services for the poor in Costa Mesa, California. It was one of those dispiriting situations where trying to help people involved dehumanizing them, and yourself; there seemed no way around it. In this case the clients, people in need of food and money and in some cases shelter, sat in rows in a windowless room and waited for their names to be called—Martinez, Rodriguez—so they could receive a bag of groceries or, in special instances, see the lady in the back room who gave out money for electric bills and bus fares.

One day, while filing slips of paper so the people from Costa Mesa (which helped support the center) wouldn't get counted with the people from Santa Ana and other municipalities (which didn't), I noticed a man deeply absorbed in a novel. It was *Fort Everglades* by Frank Slaughter, who wrote adventure stories some decades ago. I asked the man if he'd ever read Louis L'Amour. "Oh yes," he said. At the time, L'Amour had died less than a year before. The man paused and said to me glumly, "You know about L'Amour, don't you?" "Yes," I said, and he replied, "Some people should live forever."

The reverence and respect his words conveyed, their spare eloquence and strength of conviction, reminded me of L'Amour's best writing and of the tough-it-out-against-all-odds philosophy his writing stood for. To the man who spoke them—his name was Roland Bennett—L'Amour was a hero. No difference, finally, between the writer and his work. There's something about L'Amour's work—the solemnity of living and dying that it captures—that makes you want to pay tribute. Especially now that L'Amour himself has gone west of everything. I never would have gotten involved with Westerns if it hadn't been for L'Amour; his books inspired this book [*West of Everything: The Inner Life of Westerns*, Oxford University Press, 1992], and his spirit runs through it. L'Amour in his way was a great writer; his works spoke and still speak to millions of people. He has had the praise and gratitude of millions, and so he doesn't really need the words of critics. Still, he deserves critical attention, and certainly he rewards it.

Toward the end of his long career, L'Amour wrote a best-selling novel that was not a Western—not set in the American West or in the nineteenth century. It was called *The Last of the Breed*. The novel is a kind of summa of the books L'Amour had written all his life. Containing the elements normally found in Westerns, it removes them from their usual location in time and space and pushes them to an extreme, as if driving the genre to its lair once and for all, closing in for the kill.

The story is about Major Joseph Makatozi of the U.S. Army Air Force, a test pilot shot down by the Russians, who are after information on the latest experimental aircraft. The flyer is captured, imprisoned, and about to be questioned under torture by his nemesis, Colonel Zamatev, when he escapes into the forest; the rest of the novel consists of his trek across Siberia to the Bering Strait, which he intends to cross as his ancestors had done thousands of years before. For Joe Mack, as he is familiarly known, is mostly Indian—part Sioux, part Cheyenne, and part Scots.

I picked up this book because it had been recommended to me by Rick Hanson, a L'Amour fan I talk to sometimes in a homeless shelter in Durham, North Carolina, the state where I live. I'll return to the shelter later because it's connected to my sense of L'Amour as a writer for Americans, homeless and presidents alike. First, though, I want to explain why I'm writing about this novel.

I'd begun *The Last of the Breed* on a flight to California. As airplane reading it was ideal, immediately replacing my other novel, an appealing story about the life of an Appalachian woman, full of lyric prose, the love of nature, grief, longing, women who endured. It was no contest. Every time I had to decide what to read for the next several days, *The Last of the Breed* won hands down. And this continued. When in preparation for a course I was teaching I began reading another book, *The Education of Little Tree* by Forrest Carter, it was the same. This was arguably a great book, the fictional autobiography of a Cherokee boy growing up in Appalachia during the Depression. It was poetic, it was deeply wise, it was eloquent and moving. It didn't have a chance. I was out there in the *taiga* at sixty degrees below zero with Joe Makatozi, trying to stay alive. No way could I be tempted by an Appalachian spring.

Day after day and night after night I followed him up goat tracks, through forests, across frozen rivers, camping in lean-tos cleverly put together out of blow-downs, sheltered under giant spruces, hidden from pursuers and providing some small respite from the cold. I drank black tea (when he had any tea) made from melted snow boiled over a small fire whose smoke no one would detect because it was diffused by tree branches. I ate strips of broiled meat cut from the carcass of his latest kill—a moose, a deer, a bear (I am a vegetarian)—and shivered with him (though *he* never shivered) as he looked out across the vast territories he had yet to cross, snow-covered, mountainous, uninhabited by men. I curled up with him in caves, scraped animal hides for moccasins, sewed goatskin jackets with stiff fingers, let stone-tipped arrows fly at the throats of would-be assassins. I loved it. I would rather be out there with Joe Makatozi, listening for telltale sounds, running swiftly down forest paths at night, crouching in the brush while his enemies passed by all unsuspecting, than doing almost anything else. I'm sorry I finished the novel. Not even Siberia was large enough to satisfy my hunger for these things.

I know that *The Education of Little Tree* is a better book than *The Last of the Breed*, better for me, and better, I should think, for most people I know. It reflects a truer, more helpful vision of the world than L'Amour's novel. When I put *Little Tree* down, I felt reassured that the world is a safe place to be—not because the book avoids pain, death, cruelty, and human meanness, but because its vision embraces these things, making them part of a larger whole. Forrest Carter lets you feel the goodness in nature and in human beings and lets you see that they are connected. Still, though I know I'm in need of this wisdom, when given a choice, it seems, I go for the ordeal, the long-drawn-out desperate effort, the close calls, the staying power of the determined man. I want the thrill and the risk and the satisfaction that comes from striving against odds. I want the fear.

By which I mean I want the sexiness of it, the titillation you get from reading books where excitement is so acute it becomes a physical sensation. It pulls you in against your will and better judgment. Knowing you should be answering mail, sleeping, washing your hair, you read anyway and keep on reading. You want the adrenaline rush, the stirred-up feeling, the sense, not consciously registered but strongly apprehended nonetheless, that your mind is totally absorbed, occupied by a form of experience that originates outside itself: consciousness traveling at speed down a track it can't get free of without a powerful jolt. To be a prisoner of adventure in this way is to be free—free of the present moment with the burden of consciousness it holds.

Fear is the emotion that most often triggers this intense absorption; that is the first lesson I learned from *The Last of the Breed*. When I finished this book I was really scared. Usually, at the end of a L'Amour novel I feel invigorated, ready to tackle any task at hand, because, with the hero, I've just won out over long odds. But in *The Last of the Breed*, though it's strongly implied that the hero will finally escape, it's not absolutely certain (and the title, with its double meaning, makes you wonder). The last we see of Joe Mack, he has arranged for a kayak to cross the Bering Strait, and he is about to fight the man who has been tracking him for the entire novel—a bearlike Yakut tribesman named Alekhin, said never to have let a prisoner escape. But instead of giving us the fight we've been waiting for, L'Amour cuts to Colonel Zamatev, the man who had arranged to have Joe Mack shot down in the first place and who has masterminded the yearlong manhunt for him. In the final scene, Zamatev opens a package strangely wrapped in animal skin and sewn together with thongs. It contains the scalp of Alekhin, who was supposed to kill Joe Mack; now we know who has won that one. Included in the package is a note, neatly lettered on birchbark, referring to the contents. It reads:

THIS WAS ONCE A CUSTOM OF MY PEOPLE. IN MY LIFETIME I SHALL TAKE TWO. THIS IS THE FIRST.

These are the novel's last words. I still feel in my stomach the fear they inspired in me when I read them.

What was I afraid of? That the hero wouldn't escape after all? That the kayak wouldn't be waiting and he would have to endure another winter inside the Arctic Circle? No, it was the other way around. I was afraid for Zamatev, whose scalp Joe Mack meant to take when he returned. (I identified with Zamatev when the story unfolded from his point of view.) And I was upset because of what the note revealed about the hero and, by extension, me. This man, whom I had identified with for most of the novel, slept with, ate with, suffered with, thought with, was really a horror. He wasn't just escaping persecution, he wanted blood. Before, his killing of soldiers had seemed necessary for his own survival. This was different. But it was too late to separate from him there at the last moment, to pretend that I didn't write those words on the birchbark. Suddenly I am a scalper, and I will return to the Soviet Union to claim my next victim. This is who I have been all along without knowing it. So I am afraid at the end, afraid for myself as Zamatev, over whose drab shoulder I read the note, and afraid for myself as Joe Mack, the avenger, who will come in his creamy-white goatskin jacket and leggings to slit Zamatev's throat.

The fear I felt at the end of *The Last of the Breed* is an extreme form of the excitement, tinged with apprehension, that accompanies my reading of most Westerns. It exaggerates something that is always there but not clearly seen. You go to a Western for adventure, or rather for the feeling that adventure stimulates, a feeling of being on the edge, at risk, without guarantee. First the narrow rivulet of fear running inside you that widens or narrows depending on how close the danger is. Then moments of excited dread—dry throat, tingling palms, accelerated heartbeat—the high. Then moments of relief, the body at ease, comforted, letting go. But it's the fear that keeps you on—there, totally in the moment with the hero in his trial. It's what keeps him going, too, makes him build that lean-to, find a way to muffle his horse's hooves, detect the rifle barrel's glint among the rocks. Fear heightens his perceptions and sends him superhuman strength in the hour of need. When he survives, and your muscles relax, you know that you too will survive, because you feel it in your gut. And you feel once more the feeling that you need to feel—I am safe, I am OK, I will not die.

———◆◆———

The cycle of fear and release from fear that the reader goes through is an end in itself, enough of a reason for reading the book. The text turns you on, you get off on it. Carried along by the momentum of the plot and the emotions it arouses, you don't have time to notice too much else. Yet there are things to notice. The world of the Western, as of the spy novel, the detective story, the science fiction adventure, is packed with messages. There is never a moment when you aren't being programmed to believe, act, or feel a certain way. The feelings that reading or seeing a Western excites are related to the principal messages it sends. Intended for men primarily, they are messages about what it means to be a successful adult in our society.

Though *The Last of the Breed* is about an American airman shot down on Russian soil, the real opposition in the novel is not between the United States and the Soviet Union but between the life Joe Mack stands for and the lives of all of us. Joe Mack tells his captors that his only allegiance is to his country, for he has no wife, no children, no living kin. But his patriotism is neither national nor racial nor tribal. Joe Mack is a patriot because he lives close to his instincts, close to the land, and close to the spirit of his ancestors. (His bloodlines give him ancestors on three continents—Asia, Europe, and North America—the Indians migrating to America from eastern Siberia, the Scots from Europe). He belongs to the past of the species, to the planet, to earth. His enemies, with one exception, are not defined by language or skin color or ethnic affiliation, but by the way they live—as parts of a bureaucracy, a centralized government, and a giant military machine, flesh and spirit trapped inside huge, complicated organizations of men and equipment. They live like us, the slip-filers.

By contrast, Joe Mack is pure purpose and unadulterated will. An atavistic redeemer, without gospel or program, stripped of everything associated with the name of civilization, he comes to rekindle the will. His mission is to return us to zero, to a state of utter purity before the elements, where essence fronts essence, and there is nothing to get in the way. Joe Mack must stay alive in the Siberian forest in the dead of winter with nothing but his hands and feet. No weapons, no tools, no shelter, no clothing, no food, not even a horse or dog for companionship. (Joe Mack has no animal companions because he *is* the animal, hunted and in hiding, dressed in skins, crouching, eating only the flesh of living things.) His being bereft of everything is essential. It burns away all the accumulated garbage of living: material baggage, mental clutter, emotional entanglements. Joe Mack is naked, free of the past's contamination. His deprivation is ecstatic.

This is how it works. When Joe Mack is almost at the end of his journey, he is captured and beaten and escapes once more, to start again with nothing, a struggle L'Amour describes—and you can feel the accumulated momentum of the narrative pushing the pace along—in a passage that is a mini-version of the whole novel:

Day after day he had slogged along through storm and sun, working his way, mostly by night when there was any night, toward the east. He had camped in the cold, slept on boughs over icy ground. His feet were in terrible shape, and desperately he needed moccasins.

When the emergency rations taken from the Volga [a Soviet automobile] had given out, he had subsisted on marmots, even voles, and occasionally a ptarmigan.

Shortly after he abandoned the Volga the country had been crisscrossed by helicopters and planes, and during most of that time he had huddled in a niche in a clay bank behind some dead poplars and a few straggling willows, a place planes flew over time and again, the searchers never imagining that even a marmot might conceal itself there. For three days he had had nothing to eat; then he caught some fish in a trap he had woven from plant fibers.

Spring was here, and the tundra was aglow with wildflowers.
They were flowers found above timberline in his own country.
(359)

The sufferings this passage depicts—the bruised feet, the cold, the
uncomfortable boughs—are elixir in the cup of life. This and eating
ptarmigan, though we may not be sure what ptarmigan is. Not knowing
makes it more delicious. And the trap "woven from plant fibers"—a perfect touch—better than catching fish with bare hands would have been,
since it shows more craft and ingenuity. Not to mention his hiding under
the enemies' noses for three days. He may be cramped and starving, but
he has made fools of them again, with their clumsy technology. Give me
a marmot-skin moccasin and some dead poplars to hide under any day
and I'll be happy. The joy is in the pain and in the prowess.

Even the reward for staying close to nature and needing nothing—
the wildflowers—cannot be enjoyed from a pleasant vantage. They
must be seen, as they are here, through a film of pain. And they never
will be gathered. For renunciation and denial and doing without are
the essence of this life, the guarantors of vitality. Joe Mack rubs stolen
vodka on his wounds; he doesn't drink any. He lives as close to the bone
as it is possible for a human to live and still survive. "He was always
cold." The suffering is relentless.

Rick Hanson, the homeless man, loved it. So, I am sure, did President
Reagan, who read *Jubal Sackett* (another L'Amour bestseller) while
recovering from cancer; he must have had time to read *The Last of the
Breed*, now that he is out of office.

What does this mean? I argued before that the ordeal dramatized
in L'Amour's fiction satisfies the modern reader's desire for seriousness, for a life where something really is at stake; that the Western is
not an escape from reality but an attempt to get as close to the marrow of things as possible. There is something else involved as well. To
live only in the moment on nothing but your nerve is like trying to do
without a body at all. To press your soul against the windowpane of
being and hold it there. Though the Western hero thrives on physical
sensations, the thrill of facing death challenges the mind above all. He
goes *through* the body to the mind. The faculty of attention, always

operating at capacity, at the crucial moments becomes so concentrated that consciousness is all there is, as if one were lifted out of the body entirely and made into pure awareness.

Body and mind operating at capacity, going beyond their limits into moments of self-transcendence—these are the wished-for experiences that motivate adventure narratives, visitations of the sublime. But these brushes with glory, I am convinced, have a double impact on the reader or viewer only one aspect of which is revealed to casual reflection. Heroic narrative instills a spirit of emulation; you can fight the dragon with Beowulf or swell in righteous anger with the Incredible Hulk and feel motivated to go beyond yourself. But these experiences are purchased at a price. The very process that brings the hero and his reader to moments of exquisite excitement and superhuman concentration has, ultimately, a deadening effect. The hero who is pushed beyond his limits again and again eventually loses the capacity to feel. The result is a gradual etiolation of the nerves whose end point, for the Western hero, is foreshadowed in the desert landscape.

I've said that the hero's trial takes place characteristically within a hostile setting and that the hero's physical body seems sometimes to be an emanation of the land. The harshness of that setting as it's represented in *The Last of the Breed* exceeds the normal limit. The cold that dominates the book from beginning to end is the symbol of this harshness and its embodiment as well. The earth is so cold it is numb. Its body cannot feel anymore. Everything is petrified—the needles of the spruces, the moss underfoot, the rivers, the bark of trees, even the sky. Encased in freezing air, nature is made inaccessible by the cold. The hero's traditional bedding down in nature, nestling into the land's breast, is thwarted by the frigid temperatures. The best he can do is burrow in dank caves or huddle under dead poplars. He feels the cold more as the book progresses, and so do we; the primary physical sensation the book offers is the combined pain and lack of pain produced by slowly freezing.

The hero's body imitates the frozenness of the land by becoming progressively less able to register feeling and reaches the condition of flayed stupor achieved when the body has been driven relentlessly by the will. Victory, in the *The Last of the Breed*, means becoming insensate—the freezing, a metaphor for the numbness necessary to withstand circumstances so appalling that to *feel* them would be to wipe out consciousness altogether. The representative episode from L'Amour's *Heller with a Gun* ends on the note of numbness:

> His mind was empty. He did not think. Only the occasional tug on the lead rope reminded him of the man who rode behind him.
>
> It was a hard land, and it bred hard men to hard ways. (15)

And this anesthetization of the hero is present in Westerns generally. The ethic of self-denial—denial of the needs of the flesh for warmth and comfort, succor, ease, and pleasure; and denial of the needs of the spirit for companionship, affection, love, dependency, exchange—turns the hero to stone in the end. He becomes the desert butte.

This mortification of feeling—both the need to mortify feeling and the effect of having done so—motivates much of the Western hero's typical behavior: his impassivity, inexpressive features, the monolithic character of his presence, his stunted language and non-conversational style of speaking. It is not only the need to maintain a power position that makes him a silent interlocutor but the absolute necessity of protecting himself from his own pain. The hero's throat is closed because if he were to open it and speak he would risk letting his feelings out; they might rise to the surface and flood his face, and he would "play the baby" as Steve, the Virginian's bosom friend, so feared to do that even in death he withheld any sign of his affection. For speech is attended by a double risk: pain and the shame of showing that you feel it. So silence and numbness are two aspects of the same thing—the fear of feeling— and they reinforce each other. Afraid of what would come out if he opened up, the hero remains mute and, not speaking, eventually loses touch with the springs of feeling. His humanness then begins to suffer a slow death, and the fate he avoided by surviving the ordeal overtakes him from another quarter unaware.

While he was in the army L'Amour was assigned to Camp McCoy in the Upper Peninsula of Michigan to give instruction in winter survival.

It was one of the few army assignments for which he felt "thoroughly equipped." He wrote: "I understood the cold. . . . Several times in Oregon I had taken a rifle or a shotgun and gone into the woods in the depth of winter to spend a week or more just knocking about and camping out. Such forays had taught me a great deal about survival in the cold . . ." (*Education of a Wandering Man*, 139, 140). Elsewhere he writes: "As much time as I have spent in cities . . . I liked the wild country the best. Again and again I returned to the desert or the mountains, seeking out the lonely water holes, studying the wildlife, learning to exist on the outer margins" (130).

L'Amour likes the cold, he likes the wild, and he likes to be alone. He finds something to savor in it. The first nonfiction book he read was called *The Genius of Solitude*, and it made a big impression. At the age of fifteen he left school forever. When his classmates were graduating from Jamestown High, in North Dakota, he was buying Kipling's *Departmental Ditties* at Muhammad Dufalkir's bookshop on High Street in Singapore. In his autobiography, *The Education of a Wandering Man*, L'Amour tells a story about loneliness that reveals something of his attitude toward it. A young teacher L'Amour met who thought he wanted to be alone took a job as caretaker of a mine, miles from anywhere. He brought with him a box full of books—Shakespeare, *The Anatomy of Melancholy*, O. Henry's short stories. He lasted two weeks. L'Amour comments:

> The difficulty was that few people know what it means to be absolutely alone. Even fewer know what silence is. Our lives are filled with the coming and going of people and vehicles, so much so that our senses scarcely notice the sounds. . . . Suddenly, here, the man was *alone*. There was no sound. Occasionally, during the day, a hen might cackle, a loosened pebble might rattle down the rocks. Otherwise, nothing. . . . It was not Walden Pond. (42)

L'Amour likes the sound of that loosened pebble, the silence it implies, and the image of profound tedium accentuated by the cackle of a hen. He took the job and stayed. He found it enjoyable.

There is something in the deliberate loneliness of the life L'Amour lets us glimpse in his memoir, the mining claim vigils, the solitary trips in northern forests, the rented rooms near libraries where he holed up to read, that mirrors the Western hero's isolation. Physically comfortless, without close human ties, dedicated to some nameless goal, it is a monastic existence, but without the communitarian aspects of monastic life and apparently without the introspection. This double denial—denial of intimacy either with other people or with one's self—makes the hero's isolation tremendous.

Except for a brief period in the dead of winter, when he associates with some political exiles in a forest camp (and even then he sleeps in a secret lair he's made for himself in the woods), Joe Makatozi spends the entire novel alone. The only human being in vast stretches of wilderness, he is also in a foreign country. Add to this the gelid air that freezes nature's body against him, and his loneliness would seem unendurable. His only relations are with men who want to kill him and whom he wants to kill. He communicates with them, indirectly, through the traces he leaves of his passage over the earth's surface, though typically he leaves no marks, it being a sign of his prowess to leave none. I believe that this image of the hero, isolated, in pain, involved in an endless kill-or-be-killed struggle for existence, reflects and magnifies the emotional reality of many readers' lives. But it is a reality that the hyperbolic action of the story prevents the reader from having to face.

I never feel lonely when reading L'Amour. I'm too busy trying to stay alive. I never think about the fact that this hero has no friends, just temporary allies, no family, only some shadowy people back home or dead. The excitement of hunting or being hunted, of living close to the land, is enough for him, and me. The thrill of the story and the cycle of fear and relief from fear keep the isolation from appearing. And they keep at bay the entire range of feelings that normally arise in the course of any day. The Western's exclusive focus on do-or-die situations doesn't simply represent life without birth and marriage, growing up, finding a place in the world, and growing old; it leaves out all the emotions that are associated with day-to-day living. If you are always fighting off men with guns or trying not to die from thirst in the desert, it isn't possible to entertain other kinds of feelings. As long as you are reading a story where life hangs in the balance, the tremendous pull of the narrative line guarantees that there will be no mental space for anything else.

While exposing you to death the Western insulates you from life, from the mental clutter and emotional turmoil that attend everyday experience. It is not so much the facts of life the story shields you from as their psychological fallout. In this sense, the reader's experience and the hero's go hand in hand. Forced to confront death on a regular basis, the hero steels himself against all emotions and perceptions that do not lead directly to his conquering. Meanwhile, his wounds ache unattended inside. In a parallel fashion, the reader who stares down the barrel of the enemy's gun becomes familiar with the feelings that accompany life-or-death situations, but remains a comparative stranger in his or her own emotional backyard. The hardened-by-suffering hero and the temporarily anesthetized reader are one.

When seen from this vantage, the message that Westerns are sending their audiences seems to center on the need for numbness. Over and over again in countless Westerns we watch the hero swallow his feelings in order to carry out his difficult and distasteful tasks. The numbing process gathers momentum in post-Western cop narratives like the Dirty Harry series, where the hero has to kill so much he becomes a zombielike extension of his hypertrophied gun; and it ends in robotization in science fiction extensions of this line of development such as *The Terminator*, *RoboCop*, and *Total Recall*. But I never realized how central the process of anesthetization was to establishing the hero's claim to heroism until seeing Anthony Mann's aptly titled *Man of the West* (1958), where the main character, played by Gary Cooper, kills almost every other character in the film, performing progressively more terrible acts until in the end he is completely dehumanized. Repeatedly this character finds himself in situations where, we are supposed to believe, he has no choice but to kill or hurt another person, though in doing so he must quell his humanitarian instincts. In the last scene, when the female lead tells him that she loves him and he meets her declaration with stony silence, he has become incapable of any relationship at all.

What is especially revealing about this film is the expression on Gary Cooper's face as he performs his deadly duties. It is the characteristic Gary Cooper grimace—the same one he wears all the way through *High Noon*—a compound of pain, disgust, and determination: pain at the horror of what he has to do, disgust at the venality of his fellow humans for forcing him to do it, and determination to do it anyway, despite his softer feelings. His face, twisted so often into this expression, is the visible sign of his condition, of the fallenness of the world he inhabits, of his own distance from and implication in its fallenness, and of how much it hurts him to do what he has to do.

The expression is also the sign that he is not completely callous, not totally inured to the brutality he witnesses and shares in against his will. For what distinguishes the hero from the villains in a Western is that *he still feels* despite all the horror he has seen and all the horror he has perpetrated. In fact, that is how we know he is tough in the way a hero has to be, for his face shows that he has had to harden himself against his own feelings. His heart is not dead; it is battered and bruised inside the casing of his chest. This, his bruised and bleeding heart, hidden behind his leathery exterior and signaled only by the grimness of his face, his heart which is never heard to utter any sound, is what he carries with him back into the wilderness at the end. It is his sacrifice, bound and smoking on the altar of his principles, the thing without which what he did would have no weight at all.

The death of the heart, or, rather, its scarification and eventual sacrifice, is what the Western genre, more than anything else, is about. The numbing of the capacity to feel, which allows the hero to inflict pain on others, requires the sacrifice of his own heart, a sacrifice kept hidden under his toughness, which is inseparable from his heroic character. At this point, we come upon one of the underlying continuities that link Westerns to the sentimental domestic novels that preceded them. For the hero, who offers himself as a savior of his people, sacrificing his heart so that they can live, replicates the Christian ideal of behavior, giving the self for others, but in a manner that is distorted and disguised so that we do not recognize it. Outwardly the Western hero is the opposite of the sacrificial lamb: he fights, he toughs it out, he seeks the showdown. Instead of dying, he rides out of town alive, a strong man, stronger than the rest, strong enough to do what the others couldn't (kill somebody), strong enough to take his perpetual exile. But inwardly the hero has performed a sacrifice—an ironic and a tragic sacrifice—for the very things he offers up, his heart, his love, his feelings, are what Christ in the trinitarian division of labor has come to represent. It is also the feminine part of himself, the part that opens him to intimate relations to other people, the part that "plays the baby."

Having renounced his heart so that others might keep theirs (even his physique betrays the truth, the slouch from head to hip, chest concave where the heart had been), he rides away alone. And he must do this not because he is a murderer and therefore not to be trusted, but because having hardened himself to do murder, he can no longer open his heart to humankind. His love is aborted, cut off. When I think of the hero in this way, when I think of Shane or Thomas Dunson or Ethan Edwards, the tough lonely men who lord it over others in countless films, my throat constricts. So much pain sustained internally and denied. So much suffering not allowed to speak its name. When he rides out of town at the end, the hero bears his burdens by himself. When I think of how he feels, no words coming out, everything closed inside, the internal bleeding, the sadness of the genre is terrible, and I want to cry. Instead of emulation or outrage, it's compassion the hero deserves, and compassion alone. I would not trade places with him for anything.

Frankenstein's Fallen Angel

JOYCE CAROL OATES

> "*Am I to be thought the only criminal, when all human kind sinned against me?*"
>
> —Frankenstein's demon

Quite apart from its enduring celebrity, and its proliferation in numberless extraliterary forms, Mary Shelley's *Frankenstein; or, The Modern Prometheus* is a remarkable work: a novel sui generis—if a novel at all—and a unique blending of Gothic, fabulist, allegorical, and philosophical materials. Though certainly one of the most calculated and *willed* of fantasies, being in large part a kind of gloss upon or rejoinder to Milton's *Paradise Lost, Frankenstein* is fueled by the kind of grotesque, faintly absurd, and wildly inventive images that spring direct from the unconscious—the eight-foot creature designed to be "beautiful" who turns out almost indescribably repulsive (yellow-skinned, shriveled of countenance, with straight black lips and near-colorless eyes); the cherished cousin bride who *is* beautiful but, in the mind's dreaming, yields horrors ("as I imprinted the first kiss on her lips, they became livid with the hue of death; her features appeared to change, and I thought that I held the corpse of my dead mother in my arms; a shroud enveloped her form, and I saw the grave-worms crawling in the folds"); the mad dream of the Arctic as a country of "eternal light" that will prove, of course, only a place of endless ice, the appropriate land-scape for Victor Frankenstein's death and his demon's self-immolation.

Central to *Frankenstein*—as it is central to a vastly different nine-teenth-century romance, *Jane Eyre*—is a stroke of lightning that appears to issue in a dazzling "stream of fire" from a beautiful old oak tree ("so soon the light vanished, the oak had disappeared, and nothing remained but a blasted stump"): the literal stimulus for Frankenstein's subsequent discovery of the cause of generation and life. And according to Mary Shelley's account of the origin of her "ghost story," the very image of Frankenstein and his demon creature spring from a waking dream of extraordinary vividness:

> I did not sleep, nor could I be said to think. My imagination, unbidden, possessed and guided me, gifting the successive images that arose in my mind with a vividness far beyond the usual bound of reverie. I saw—with shut eyes, but acute mental vision—I saw the pale student of unhallowed arts kneeling beside the thing he had put together. I saw the hideous phantasm of a man stretched out, and then, on the working of some powerful engine, show signs of life, and stir with an uneasy, half-vital motion. . . . [The student] sleeps; but he is awakened; he opens his eyes; behold the horrid thing stands at his bedside, opening his curtains, and looking on him with yellow, watery, but speculative eyes.

Hallucinatory and surrealist on its deepest level, *Frankenstein* is of course one of the most self-consciously literary "novels" ever writ-ten: its awkward form is the epistolary Gothic, its lyric descriptions of natural scenes (the grandiose Valley of Chamounix in particular) spring from Romantic sources, its speeches and monologues echo both Shakespeare and Milton, and, should the author's didactic intention not be clear enough, the demon creature educates himself by studying three books of symbolic significance—Goethe's *The Sorrows of Young Werther*, Plutarch's *Lives*, and Milton's *Paradise Lost*. (The last-named conveniently supplies him with a sense of his own predicament, as Mary Shelley hopes to dramatize it. He reads Milton's great epic as if it were a "true history" giving the picture of an omnipotent God warring with his creatures; he identifies himself with Adam except so far as Adam had come forth from God a "perfect creature, happy and prosperous." Finally, of course, he identifies with Satan: "I am thy creature: I ought to be thy Adam; but I am rather the fallen angel, whom thou drivest from joy for no misdeed. Everywhere I see bliss, from which I alone am irrevocably excluded. I was benevolent and good; misery made me a fiend. Make me happy, and I shall again be virtuous.")

The search of medieval alchemists for the legendary Philosopher's Stone (the talismanic process by which base metals might be transformed into gold or, in psychological terms, the means by which the individual might realize his destiny)—Faust's reckless defiance of human limitations and his willingness to barter his soul for knowledge; the fatal search for answers to the mysteries of their lives of such tragic figures as Oedipus and Hamlet—these are the archetypal dramas to which *Frankenstein* bears an obvious kinship. Yet, as one reads, as Frankenstein and his despised shadow self engage in one after another of the novel's many dialogues, it begins to seem as if the nineteen-year-old author is discovering these archetypal elements for the first time. Frankenstein "is" *Prometheus plasticator*, the creator of mankind; but at the same time, by his own account, he is totally unable to control the behavior of his demon (variously called "monster," "fiend," "wretch," but necessarily lacking a name). Surprisingly, it is not by way of the priggish and "self-devoted" young scientist that Mary Shelley discovers the great power of her narrative, but by way of the misshapen demon, with whom most readers identify: "My person was hideous, and my stature gigantic: what did this mean? Who was I? What was I? Whence did I come? What was my destination?" It is not simply the case that the demon—like Satan and Adam in *Paradise Lost*—has the most compelling speeches in the novel and is far wiser and more magnanimous than his creator: he is also the means by which a transcendent love—a romantically *unrequited* love—is expressed. Surely one of the secrets of *Frankenstein*, which helps to account for its abiding appeal, is the demon's patient, unquestioning, utterly faithful, and utterly *human* love for his irresponsible creator.

(For instance, when Frankenstein is tracking the demon into the Arctic regions, it is clearly the demon who is helping him in his search and even leaving food for him; but Frankenstein is so blind—in fact, so comically blind—he believes that "spirits" are responsible. "Yet still a spirit of good followed and directed my steps, and, when I most murmured, would suddenly extricate me from seemingly insurmountable difficulties. Sometimes, when nature, overcome by hunger, sunk under the exhaustion, a repast was prepared for me in the desert, that restored and inspirited me. . . . I may not doubt that it was set there by the spirits that I had invoked to aid me.")

By degrees, with the progression of the fable's unlikely plot, the inhuman creation becomes increasingly human while his creator becomes increasingly inhuman, frozen in a posture of rigorous denial. (*He* is blameless of any wrongdoing in terms of the demon; and even dares to tell Walton, literally with his dying breath, that another scientist might succeed where he had failed!—so that the lesson of the "Frankenstein monster" is revealed as totally lost on Frankenstein himself.) The demon is (sub)human consciousness-in-the-making, naturally benevolent as Milton's Satan is not, and received with horror and contempt solely because of his physical appearance. He is sired without a mother in defiance of nature but he is in one sense an infant—a comically monstrous eight-foot baby—whose progenitor rejects him immediately after creating him, in one of the most curious (and dreamlike) scenes in the novel:

> How can I describe my emotions at this catastrophe, or how delineate the wretch whom, with such infinite pains and care, I had endeavored to form? [says Victor Frankenstein]. . . . I had worked hard for nearly two years, for the sole purpose of infusing life into an inanimate body. For this I had deprived myself of rest and health. I had desired it with an ardor that far exceeded moderation; but now that I had finished, the beauty of the dream vanished, and breathless horror and disgust filled my heart. Unable to endure the aspect of the being I had created, I rushed out of the room, and continued a long time traversing my bed-chamber, unable to compose my mind to sleep.

Here follows the nightmare vision of Frankenstein's bride-to-be Elizabeth as a form of his dead mother, with "grave-worms crawling" in her shroud; and shortly afterward the "wretch" himself appears at Frankenstein's bed, drawing away the canopy as Mary Shelley had imagined. But Frankenstein is so cowardly he runs away again; and this time the demon is indeed abandoned, to reappear after the first of the "murders" of Frankenstein's kin. On the surface Frankenstein's behavior is preposterous, even idiotic, for he seems blind to the fact that is apparent to any reader: that he has loosed a fearful power into the world, whether it strikes his eye as aesthetically pleasing or not, and he *must* take responsibility for it. Except, of course, he does not. For, as he keeps telling himself, he is blameless of any wrongdoing apart from the act of creation itself. The emotions he catalogues for us—gloom, sorrow, misery, despair—are conventionally Romantic attitudes, mere luxuries in a context that requires action and not simply response.

By contrast the demon is all activity, all yearning, all hope: his love for his maker is unrequited and seems incapable of making any impression upon him, yet he never gives it up, even when he sounds most threatening. ("Beware," says the demon midway in the novel, "for I am fearless, and therefore powerful. I will watch with the wiliness of a snake, that I may sting with its venom. Man, you shall repent of the injuries you inflict.") His voice is very like his creator's—indeed, everyone in *Frankenstein* sounds alike—but his posture is always one of simple need; he requires love in order to become less monstrous, but, as he *is* a monster, love is denied him; and the man responsible for this comically tragic state of affairs says repeatedly that he is not to blame. (Frankenstein's typical response to the situation is: "I felt as if I had committed some great crime, the consciousness of which haunted me. I was guiltless, but I had indeed drawn a horrible curse upon my head, as mortal as that of crime.") But if Frankenstein is not to blame for the various deaths that occur, who is? Has he endowed his creation, as God endowed Adam in Milton's epic, with free will? Or is the demon psychologically his creature, committing the forbidden acts he wants committed—so long as he himself remains "guiltless"?

It is a measure of the subtlety of this moral parable that the demon strikes so many archetypal chords and suggests so many variant readings.

He recapitulates in truncated form the history of consciousness of his race (learning to speak, read, write, etc., by closely watching the De Lacey family); he is an abandoned child, a parentless orphan; he takes on the voices of Adam, Satan ("Evil thenceforth became my good," he says, as Milton's fallen angel says, "Evil be thou my good"), even our "first mother" Eve. When the demon terrifies himself by seeing his reflection in a pool and grasping at once the nature of his own deformity, he is surely not mirroring Narcissus, as some commentators have suggested, but Milton's Eve in her surprised discovery of her own beauty, in Book IV of *Paradise Lost*.[1] He is Shakespeare's Edmund, though *unloved*; a shadow figure more tragic, because more "conscious," than the hero he represents. Most suggestively he has become by the novel's melodramatic conclusion a form of Christ: sinned against by all humankind, yet fundamentally blameless, and *yet* quite willing to die as a sacrifice. He speaks of his death as a "consummation"; he is going to burn himself on a funeral pyre somewhere in the Arctic wastes. Unlikely, certainly, but a fitting end to a life conceived by way of lightning and electricity:

"But soon," he cried with sad and solemn enthusiasm, "I shall die, and what I now feel be no longer felt. Soon these burning miseries will be extinct. I shall ascend my funeral pile triumphantly, and exult in the agony of the torturing flames. The light of that conflagration will fade away; my ashes will be swept into the sea by the winds. My spirit will sleep in peace; or, if it thinks, it will not surely think thus."

But the demon does not die within the confines of the novel, so perhaps he has not died after all. He is a "modern" species of shadow or

1 The influence of Milton on *Frankenstein* is so general as to figure on nearly every page; and certainly the very conception of the monumental *Paradise Lost* stands behind the conception of Mary Shelley's "ghost story." According to Christopher Small's excellent *Ariel Like a Harpy: Shelley, Mary, and Frankenstein* (New York: Humanities Press, 1974), Mary Shelley's booklist notes *Paradise Regained* as read in 1815, and in 1816 she and Shelley were both reading *Paradise Lost* at intervals during the year. At one point Shelley read the long poem aloud to her, finishing it in a week in November of 1816.

doppelgänger—*the nightmare that is deliberately created by man's inge-nuity* and not a mere supernatural being or fairy-tale remnant.

Frankenstein's double significance as a work of prose fiction and a cul-tural myth—as "novel" of 1818 and timeless "metaphor"—makes it a highly difficult story to read directly. A number of popular miscon-ceptions obscure it for most readers: Frankenstein is of course not the monster but his creator; nor is he a mad scientist of genius—he is in fact a highly idealistic and naïve youth in the conventional Romantic mode (in Walton's admiring eyes "noble," "cultivated," a "celestial spirit" who has suffered "great and unparalleled misfortunes"), not unlike Mary Shelley's fated lover Shelley. Despite the fact that a number of catastrophes occur around him and indirectly because of him, Victor Frankenstein is well intentioned, gentlemanly, *good*; he is no sadist like H. G. Wells's exiled vivisectionist Dr. Moreau (who boasts, "You cannot imagine the strange colorless delight of these intellectual desires. The thing before you is no longer an animal, a fellow-creature, but a prob-lem.")[2] Frankenstein's mission is selfless, even messianic:

> No one can conceive the variety of feelings which bore me onwards, like a hurricane, in the first enthusiasm of success. Life and death appeared to me ideal bounds, which I should first break through, and pour a torrent of light into our dark world. A new species would bless me as its creator and source; many happy and excellent natures would owe their being to me. No father could claim the gratitude of his child so completely as I should deserve theirs. . . . If I could bestow animation upon lifeless matter, I might in process of time . . . renew life where death had apparently devoted the body to corruption.

---

2 H. G. Wells's *The Island of Dr. Moreau* (1896) is a savage variant on the Frankenstein legend. Moreau experiments on living animals, trying to make them "human" or humanoid; he succeeds in creating a race of Beast Folk who eventually rise up against him and kill him. Moreau's beliefs strike a more chilling—and more contemporary—note than Frankenstein's idealism: "To this day I have never troubled about the ethics of the matter. The study of Nature makes a man at last as remorseless as Nature," boasts Moreau.

It is a measure of the novel's extraordinary fame that the very name "Frankenstein" has long since supplanted "Prometheus" in popular usage, and the "Frankenstein legend" retains a significance for our time as the "Prometheus legend" does not.

How many fictional characters after all have made the great leap from literature to mythology; how many creations of sheer language have stepped from the rhythms of their authors' unique voices into what might be called a collective cultural consciousness? Don Quixote, Dracula, Sherlock Holmes, Alice (in Wonderland), certain figures in the fairy tales of Hans Christian Andersen . . . and of course Frankenstein's "monster." Virtually millions of people who have never heard of the novel *Frankenstein*, let alone that a young Englishwoman named Mary Shelley (in fact, Godwin) wrote it at the age of nineteen, are well acquainted with the image of Frankenstein popularized by Boris Karloff in the 1930s; and understand at least intuitively the ethical implications of the metaphor. (As in the expression, particularly relevant for our time, "We have created a Frankenstein monster.") The more potent the archetype evoked by a work of literature, the more readily its specific form slips free of the time-bound *personal* work. On the level of cultural myth the figures of Dracula, Sherlock Holmes, Alice, and the rest are near-autonomous beings, linked to no specific books and no specific authors. They have become communal creations; they belong to us all. Hence the very real difficulty in reading Mary Shelley's novel for the first time. (Subsequent readings are far easier and yield greater rewards.)

Precisely because of this extraordinary fame, one should be reminded of how original and unique the novel was at the time of its publication. Can it even be read at the present time in a context hospitable to its specific allusions and assumptions—one conversant with the thorny glories of *Paradise Lost*, the sentimental ironies of Coleridge's "The Rime of the Ancient Mariner," the Gothic conventions of tales-within-tales, epistolary frames, and histrionic speeches delivered at length? In a more accomplished work, *Wuthering Heights*, the structural complexities of tales-within-tales are employed for artistic ends; the ostensible fracturing of time yields a rich poetic significance; characters grow and change like people whom we have come to know. In

Mary Shelley's *Frankenstein* the strained conventions of the romance are mere structural devices to allow Victor Frankenstein and his demon their opposing—but intimately linked—"voices." Thus abrupt transitions in space and time take place in a kind of rhetorical vacuum: all is summary, past history, exemplum.

But it is a mistake to wish to read *Frankenstein* as a modern novel of psychological realism, or as a "novel" at all. It contains no characters, only points of view; its concerns are pointedly moral and didactic; it makes no claims for verisimilitude of even a poetic Wordsworthian nature. (The Alpine landscapes are all self-consciously sublime and theatrical; Mont Blanc, for instance, suggests "another earth, the habitations of another race of beings.") If one were pressed to choose a literary antecedent for *Frankenstein* it might be, surprisingly, Samuel Johnson's *Rasselas*, rather than a popular Gothic like Mrs. Radcliffe's *Mysteries of Udolpho*, which allegedly had the power to frighten its readers. (A character in Jane Austen's *Northanger Abbey* says of this once-famous novel: "I remember finishing it in two days—my hair standing on end the whole time.") Though *Frankenstein* and *Dracula* are commonly linked, Bram Stoker's tour de force of 1897 is vastly different in tone, theme, and intention from Shelley's novel: its "monster" is not at all monstrous in appearance, only in behavior; and he is thoroughly and irremediably evil by nature. But no one in *Frankenstein* is evil—the universe is emptied of God and of theistic assumptions of "good" and "evil." Hence its modernity.

Tragedy does not arise spontaneous and unwilled in so "modern" a setting, it must be made—in fact, manufactured. The Fates are not to blame; there *are* no Fates, only the brash young scientist who boasts of never having feared the supernatural. ("In my education my father had taken the greatest precautions that my mind should be impressed with no supernatural horrors. I do not ever remember to have trembled at a tale of superstition, or to have feared the apparition of a spirit. . . . A churchyard was to me merely the receptacle of bodies deprived of life, which, from being the seat of beauty and strength, had become food for the worm.") Where *Dracula* and other conventional Gothic works are fantasies, with clear links to fairy tales and legends, and even popular ballads, *Frankenstein* has the theoretical and cautionary tone of science fiction. It is meant to prophesize, not to entertain.

Another aspect of *Frankenstein*'s uniqueness lies in the curious bond between Frankenstein and his created demon. Where by tradition such beings as doubles, shadow selves, "imps of the perverse," and classic doppelgängers (like poor Golyadkin's nemesis in Dostoyevsky's "The Double," of 1846) spring full grown from supernatural origins—that is, from unacknowledged recesses of the human spirit—Frankenstein's demon is *natural* in origin: a manufactured nemesis. He is an abstract idea made flesh, a Platonic essence given a horrific (and certainly ludicrous) existence. Yet though he is meant to be Frankenstein's ideal, a man-made miracle that would "pour a torrent of light into our dark world," he is only a fragment of that ideal—which is to say, a mockery, a parody, a joke. The monsters we create by way of an advanced technological civilization "are" ourselves as we cannot hope to see ourselves—incomplete, blind, blighted, and, most of all, self-destructive. For it is the forbidden wish for death that dominates. (In intention it is customarily the deaths of others, "enemies"; in fact it may be our own deaths we plan.) Hence the tradition of recognizing Faustian pacts with the Devil as acts of aggression against the human self—the very "I" of the rational being.

Since Frankenstein's creature is made up of parts collected from charnel houses and graves, and his creator acknowledges that he "disturbed, with profane fingers, the tremendous secrets of the human frame," it is inevitable that he be a profane thing. He cannot be blessed or loved: he springs not from a natural union but has been forged in what Frankenstein calls a "workshop of filthy creation." One of the brilliant surrealist touches of the narrative is the fact that Frankenstein's shadow self is a giant; even the rationalization for this curious decision is ingenious. "As the minuteness of the parts formed a great hindrance to my speed," Frankenstein explains to Walton, "I resolved, contrary to my first intention, to make the being of a gigantic stature; that is to say, about eight feet in height, and proportionably large." A demon of mere human size would not have been nearly so compelling.

(The reader should keep in mind the fact that, in 1818, the notion that "life" might be galvanized in laboratory conditions was really not so farfetched; for the properties of electricity were not commonly understood and seem to have been bound up magically with what might be called metaphorically the "spark" of life.[3] Again, in our own time, the possibility of artificially induced life, human or otherwise, does not seem especially remote.)

Because in one sense the demon is Frankenstein's deepest self, the relationship between them is dreamlike, fraught with undefined emotion. Throughout the novel Frankenstein is susceptible to fainting fits, bouts of illness and exhaustion, and nightmares of romantic intensity, less a fully realized personality than a queer stunted half-self (rather like Roderick Usher, whose sister, Madeleine, *his* secret self, is buried alive). It is significant that as soon as Frankenstein induces life in his eight-foot monster he notices *for the first time* what he has created. "His limbs were in proportion," Frankenstein testifies, "and I had selected his features as beautiful." But something has clearly gone wrong:

> Beautiful! Great God! His yellow skin scarcely covered the work of muscles and arteries beneath; his hair was of a lustrous black, and flowing; his teeth of a pearly whiteness; but these luxuriances only formed a more horrid contrast with his watery eyes, that seemed almost of the same color as the dun white sockets in which they were set, his shrivelled complexion, and straight black lips.

Significant too is the fact that Frankenstein retreats from this vision and falls asleep—an unlikely response in naturalistic terms, but quite appropriate symbolically—so that, shortly afterward, his demon can arouse *him* from sleep:

> I started from my sleep with horror; a cold dew covered my forehead, my teeth chattered, and every limb became convulsed;

---

3 In Thomas Hogg's *The Life of Percy Bysshe Shelley* (1858) Shelley's lifelong fascination with lightning, electricity, and galvanism is discussed at some length. As a boy he owned something called an "electrical machine" with which he amused himself with experiments; as a young man he was mesmerized by lightning and thunder and made it a point to "enjoy" electrical storms.

when, by the dim and yellow light of the moon, as it forced
its way through the window-shutters, I beheld the wretch, the
miserable monster whom I had created. He held up the curtain
of the bed; and his eyes, if eyes they may be called, were fixed on
me. His jaws opened, and he muttered some inarticulate sounds,
while a grin wrinkled his cheeks. . . .

Oh! no mortal could support the horror of that countenance. A
mummy again endued with animation could not be so hideous as
that wretch. I had gazed on him while unfinished: he was ugly then;
but when those muscles and joints were rendered capable of motion,
it became a thing such as even Dante could not have conceived.

Frankenstein's superficial response to the "thing" he has created is solely
in aesthetic terms, for his atheistic morality precludes all thoughts of
transgression. (Considering the fact that the author of *Frankenstein* is
a woman, a woman well acquainted with pregnancy and childbirth at
a precocious age, it is curious that nowhere in the novel does anyone
raise the issue of the demon's "unnatural" genesis; he is a monster son
born of Man exclusively, a parody of the Word or the Idea made flesh.)
Ethically, Frankenstein is "blameless"——though he is haunted by the
suspicion throughout that he has committed a crime of some sort, with
the very best of intentions.

Where the realistic novel presents characters in a more or less coherent "field," as part of a defined society, firmly established in time and
place, romance does away with questions of verisimilitude and plau-
sibility altogether and deals directly with the elements of narrative:
it might be said to be an "easier" form psychologically, since it evokes
archetypal responses on its primary level. No one expects of Victor
Frankenstein that he behave plausibly when he is a near-allegorical
figure; no one expects of his demon that he behave plausibly since he is
a demonic presence, an outsized mirror image of his creator. When the
demon warns Frankenstein (in traditional Gothic form, incidentally),
"I shall be with you on your wedding-night," it seems only natural,
granted Frankenstein's egocentricity, that he worry about his own
safety and not his bride's; and that, despite the warning, Frankenstein
allows Elizabeth to be murdered. His wish is his demon self's command,

though he never acknowledges his complicity. Indeed, *Frankenstein* begins to read as an antiromance, a merciless critique of Romantic attitudes—sorrow, misery, self-loathing, despair, paralysis, etc.—written, as it were, from the inside, by a young woman who had already lost a baby in infancy (in 1815, a girl); would lose another, also a girl, in 1817; and, in 1819, a third—named, oddly, William (the very name of the little boy murdered early on in the narrative by Frankenstein's demon).[4] Regardless of the sufferings of others, the romantically "self-devoted" hero responds solely in terms of his own emotions. He might be a lyric poet of the early 1800s, for all his preoccupation with self: everything refers tragically to him, everything is rendered in terms of *his* experience:

> Great God! why did I not then expire? Why am I here to relate the destruction of the best hope, and the purest creature of earth? [Elizabeth] was there, lifeless and inanimate, thrown across the bed, her head hanging down, and her pale and distorted features half covered by her hair. Everywhere I turn I see the same figure—her bloodless arms and relaxed form flung by the murderer on its bridal bier. Could I behold this, and live? (Alas, life is obstinate, and clings closest where it is most hated.) For a moment only, and I lost recollection: I fainted.

Frankenstein grapples with the complex moral issues raised by his demonic creation by "fainting" in one way or another throughout the novel. And in his abrogation of consciousness and responsibility, the

---

4 The feminist critic Ellen Moers interprets *Frankenstein* solely in terms of a birth myth "that was lodged in the novelist's imagination . . . by the fact that she was herself a mother." Though her argument certainly aids in understanding some of the less evident motives for the composition of *Frankenstein*, it reduces a complex philosophical narrative to little more than a semiconscious fantasy, scarcely a *literary* work at all. Did Mary Shelley's womb, or her brain, write *Frankenstein*? In virtually a parody of feminist myth-making, Moers argues that Shelley's book is "most powerful" where it is "most feminine": "in the motif of revulsion against newborn life, and the drama of guilt, dread, and flight surrounding birth and its consequences." See Ellen Moers, "Female Gothic," in *Literary Women* (Garden City, N.Y.: Doubleday & Co., 1974).

demon naturally acts: for this is the Word, the secret wish for destruction, made Flesh.

The cruelest act of all is performed by Frankenstein before the very eyes of his demon: this is the sudden destruction of the partly assembled "bride." He makes the creature at the bidding of his demon, who has promised, most convincingly, to leave Europe with her and to live "virtuously," but, suddenly repulsed by the "filthy process" he has undertaken, Frankenstein destroys his work. ("The wretch saw me destroy the creature on whose future existence he depended for happiness, and, with a howl of devilish despair and revenge, withdrew.") Afterward he thinks, looking at the remains of the half-finished creature, that he has almost mangled the living flesh of a human being; but he never feels any remorse for what he has done and never considers that, in "mangling" the flesh of his demon's bride, he is murdering the pious and rather too perfect Elizabeth, the cousin bride whom he professes to love. "Am I to be thought the only criminal," the demon asks, "when all human kind sinned against me?" He might have said, as reasonably, *when all human kind conspired in my sin.*

While *Paradise Lost* is to Frankenstein's demon (and very likely to Mary Shelley as well) the picture of an "omnipotent God warring with his creatures," *Frankenstein* is the picture of a finite and flawed god at war with, and eventually overcome by, his creation. It is a parable for our time, an enduring prophecy, a remarkably acute diagnosis of the lethal nature of *denial*: denial of responsibility for one's actions, denial of the shadow self locked within consciousness. Even in the debased and sensational form in which Frankenstein's monster is known by most persons—as a kind of retarded giant, one might say, with electrodes in his neck—his archetypal significance rings true. "My form," he says eloquently, "is a filthy type of yours."

Philip Larkin 1922–1985

MARTIN AMIS

Philip Larkin was not an inescapable presence in America, as he was in England; and to some extent you can see America's point. His Englishness was so desolate and inhospitable that even the English were scandalized by it. Certainly, you won't find his work on the Personal Growth or Self-Improvement shelves in your local bookstore. "Get out as early as you can," as he once put it. "And don't have any kids yourself."

All his values and attitudes were utterly, even fanatically "negative." He really was "anti-life"—a condition that many are accused of but few achieve. To put it at its harshest, you could say that there is in his ethos a vein of spiritual poverty, almost of spiritual squalor. Along with John Betjeman, he was England's best-loved postwar poet; but he didn't love postwar England, or anything else. He didn't love—end of story—because love seemed derisory when set against death. "The past is past and the future neuter"; "Life is first boredom, then fear" . . . That these elements should have produced a corpus full of truth, beauty, instruction, delight—and much wincing humor—is one of the many great retrievals wrought by irony. Everything about Larkin rests on irony, that English specialty and vice.

Anti-intellectual, incurious and reactionary ("Oh, I adore Mrs Thatcher"), Larkin was himself an anti-poet. He never wanted to go anywhere or do anything. "I've never been to America, nor to anywhere else, for that matter." Asked by an interviewer whether he would like to visit, say, China, he replied, "I wouldn't mind seeing China if I could come back the same day." He never read his poems in public, never lectured on poetry, and "never taught anyone how to write it." He lived in Hull, which is like living in Akron, Ohio, with the further advantage that it is more or less impossible to get to.

His meanness was legendary, and closely connected to the solitude he built around himself. It is said that he never owned more than one kitchen chair, to make sure that no one could stop by for lunch—or, worse, come to stay. Christmas shopping was, for him, "that annual conversion of one's indifference to others into active hatred." Sometimes, though, he weakened:

> Finding Stevie Smith's *Not Waving but Drowning* in a bookshop one Christmas some years ago, I was sufficiently impressed by it to buy a number of copies for random distribution among friends. The surprise this caused them was partly, no doubt, due to the reaction that before the war led us to amend the celebrated cigarette advertisement "If So-and-So, usually a well-known theatrical personality, offered you a cigarette it would be a Kensitas" by substituting for the brand name the words "bloody miracle."

His feelings about money were complicated and pleasureless. He pronounced the word *bills* as if it were a violent obscenity. (He brooded deeply about his bills.) He always had enough money and, anyway, there was nothing he wanted to spend it on.

> Quarterly, is it, money reproaches me:
> "Why do you let me lie here wastefully?
> I am all you never had of goods and sex.
> You could get them still by writing a few cheques". . .
> . . . I listen to money singing. It's like looking down
> From long french windows at a provincial town,
> The slums, the canal, the churches ornate and mad
> In the evening sun. It is intensely sad.

Money meant work, and there was a priestly stoicism in Larkin's devotion, or submission, to his job as University Librarian at Hull. He supervised a staff of over a hundred; typically he was a brilliant administrator, with a great talent for drudgery. Work was the "toad" that he let "squat on my life." In the last decade he didn't need the job any longer, but he thought (with maximum lack of glamor), "Well, I might as well get my pension, since I've gone so far."

What else can I answer,

When the lights come on at four
At the end of another year?
Give me your arm, old toad,
Help me down Cemetery Road.

He never married, naturally, and made a boast of his aversion to children. "Children are very horrible, aren't they? Selfish, noisy, cruel, vulgar little brutes." As a child himself, he has said, he thought he hated everybody: "but when I grew up I realized it was just children I didn't like." His own childhood he repeatedly dismissed as "a forgotten boredom" ("Nothing, like something, happens anywhere"). You feel that the very notion of childhood, with all its agitation and enchantment, was simply too sexy for Larkin. He regarded married life as a terrible mystery, something that other people did (and "'Other People are Hell"), a matter for appalled—and double-edged—ridicule:

He married a woman to stop her getting away
Now she's there all day,
And the money he gets for wasting his life on work
She takes as her perk
To pay for the kiddies' clobber and the drier
And the electric fire . . .

And so on, until the inexorable revenge:

So he and I are the same,

Only I'm a better hand
At knowing what I can stand

Without them sending a van—
Or I suppose I can.

The clinching paradox may be, however, that Larkin will survive as
a romantic poet, an exponent of the ironic romance of exclusion, or
inversion. One review of *High Windows* (his last book of poems, and
his best by some distance) was headed "Don Juan in Hull"; and this
says a great deal, I think, about the currents of thwarted eroticism in
his work. Of the shopping-center, the motorway cafe, the old people's
home, the madman-haunted park, the ambulance, the hospital, Larkin
sang. Even his own inner ugliness ("monkey-brown, fish-grey") he
made beautiful:

For something sufficiently toad-like
Squats in me, too;
Its hunkers are heavy as hard luck,
And cold as snow...

"Do you feel you could have had a much happier life?" an interviewer
once asked. "Not without being someone else." What we are left with is
the lyricism that Larkin seemed to be shedding or throwing away as he
moved towards death. From "The Trees":

Yet still the unresting castles thresh
In fullgrown thickness every May.
Last year is dead, they seem to say,
Begin afresh, afresh, afresh.

It was in my capacity as a cruel and vulgar little brute that I first met
Larkin—at the age of four or five. He was my elder brother's godfather and namesake, and, to my brother and me (true to type: indeed,
it might have been us who put him off), visits from godfathers meant
money. *My* godfather was rich, generous, and seldom sober when he
came to stay: half-crowns and ten-shilling notes dropped from his hand
into ours. But it was always a solemn moment when it came for Larkin
to "tip the boys"—almost a religious experience, as I remember it. At

first it was sixpence for Philip against threepence for Martin; years later it was tenpence against sixpence; later still it was a shilling against ninepence: always index-linked and carefully graded. Other poets I came across during that time—notably Robert Graves—tended to be ebullient, excitable, candidly bardic. Larkin was simply a melancholy man, prematurely bald and with the remains of a stutter. In my later dealings with him, he was always quietly amusing, doggedly honest and (in the widest sense) exceptionally well-mannered. Larkin may have written poetry, but he spent no time "being a poet."

The death was as comfortless as the life. And it had its element of ironic heroism. There was no real family, of course, and visits from friends were not encouraged. All his life he had girded himself for extinction; but when it came (and this is appropriate and consistent) he was quite unprepared, resolutely helpless, having closed no deal with death. He instructed his doctors to tell him nothing—to tell him lies. It is said that Evelyn Waugh died of snobbery. Philip Larkin died of shame: mortal, corporeal shame.

He made no effort to prolong matters. In the last year of his life he used to start the day with three glasses of supermarket port ("Well," he explained to my father, "you've got to have some fucking reason for getting up in the morning"). In the last week he was subsisting on "gin, Complan and cheap red wine." "Couldn't you at least get some *expensive* red wine?" my mother suggested on the telephone, three days before his death. But no. Live out the comfortlessness, in fear and bafflement—that was the strategy. Although he was Larkin's best friend, my father saw him infrequently and now wonders if he ever really knew him.

Ten Ways of Looking at *The Island of Doctor Moreau* by H. G. Wells

MARGARET ATWOOD

H. G. Wells's *The Island of Doctor Moreau* is one of those books that, once read, is rarely forgotten. Jorge Luis Borges called it an "atrocious miracle," and made large claims for it. Speaking of Wells's early tales—*The Island of Doctor Moreau* among them—he said, "I think they will be incorporated, like the fables of Theseus or Ahasuerus, into the general memory of the species and even transcend the fame of their creator or the extinction of the language in which they were written."[1]

This has proved true, if film may be considered a language unto itself. *The Island of Doctor Moreau* has inspired three films—two of them quite bad—and doubtless few who saw them remembered that it was Wells who authored the book. The story has taken on a life of its own, and, like the offspring of Mary Shelley's *Frankenstein*, has acquired attributes and meanings not present in the original. Moreau himself, in his filmic incarnations, has drifted toward the type of the Mad Scientist, or the Peculiar Genetic Engineer, or the Tyrant-in-Training, bent on taking over the world; whereas Wells's Moreau is certainly not mad, is a mere vivisectionist, and has no ambitions to take over anything whatsoever.

---

1 Borges, Jorge Luis. Weinberger, Eliot (ed.), Allen, Esther (trans.), *The Total Library: Non-Fiction 1922–1986* (London: Allen Lane, Penguin Press, 1999).

Borges's use of the word "fable" is suggestive, for—despite the realistically rendered details of its surface—the book is certainly not a novel, if by that we mean a prose narrative dealing with observable social life. "Fable" points to a certain folkloric quality that lurks in the pattern of this curious work, as animal faces may lurk in the fronds and flowers of an Aubrey Beardsley design. The term may also indicate a lie—something fabulous or invented, as opposed to that which demonstrably exists—and employed this way it is quite apt, as no man ever did or ever will turn animals into human beings by cutting them up and sewing them together again. In its commonest sense, a fable is a tale—like those of Aesop—meant to convey some useful lesson. But what is that useful lesson? It is certainly not spelled out by Wells.

"Work that endures is always capable of an infinite and plastic ambiguity; it is all things for all men," says Borges, ". . . and it must be ambiguous in an evanescent and modest way, almost in spite of the author; he must appear to be ignorant of all symbolism. Wells displayed that lucid innocence in his first fantastic exercises, which are to me the most admirable part of his admirable work."[2] Borges carefully did not say that Wells employed no symbolism, only that he appeared to be ignorant of doing so.

Here follows what I hope will be an equally modest attempt to probe beneath the appearance, to examine the infinite and plastic ambiguity, to touch on the symbolism that Wells may or may not have employed deliberately, and to try to discover what the useful lesson—if there is one—might be.

TEN WAYS OF LOOKING AT THE ISLAND OF DOCTOR MOREAU

1. ELOIS AND MORLOCKS

The Island of Doctor Moreau was published in 1896, when H. G. Wells was only thirty years old. It followed *The Time Machine*, which had appeared the year before, and was to be followed two years later by *The War of the Worlds*, this being the book that established Wells as a force to be reckoned with at a mere thirty-two years of age.

---

2 Borges, Jorge Luis, *Other Inquisitions 1937–1952* (New York: Clarion, 1968).

To some of literature's more gentlemanly practitioners—those, for instance, who had inherited money, and didn't have to make it by scribbling—Wells must have seemed like a puffed-up little counter-jumper, and a challenging one at that, because he was bright. He'd come up the hard way. In the stratified English social world of the time, he was neither working-class nor top crust. His father was an unsuccessful tradesman; he himself apprenticed with a draper for two years before wending his way, via school-teaching and a scholarship, to the Normal School of Science. Here he studied under Darwin's famous apologist Thomas Henry Huxley. Wells graduated with a first-class degree, but he'd been seriously injured by one of the students while teaching, an event that put him off school-mastering. It was after this that he turned to writing.

The Time Traveler in *The Time Machine*—written just before *The Island of Doctor Moreau*—finds that human beings in the future have split into two distinct races. The Eloi are pretty as butterflies, but useless; the grim and ugly Morlocks live underground, make everything, and come out at night to devour the Eloi, whose needs they also supply. The Upper Classes, in other words, have become a bevy of Upper-Class Twitterers and have lost the ability to fend for themselves, and the working classes have become vicious and cannibalistic.

Wells was neither an Eloi or a Morlock. He must have felt he represented a third way, a rational being who had climbed up the ladder through ability alone, without partaking of the foolishness and impracticality of the social strata above his nor of the brutish crudeness of those below.

But what about Prendick, the narrator of *The Island of Doctor Moreau*? He's been pootling idly about the world—for his own diversion, we assume—when he's shipwrecked. The ship is called the *Lady Vain*, surely a comment on the snooty aristocracy. Prendick himself is a "private gentleman" who doesn't have to work for a living, and, though he—like Wells—has studied with Huxley, he has done so not out of necessity but out of dilettantish boredom—"as a relief from the dullness of [his] comfortable independence." Prendick, though not quite as helpless as a full-fledged Eloi, is well on the path to becoming one. Thus his hysteria, his lassitude, his moping, his ineffectual attempts at fair play, and his lack of common sense—he can't figure out how to make a raft because he's never done "any carpentry or suchlike work" in his life, and when he does manage to patch something together, he's situated it too far from the sea and it falls apart when he's dragging it. Although Prendick is not a complete waste of time—if he were, he wouldn't be able to hold our attention while he tells his story—he's nonetheless in the same general league as the weak-chinned curate in the later *War of the Worlds*, that helpless and driveling "spoiled child of life."[3]

His name—Prendick—is suggestive of "thick" coupled with "prig," this last a thing he is explicitly called. To those versed in legal lore, it could suggest "prender," a term for something you are empowered to take without it having been offered. But it more nearly suggests "prentice," a word that would have been floating close to the top of Wells's semiconsciousness, due to his own stint as an apprentice. Now it's the Upper Class's turn at apprenticeship! Time for one of them to undergo a little degradation and learn a thing or two. But what?

2. SIGNS OF THE TIMES

The Island of Doctor Moreau comes not only midway in Wells's most fertile period of fantastic inventiveness; it also comes during such a period in English literary history. Adventure romance had taken off with Robert Louis Stevenson's *Treasure Island* in 1882, and Rider Haggard had done him one better with *She*, in 1887. This latter coupled straight adventure—shipwreck, tramps through dangerous swamps and nasty shrubbery, encounters with bloody-minded savages, fun in steep ravines and dim grottoes—with a big dollop of weirdness carried over from earlier gothic traditions, done up this time in a package labeled "Not Supernatural." The excessive powers of She are ascribed not to a close encounter with a vampire or god, but to a dip in a revolving pillar of fire, no more supernatural than lightning. She gets her powers from Nature.

It's from this blend—the grotesque and the "natural"—that Wells took his cue. An adventure story that would once have featured battles

3 Wells, H. G., *The War of the Worlds* (New York: Airmont, 1964).

with fantastic monsters—dragons, gorgons, hydras—keeps the exotic scenery, but the monsters have been produced by the very agency that was seen by many in late Victorian England as the bright, new, shiny salvation of mankind: science.

The other blend that proved so irresistible to readers was one that was developed much earlier, and to singular advantage, by Jonathan Swift: a plain, forthright style in the service of incredible events. Poe, that master of the uncanny, piles on the adjectives to create "atmosphere"; Wells, on the other hand, follows R. L. Stevenson and anticipates Hemingway in his terse, almost journalistic approach, usually the hallmark of the ultrarealists. *The War of the Worlds* shows Wells employing this combination to best effect—we think we're reading a series of news reports and eyewitness accounts, but he's already honing it in *The Island of Doctor Moreau*. A tale told so matter-of-factly and with such an eye to solid detail surely cannot be—we feel—either an invention or a hallucination.

3. SCIENTIFIC

Wells is acknowledged to be one of the foremost inventors in the genre we now know as "science fiction." As Robert Silverberg has said, "Every time-travel tale written since *The Time Machine* is fundamentally indebted to Wells. . . . In this theme, as in most of science fiction's great themes, Wells was there first."[4]

"Science fiction" as a term was unknown to Wells; it did not make its appearance until the 1930s, in America, during the golden age of bug-eyed monsters and girls in brass brassieres.[5] Wells himself referred to his science-oriented fictions as "scientific romances"—a term that did not originate with him, but with a lesser-known writer named Charles Howard Hinton.

There are several interpretations of the term "science." If it implies the known and the possible, then Wells's scientific romances are by no

4 Silverberg, Robert (ed.), *Voyages in Time: Twelve Great Science Fiction Stories* (New York: Tempo, 1970).

5 The "brass brassiere" is from an oral history of science fiction prepared by Richard Wolinsky for Berkeley's KPFA-FM.

means scientific; he paid little attention to those boundaries. As Jules Verne remarked with displeasure, "*Il invente!*" The "science" part of these tales is embedded instead in a worldview that derived from Wells's study of Darwinian principles under Huxley, and has to do with the grand study that engrossed Wells throughout his career: the nature of man. This, too, may account for his veering between extreme Utopianism (if man is the result of evolution, not of Divine creation, surely he can evolve yet further?) and the deepest pessimism (if man came from the animals and is akin to them, rather than to the angels, surely he might slide back the way he came?). *The Island of Doctor Moreau* belongs to the debit side of the Wellsian account book.

Darwin's *On the Origin of Species* and *The Descent of Man* were profound shocks to the Victorian system. Gone was the God who spoke the world into being in seven days and made man out of clay; in its place stood millions of years of evolutionary change, and a family tree that included primates. Gone, too, was the kindly Wordsworthian version of Mother Nature that had presided over the first years of the century; in her place was Tennyson's "Nature, red in tooth and claw / With ravine." The devouring femme fatale that became so iconic in the 1880s and 1890s owes a lot to Darwin. So does the imagery and cosmogony of *The Island of Doctor Moreau.*

4. ROMANCE

So much for the "scientific" in "scientific romance." What about the "romance"?

In both "scientific romance" and "science fiction," the scientific element is merely an adjective; the nouns are "romance" and "fiction." In respect to Wells, "romance" is more helpful than "fiction."

"Romance," in today's general usage, is what happens on Valentine's Day. As a literary term it has slipped in rank somewhat—being now applied to such things as Harlequin Romances—but it was otherwise understood in the nineteenth century, when it was used in opposition to the term "novel." The novel dealt with known social life, but a romance could deal with the long ago and the far away. It also allowed much more latitude in terms of plot. In a romance, event follows exciting event at breakneck pace. As a rule, this has caused the romance to be viewed by the high literati—those bent more on instruction than on delight—as escapist and vulgar, a judgment that goes back at least two thousand years.

In *The Secular Scripture*, Northrop Frye provides an exhaustive analysis of the structure and elements of the romance as a form. Typically a romance begins with a break in ordinary consciousness, often—traditionally—signaled by a shipwreck, frequently linked with a kidnapping by pirates. Exotic climes are a feature, especially exotic desert islands; so are strange creatures.

In the sinister portions of a romance, the protagonist is often imprisoned or trapped, or lost in a labyrinth or maze, or in a forest that serves the same purpose. Boundaries between the normal levels of life dissolve: vegetable becomes animal, animal becomes quasi-human, human descends to animal. If the lead character is female, an attempt will be made on her virtue, which she manages miraculously to preserve. A rescue, however improbable, restores the protagonist to his or her previous life and reunites him or her with loved ones. *Pericles, Prince of Tyre* is a romance. It's got everything but talking dogs.

The Island of Doctor Moreau is also a romance, though a dark one. Consider the shipwreck. Consider the break in the protagonist's consciousness—the multiple breaks, in fact. Consider the pirates, here supplied by the vile captain and crew of the *Ipecacuanha*. Consider the name *Ipecacuanha*, signifying an emetic and purgative: the break in consciousness is going to have a nastily physical side to it, of a possibly medicinal kind. Consider the fluid boundaries between animal and human. Consider the island.

5. THE ENCHANTED ISLAND

The name given to the island by Wells is Noble's Island, a patent irony as well as another poke at the class system. Say it quickly and slur a little, and it's *no blessed island*.

This island has many literary antecedents and several descendants. Foremost among the latter is William Golding's island in *Lord of the Flies*—a book that owes something to *The Island of Doctor Moreau*, as well as to those adventure books *Coral Island* and *The Swiss Family Robinson*, and of course to the great original shipwreck-on-an-island

classic, *Robinson Crusoe. Moreau* could be thought of as one in a long
line of island-castaway books.

All those just mentioned, however, keep within the boundaries set
by the possible. *The Island of Doctor Moreau* is, on the contrary, a work
of fantasy, and its more immediate grandparents are to be found elsewhere. *The Tempest* springs immediately to mind: here is a beautiful
island, belonging at first to a witch, then taken over by a magician who
lays down the law, particularly to the malignant, animal-like Caliban,
who will obey only when pain is inflicted on him. Doctor Moreau could
be seen as a sinister version of Prospero, surrounded by a hundred or so
Calibans of his own creation.

But Wells himself points us toward another enchanted island. When
Prendick mistakenly believes that the beast-men he's seen were once
men, he says: "[Moreau] had merely intended. . . . to fall upon me with
a fate more horrible than death, with torture, and after torture the most
hideous degradation it was possible to conceive—to send me off, a lost
soul, a beast, to the rest of [the] Comus rout."

Comus, in the masque of that name by Milton, is a powerful sorcerer who rules a labyrinthine forest. He's the son of the enchantress
Circe, who in Greek myth was the daughter of the Sun and lived on
the island of Aeaea. Odysseus landed there during his wanderings, and
Circe transformed his crew into pigs. She has a whole menagerie of
other kinds of animals—wolves, lions—that were also once men. Her
island is an island of transformation: man to beast (and then to man
again, once Odysseus gets the upper hand).

As for Comus, he leads a band of creatures, once men, who have
drunk from his enchanted cup and have turned into hybrid monsters.
They retain their human bodies, but their heads are those of beasts
of all kinds. Thus changed, they indulge in sensual revels. Christina
Rosetti's *Goblin Market*, with its animal-form goblins who tempt chas-
tity and use luscious edibles as bait, is surely a late offshoot of Comus.

As befits an enchanted island, Moreau's island is both semi-alive and
female, but not in a pleasant way. It's volcanic, and emits from time to
time a sulfurous reek. It comes equipped with flowers, and also with
clefts and ravines, fronded on either side. Moreau's beast-men live in
one of these, and since they do not have very good table manners, it has

rotting food in it and it smells bad. When the beast-men start to lose their humanity and revert to their beast natures, this locale becomes the site of a moral breakdown that is specifically sexual.

What is it that leads us to believe that Prendick will never have a girlfriend?

6. THE UNHOLY TRINITY

Nor will Doctor Moreau. There is no Mrs. Moreau on the island. There are no female human beings at all.

Similarly, the God of the Old Testament has no wife. Wells called *The Island of Doctor Moreau* "a youthful piece of blasphemy," and it's obvious that he intended Moreau—that strong, solitary gentleman with the white hair and beard—to resemble traditional paintings of God. He surrounds Moreau with semi-Biblical language as well: Moreau is the lawgiver of the island; those of his creatures who go against his will are punished and tortured; he is a god of whim and pain. But he isn't a real God, because he cannot really create; he can only imitate, and his imitations are poor.

What drives him on? His sin is the sin of pride, combined with a cold "intellectual passion." He wants to know everything. He wishes to discover the secrets of life. His ambition is to be as God the Creator. As such, he follows in the wake of several other aspirants, including Doctor Frankenstein and Hawthorne's various alchemists. Doctor Faustus hovers in the background, but he wanted youth and wealth and sex in return for his soul, and Moreau has no interest in such things; he despises what he calls "materialism," which includes pleasure and pain. He dabbles in bodies but wishes to detach himself from his own. (He has some literary brothers: Sherlock Holmes would understand his bloodless intellectual passion. So would Oscar Wilde's Lord Henry Wooton, of that earlier fin de siécle transformation novel *The Picture of Dorian Gray*.)

But in Christianity, God is a trinity, and on Moreau's island there are three beings whose names begin with M. *Moreau* as a name combines the syllable "mor"—from *mors, mortis*, no doubt—with the French for "water," suitable in one who aims at exploring the limits of plasticity. The whole word means "moor" in French. So the very white Moreau is also the Black Man of witchcraft tales, a sort of anti-God.

Montgomery, his alcoholic assistant, has the face of a sheep. He acts as the intercessor between the beast folk and Moreau, and in this function stands in for Christ the Son. He's first seen offering Prendick a red drink that tastes like blood, and some boiled mutton. Is there a hint of an ironic Communion service here—blood drink, flesh of the Lamb? The communion Prendick enters into by drinking the red drink is the communion of carnivores, that human communion forbidden to the beast folk. But it's a communion he was part of anyway.

The third person of the Trinity is the Holy Spirit, usually portrayed as a dove—God in living but nonhuman form. The third M creature on the island is M'Ling, the beast creature who serves as Montgomery's attendant. He, too, enters into the communion of blood: he licks his fingers while preparing a rabbit for the human beings to eat. The Holy Spirit as a deformed and idiotic man-animal? As a piece of youthful blasphemy, *The Island of Doctor Moreau* was even more blasphemous than most commentators have realized.

Just so we don't miss it, Wells puts a serpent beast into his dubious garden: a creature that was completely evil and very strong, and that bent a gun barrel into the letter S. Can Satan, too, be created by man? If so, blasphemous indeed.

7. THE NEW WOMAN AS CATWOMAN

There are no female human beings on Moreau's island, but Moreau is busily making one. The experiment on which he's engaged for most of the book concerns his attempt to turn a female puma into the semblance of a woman.

Wells was more than interested in members of the cat family, as Brian Aldiss has pointed out. During his affair with Rebecca West, she was "Panther," he was "Jaguar." But "cat" has another connotation: in slang, it meant "prostitute." This is Montgomery's allusion when he says— while the puma is yelling under the knife—"I'm damned . . . if this place is not as bad as Gower Street—with its cats." Prendick himself makes the connection explicit on his return to London when he shies away from the "prowling women [who] would mew after me."

"I have some hope of her head and brain," says Moreau of the puma. ". . . I will make a rational creature of my own." But the puma resists.

She's almost a woman—she weeps like one—but when Moreau begins torturing her again, she utters "a shriek almost like that of an angry virago." Then she tears her fetter out of the wall and runs away, a great bleeding, scarred, suffering, female monster. It is she who kills Moreau.

Like many men of his time, Wells was obsessed with the New Woman. On the surface of it he was all in favor of sexual emancipation, including free love, but the freeing of Woman evidently had its frightening aspects. Rider Haggard's *She* can be seen as a reaction to the feminist movement of his day—if women are granted power, men are doomed—and so can Wells's deformed puma. Once the powerful, monstrous sexual cat tears her fetter out of the wall and gets loose, minus the improved brain she ought to have courtesy Man the Scientist, look out.

8. THE WHITENESS OF MOREAU, THE BLACKNESS OF M'LING

Wells was not the only nineteenth-century English writer who used furry creatures to act out English sociodramas. Lewis Carroll had done it in a whimsical way in the *Alice* books, Kipling in a more militaristic fashion in *The Jungle Book*.

Kipling made the Law sound kind of noble in *The Jungle Book*. Not so Wells. The Law mumbled by the animal-men in Moreau is a horrible parody of Christian and Jewish liturgy; it vanishes completely when the language of the beasts dissolves, indicating that it was a product of language, not some eternal God-given creed.

Wells was writing at a time when the British Empire still held sway, but the cracks were already beginning to show. Moreau's island is a little colonial enclave of the most hellish sort. It's no accident that most (although not all) of the beast folk are black or brown, that they are at first thought by Prendick to be "savages" or "natives," and that they speak in a kind of mangled English. They are employed as servants and slaves—in a regime that's kept in place with whip and gun—they secretly hate the real "men" as much as they fear them, and they disobey the Law as much as possible, and kick over the traces as soon as they can. They kill Moreau and they kill Montgomery and they kill M'Ling, and, unless Prendick can get away, they will kill him, too, although at

first he "goes native" and lives among them, and does things that fill
him with disgust and that he would rather not mention.

White Man's Burden, indeed.

9. THE MODERN ANCIENT MARINER

The way in which Prendick escapes from the island is noteworthy. He
sees a small boat with a sail and lights a fire to hail it. It approaches,
but strangely: it doesn't sail with the wind, but yaws and veers. There
are two figures in it, one with red hair. As the boat enters the bay,
"Suddenly a great white bird flew up out of the boat, and neither of the
men stirred nor noticed it. It circled round, and then came sweeping
overhead with its strong wings outspread." This bird cannot be a gull:
it's too big and solitary. The only white seabird usually described as
"great" is the albatross.

The two figures in the boat are dead. But it is this death boat, this
life-in-death coffin boat, that proves the salvation of Prendick.

In what other work of English literature do we find a lone man reduced
to a pitiable state, a boat that sails without a wind, two death figures, one
with unusual hair, and a great white bird? The work is, of course, *The
Rime of the Ancient Mariner*, which revolves around man's proper relation to Nature, and concludes that this proper relation is one of love. It is
when he manages to bless the sea serpents that the Mariner is freed from
the curse he has brought upon himself by shooting the albatross.

The Island of Doctor Moreau also revolves around man's proper
relation to Nature, but its conclusions are quite different, because
Nature itself is seen differently. It is no longer the Nature eulogized by
Wordsworth, that benevolent motherly entity who never did betray that
heart that loved her, for between Coleridge and Wells came Darwin.

The lesson learned by the albatross-shooting Mariner is summed up
by him at the end of the poem:

> He prayeth well, who loveth well
> Both man and bird and beast.
>
> He prayeth best, who loveth best
> All things both great and small;

For the dear God who loveth us,
He made and loveth all.

In the Ancient Mariner–like pattern at the end of *The Island of Doctor Moreau*, the "albatross" is still alive. It has suffered no harm at the hands of Prendick. But he lives in the shadow of a curse anyway. His curse is that he can't love or bless anything living: not bird, not beast, and most certainly not man. He has another curse, too: the Ancient Mariner is doomed to tell his tale, and those who are chosen to hear it are convinced by it. But Prendick chooses not to tell because, when he tries, no one will believe him.

10. FEAR AND TREMBLING

What then is the lesson learned by the unfortunate Prendick? It can perhaps best be understood in reference to *The Ancient Mariner*. The god of Moreau's island can scarcely be described as a dear God, who makes and loves all creatures. If Moreau is seen to stand for a version of God the Creator who "makes" living things, he has done—in Prendick's final view—a very bad job. Similarly, if God can be considered as a sort of Moreau, and if the equation "Moreau is to his animals as God is to man" may stand, then God himself is accused of cruelty and indifference—making man for fun and to satisfy his own curiosity and pride, laying laws on him he cannot understand or obey, then abandoning him to a life of torment.

Prendick cannot love the distorted and violent furry folk on the island, and it's just as hard for him to love the human beings he encounters on his return to "civilization." Like Swift's Gulliver, he can barely stand the sight of his fellow men. He lives in a state of queasy fear, inspired by his continued experience of dissolving boundaries: as the beasts on the island have at times appeared human, the human beings he encounters in England appear bestial. He displays his modernity by going to a "mental specialist," but this provides only a partial remedy. He feels himself to be "an animal tormented . . . sent to wander alone."

Prendick forsakes his earlier dabblings in biology, and turns instead to chemistry and astronomy. He finds "hope"—"a sense of infinite peace and protection" in "the glittering hosts of heaven." As if to squash even this faint hope, Wells almost immediately wrote *The War of the Worlds*, in which not peace and protection, but malice and destruction, come down from the heavens in the form of the monstrous but superior Martians.

The War of the Worlds can be read as a further gloss on Darwin. Is this where evolution will lead—to the abandonment of the body, to giant, sexless, blood-sucking heads with huge brains and tentaclelike fingers? But it can also be read as a thoroughly chilling coda to *The Island of Doctor Moreau*.

Sir Gawain and the Green Knight

MICHAEL DIRDA

sk readers to choose the most delightful work of medieval literature, and odds are that *Sir Gawain and the Green Knight* would
head the list. It conveys a wonderful Mozartean lightness and wit, an air
of make-believe and festivity, tinged with real darkness. It's a perfect
adult Christmas story. Just listen:

On New Year's Day all the court of King Arthur gather together for a
holiday feast. The ladies look particularly lovely, the knights steal kisses,
and all's right with the world. But the king wishes to be told or shown some
marvel before he will sit down to eat. Almost immediately, a noise outside
the hall is followed by the entrance of a magnificent knight "the whole
of him bright green." Taller by a head than any man there, he swaggers
into the party and issues, almost playfully, a challenge. He defies any of
these supposedly brave warriors to give him a stroke from his huge ax,
with the proviso that a year and a day later he must be allowed to deliver
a similar stroke in return. Gawain agrees, and swiftly brings the ax down
through the Green Knight's neck, slicing through the white flesh as if it
were grease. Like a loose soccer ball, the severed head rolls among the
lords and ladies. But suddenly the bloody torso strides forward and picks
up its green head, which opens a pair of red eyes and speaks: Remember,
Gawain, to meet me in a year and a day at the Green Chapel.

In a strikingly beautiful passage, the author—whose identity is
unknown—describes the changing of the seasons: the shining rain of

spring, the soft winds of summer, the dust rising from the fields at harvest time, and the gradual return of winter. On All Saint's Day— November 1—Gawain sets off to locate the Green Chapel and fulfill his pledge. But what had once seemed, during a moment of high spirits, just a strange game is now a serious matter of life and death. Searching for this mysterious Green Chapel, of which no one seems to have heard, Gawain undergoes adventures with dragons, trolls, and other wild beasts, and all the while the winter days grow darker, colder, and increasingly desolate. Finally, on Christmas Eve, Gawain prays that he might discover a warm shelter for the night, and immediately glimpses a castle, covered with turrets, so perfect it might have been cut out of paper.

Once he is admitted, the knight encounters the castle's broad-shouldered, red-bearded lord; the man's wife, who seems more beautiful than Guinevere; and a hideous bent-backed old woman. With seemingly unfeigned courtesy, they all invite him to stay for the Christmas season, and the next day sweetly passes in courtly conversation and games and feasting. In the evening Gawain explains that, for reasons he doesn't care to go into, he must journey on in his search for the Green Chapel. His jovial host laughingly replies that his new guest is in luck. This very chapel is so close by that the celebrated knight should feel free to spend the next three days at the castle, taking his ease. That settled, the lord of the manor asks Gawain to enter into the spirit of the festive season by playing a little trading game: Each morning he himself will go out hunting while Gawain rests up and does as he pleases, and in the evening the two will exchange whatever they have acquired during the day.

The next dawn the host assembles his knights and they all hurry out to hunt deer while Gawain slumbers in a warm bed, snugly surrounded by curtains. Suddenly he detects the sound of his door quietly opening, peeks out, and glimpses the host's wife softly entering his room. He pretends to be asleep as she makes her way to his bed and sits down beside him. Gawain asks to be allowed to dress, but the lady laughingly tells him that he shouldn't bother to get up, as she has a much better plan in mind. Isn't he after all known far and wide as the greatest lover among the knights of the Round Table? And aren't the two of them

alone together, and her husband far away hunting, and the door shut
and locked? Surely, she adds, they could make good use of this time.
Leaning over him, she confesses that he can do anything he wants with
her, making her meaning unmistakable by saying, "You are welcome
to my body."

To reveal any more would spoil the story for new readers of this
delicious, very adult medieval romance. But think how Gawain must
feel: He knows that in three days he will be facing a murderous ax-
stroke and, unlike the Green Knight, he cannot simply put his head
back on. Meanwhile, this seductive woman beside him is so alive, so
willing, so eager. Should he not enjoy the little time left to him? But
what of his obligations as a guest, his honor as a knight, his hope of
heaven? What should he do?

Throughout *Sir Gawain and the Green Knight* the author addresses
serious questions of courtesy, reputation, and moral conduct, but
he also suffuses his poem with irony, constantly plays with the gulf
between appearance and reality, and keeps everyone guessing until the
very end. Even then he leaves open the deepest meaning of his story.
Suffice it to say that Gawain eventually does make his way to the sinister Green Chapel, an evil-looking mound in a water-splashed glen,
where one could easily picture "the devil saying his matins." As he
stands there on the appointed day, the knight hears a loud noise echo-
ing along the cliffs nearby, the whirring sound that someone would
make if he were sharpening a scythe on a grindstone. But it is not a
scythe. And Gawain strides forth to meet his destiny.

Unlike Chaucer, whose English is recognizably our own, the
Gawain-poet writes in a northern dialect that somewhat resembles
the language of *Beowulf*. What's more, he employs the Old English
alliterative line, which suggests that even in Norman Britain some of
the old poetic ways were still kept alive. The standard scholarly edition
of the poem was first prepared by none other than the young J. R. R.
Tolkien (with E. V. Gordon, later revised by Norman Davis). Today
there are several excellent translations—by the poet W. S. Merwin,
among others—as well as a good deal of academic commentary: *Sir
Gawain* is, after all, a mysterious and endlessly rewarding masterpiece.
So, too, is the same poet's lovely elegy titled *Pearl*, in which he laments

the death of his daughter and is granted a vision of heaven. *Purity* and *Patience*, his other known works, are even more religious in character and, though masterly in their way, lack the touchingly human drama of *Sir Gawain and the Green Knight*.

The Storyteller:
Reflections on the Works of Nikolai Leskov
WALTER BENJAMIN

I

Familiar though his name may be to us, the storyteller in his living immediacy is by no means a present force. He has already become something remote from us and something that is getting even more distant. To present someone like Leskov as a storyteller does not mean bringing him closer to us but, rather, increasing our distance from him. Viewed from a certain distance, the great, simple outlines which define the storyteller stand out in him, or rather, they become visible in him, just as in a rock a human head or an animal's body may appear to an observer at the proper distance and angle of vision. This distance and this angle of vision are prescribed for us by an experience which we may have almost every day. It teaches us that the art of storytelling is coming to an end. Less and less frequently do we encounter people with the ability to tell a tale properly. More and more often there is embarrassment all around when the wish to hear a story is expressed. It is as if something that seemed inalienable to us, the securest among our possessions, were taken from us: the ability to exchange experiences.

One reason for this phenomenon is obvious: experience has fallen in value. And it looks as if it is continuing to fall into bottomlessness. Every glance at a newspaper demonstrates that it has reached a new low, that our picture, not only of the external world but of the moral world as well, overnight has undergone changes which were never thought possible. With the [First] World War a process began to become apparent which has not halted since then. Was it not noticeable at the end of the war that men returned from the battlefield grown silent—not richer, but poorer in communicable experience? What ten years later was poured out in the flood of war books was anything but experience that goes from mouth to mouth. And there was nothing remarkable about that. For never has experience been contradicted more thoroughly than strategic experience by tactical warfare, economic experience by inflation, bodily experience by mechanical warfare, moral experience by those in power. A generation that had gone to school on a horse-drawn streetcar now stood under the open sky in a countryside in which nothing remained unchanged but the clouds, and beneath these clouds, in a field of force of destructive torrents and explosions, was the tiny, fragile human body.

I I

Experience which is passed on from mouth to mouth is the source from which all storytellers have drawn. And among those who have written down the tales, it is the great ones whose written version differs least from the speech of the many nameless storytellers. Incidentally, among the last named there are two groups which, to be sure, overlap in many ways. And the figure of the storyteller gets its full corporeality only for the one who can picture them both. "When someone goes on a trip, he has something to tell about," goes the German saying, and people imagine the storyteller as someone who has come from afar. But they enjoy no less listening to the man who has stayed at home, making an honest living, and who knows the local tales and traditions. If one wants to picture these two groups through their archaic representatives, one is embodied in the resident tiller of the soil, and the other in the trading seaman. Indeed, each sphere of life has, as it were, produced its own tribe of storytellers. Each of these tribes preserves some of its characteristics centuries later. Thus, among nineteenth-century German storytellers, writers like Hebel and Gotthelf stem from the first tribe, writers like Sealsfield and Gerstäcker from the second. With these tribes, however, as stated above, it is only a matter of basic types. The actual extension of the realm of storytelling in its full historical breadth is inconceivable without the most intimate interpenetration of these two archaic types. Such an interpenetration was achieved particularly by the Middle Ages in their trade structure. The resident master craftsman and the traveling journeymen worked together in the same rooms; and every master had been a traveling journeyman before he settled down in his home town or somewhere else. If peasants and seamen were past masters of storytelling, the artisan class was its university. In it was combined the lore of faraway places, such as a much-traveled man brings home, with the lore of the past, as it best reveals itself to natives of a place.

III

Leskov was at home in distant places as well as distant times. He was a member of the Greek Orthodox Church, a man with genuine religious interests. But he was a no less sincere opponent of ecclesiastic bureaucracy. Since he was not able to get along any better with secular officialdom, the official positions he held were not of long duration. Of all his posts, the one he held for a long time as Russian representative of a big English firm was presumably the most useful one for his writing. For this firm he traveled through Russia, and these trips advanced his worldly wisdom as much as they did his knowledge of conditions in Russia. In this way he had an opportunity of becoming acquainted with the organization of the sects in the country. This left its mark on his works of fiction. In the Russian legends Leskov saw allies in his fight against Orthodox bureaucracy. There are a number of his legendary tales whose focus is a righteous man, seldom an ascetic, usually a simple, active man who becomes a saint apparently in the most natural way in the world. Mystical exaltation is not Leskov's forte. Even though he occasionally liked to indulge in the miraculous, even in piousness he prefers to stick with a sturdy nature. He sees the prototype in the man who finds his way about the world without getting too deeply involved with it.

He displayed a corresponding attitude in worldly matters. It is in keeping with this that he began to write late, at the age of twenty-nine. That was after his commercial travels. His first printed work was entitled "Why Are Books Expensive in Kiev?" A number of other writings about the working class, alcoholism, police doctors, and unemployed salesmen are precursors of his works of fiction.

I V

An orientation toward practical interests is characteristic of many born storytellers. More pronouncedly than in Leskov this trait can be recognized, for example, in Gotthelf, who gave his peasants agricultural advice; it is found in Nodier, who concerned himself with the perils of gas light; and Hebel, who slipped bits of scientific instruction for his readers into his *Schatzkästlein*, is in this line as well. All this points to the nature of every real story. It contains, openly or covertly, something useful. The usefulness may, in one case, consist in a moral; in another, in some practical advice; in a third, in a proverb or maxim. In every case the storyteller is a man who has counsel for his readers. But if today "having counsel" is beginning to have an old-fashioned ring, this is because the communicability of experience is decreasing. In consequence we have no counsel either for ourselves or for others. After all, counsel is less an answer to a question than a proposal concerning the continuation of a story which is just unfolding. To seek this counsel one would first have to be able to tell the story. (Quite apart from the fact that a man is receptive to counsel only to the extent that he allows his situation to speak.) Counsel woven into the fabric of real life is wisdom. The art of storytelling is reaching its end because the epic side of truth, wisdom, is dying out. This, however, is a process that has been going on for a long time. And nothing would be more fatuous than to want to see in it merely a "symptom of decay," let alone a "modern" symptom. It is, rather, only a concomitant symptom of the secular productive forces of history, a concomitant that has quite gradually removed narrative from the realm of living speech and at the same time is making it possible to see a new beauty in what is vanishing.

V

The earliest symptom of a process whose end is the decline of storytelling is the rise of the novel at the beginning of modern times. What distinguishes the novel from the story (and from the epic in the narrower sense) is its essential dependence on the book. The dissemination of the novel became possible only with the invention of printing. What can be handed on orally, the wealth of the epic, is of a different kind from what constitutes the stock in trade of the novel. What differentiates the novel from all other forms of prose literature—the fairy tale, the legend, even the novella, is that it neither comes from oral tradition nor goes into it. This distinguishes it from storytelling in particular. The storyteller takes what he tells from experience—his own or that reported by others. And he in turn makes it the experience of those who are listening to his tale. The novelist has isolated himself. The birthplace of the novel is the solitary individual, who is no longer able to express himself by giving examples of his most important concerns, is himself uncounseled, and cannot counsel others. To write a novel means to carry the incommensurable to extremes in the representation of human life. In the midst of life's fullness, and through the representation of this fullness, the novel gives evidence of the profound perplexity of the living. Even the first great book of the genre, *Don Quixote*, teaches how the spiritual greatness, the boldness, the helpfulness of one of the noblest of men, Don Quixote, are completely devoid of counsel and do not contain the slightest scintilla of wisdom. If now and then, in the course of the centuries, efforts have been made—most effectively, perhaps, in *Wilhelm Meisters Wanderjahre*—to implant instruction in the novel, these attempts have always amounted to a modification of the novel form. The *Bildungsroman*, on the other hand, does not deviate in any way from the basic structure of the novel. By integrating the social process with the development of a person, it bestows the most frangible justification on the order determining it. The legitimacy it provides stands in direct opposition to reality. Particularly in the *Bildungsroman*, it is this inadequacy that is actualized.

VI

One must imagine the transformation of epic forms occurring in rhythms comparable to those of the change that has come over the earth's surface in the course of thousands of centuries. Hardly any other forms of human communication have taken shape more slowly, been lost more slowly. It took the novel, whose beginnings go back to antiquity, hundreds of years before it encountered in the evolving middle class those elements which were favorable to its flowering. With the appearance of these elements, storytelling began quite slowly to recede into the archaic; in many ways, it is true, it took hold of the new material, but it was not really determined by it. On the other hand, we recognize that with the full control of the middle class, which has the press as one of its most important instruments in fully developed capitalism, there emerges a form of communication which, no matter how far back its origin may lie, never before influenced the epic form in a decisive way. But now it does exert such an influence. And it turns out that it confronts storytelling as no less of a stranger than did the novel, but in a more menacing way, and that it also brings about a crisis in the novel. This new form of communication is information.

Villemessant, the founder of *Le Figaro*, characterized the nature of information in a famous formulation. "To my readers," he used to say, "an attic fire in the Latin Quarter is more important than a revolution in Madrid." This makes strikingly clear that it is no longer intelligence coming from afar, but the information which supplies a handle for what is nearest that gets the readiest hearing. The intelligence that came from afar—whether the spatial kind from foreign countries or the temporal kind of tradition—possessed an authority which gave it validity, even when it was not subject to verification. Information, however, lays claim to prompt verifiability. The prime requirement is that it appear "understandable in itself." Often it is no more exact than the intelligence of earlier centuries was. But while the latter was inclined to borrow from the miraculous, it is indispensable for information to sound plausible. Because of this it proves incompatible with the spirit of storytelling. If the art of storytelling has become rare, the dissemination of information has had a decisive share in this state of affairs.

Every morning brings us the news of the globe, and yet we are poor in noteworthy stories. This is because no event any longer comes to us without already being shot through with explanation. In other words, by now almost nothing that happens benefits storytelling; almost everything benefits information. Actually, it is half the art of storytelling to keep a story free from explanation as one reproduces it. Leskov is a master at this (compare pieces like "The Deception" and "The White Eagle"). The most extraordinary things, marvelous things, are related with the greatest accuracy, but the psychological connection of the events is not forced on the reader. It is left up to him to interpret things the way he understands them, and thus the narrative achieves an amplitude that information lacks.

VII

Leskov was grounded in the classics. The first storyteller of the Greeks was Herodotus. In the fourteenth chapter of the third book of his *Histories* there is a story from which much can be learned. It deals with Psammenitus.

When the Egyptian king Psammenitus had been beaten and captured by the Persian king Cambyses, Cambyses was bent on humbling his prisoner. He gave orders to place Psammenitus on the road along which the Persian triumphal procession was to pass. And he further arranged that the prisoner should see his daughter pass by as a maid going to the well with her pitcher. While all the Egyptians were lamenting and bewailing this spectacle, Psammenitus stood alone, mute and motionless, his eyes fixed on the ground; and when presently he saw his son, who was being taken along in the procession to be executed, he likewise remained unmoved. But when afterwards he recognized one of his servants, an old, impoverished man, in the ranks of the prisoners, he beat his fists against his head and gave all the signs of deepest mourning.

From this story it may be seen what the nature of true storytelling is. The value of information does not survive the moment in which it was new. It lives only at that moment; it has to surrender to it completely and explain itself to it without losing any time. A story is different. It does not expend itself. It preserves and concentrates its strength and is capable of releasing it even after a long time. Thus Montaigne referred to this Egyptian king and asked himself why he mourned only when he caught sight of his servant. Montaigne answers: "Since he was already overfull of grief, it took only the smallest increase for it to burst through its dams." Thus Montaigne. But one could also say: The king is not moved by the fate of those of royal blood, for it is his own fate. Or: We are moved by much on the stage that does not move us in real life; to the king, this servant is only an actor. Or: Great grief is pent up and breaks forth only with relaxation. Seeing this servant was the relaxation. Herodotus offers no explanations. His report is the driest. That is why this story from ancient Egypt is still capable after thousands of years of arousing astonishment and thoughtfulness. It resembles the seeds of grain which have lain for centuries in the chambers of the pyramids shut up air-tight and have retained their germinative power to this day.

VIII

There is nothing that commends a story to memory more effectively than that chaste compactness which precludes psychological analysis. And the more natural the process by which the storyteller forgoes psychological shading, the greater becomes the story's claim to a place in the memory of the listener, the more completely is it integrated into his own experience, the greater will be his inclination to repeat it to someone else someday, sooner or later. This process of assimilation, which takes place in depth, requires a state of relaxation which is becoming rarer and rarer. If sleep is the apogee of physical relaxation, boredom is the apogee of mental relaxation. Boredom is the dream bird that hatches the egg of experience. A rustling in the leaves drives him away. His nesting places—the activities that are intimately associated with boredom—are already extinct in the cities and are declining in the country as well. With this the gift for listening is lost and the community of listeners disappears. For storytelling is always the art of repeating stories, and this art is lost when the stories are no longer retained. It is lost because there is no more weaving and spinning to go on while they are being listened to. The more self-forgetful the listener is, the more deeply is what he listens to impressed upon his memory. When the rhythm of work has seized him, he listens to the tales in such a way that the gift of retelling them comes to him all by itself. This, then, is the nature of the web in which the gift of storytelling is cradled. This is how today it is becoming unraveled at all its ends after being woven thousands of years ago in the ambience of the oldest forms of craftsmanship.

I X

The storytelling that thrives for a long time in the milieu of work—the rural, the maritime, and the urban—is itself an artisan form of communication, as it were. It does not aim to convey the pure essence of the thing, like information or a report. It sinks the thing into the life of the storyteller, in order to bring it out of him again. Thus traces of the storyteller cling to the story the way the handprints of the potter cling to the clay vessel. Storytellers tend to begin their story with a presentation of the circumstances in which they themselves have learned what is to follow, unless they simply pass it off as their own experience. Leskov begins his "Deception" with the description of a train trip on which he supposedly heard from a fellow passenger the events which he then goes on to relate; or he thinks of Dostoyevsky's funeral, where he sets his acquaintance with the heroine of his story "À Propos of the Kreutzer Sonata"; or he evokes a gathering of a reading circle in which we are told the events that he reproduces for us in his "Interesting Men." Thus his tracks are frequently evident in his narratives, if not as those of the one who experienced it, then as those of the one who reports it.

This craftsmanship, storytelling, was actually regarded as a craft by Leskov himself. "Writing," he says in one of his letters, "is to me no liberal art, but a craft." It cannot come as a surprise that he felt bonds with craftsmanship, but faced industrial technology as a stranger. Tolstoy, who must have understood this, occasionally touches this nerve of Leskov's storytelling talent when he calls him the first man "who pointed out the inadequacy of economic progress. . . . It is strange that Dostoyevsky is so widely read. . . . But I simply cannot comprehend why Leskov is not read. He is a truthful writer." In his artful and high-spirited story "The Steel Flea," which is midway between legend and farce, Leskov glorifies native craftsmanship through the silversmiths of Tula. Their masterpiece, the steel flea, is seen by Peter the Great and convinces him that the Russians need not be ashamed before the English.

The intellectual picture of the atmosphere of craftsmanship from which the storyteller comes has perhaps never been sketched in such a significant way as by Paul Valéry. "He speaks of the perfect things in nature, flawless pearls, full-bodied, matured wines, truly developed creatures, and calls them 'the precious product of a long chain of causes similar to one another.'" The accumulation of such causes has its temporal limit only at perfection. "This patient process of Nature," Valéry continues, "was once imitated by men. Miniatures, ivory carvings, elaborated to the point of greatest perfection, stones that are perfect in polish and engraving, lacquer work or paintings in which a series of thin, transparent layers are placed one on top of the other—all these products of sustained, sacrificing effort are vanishing, and the time is past in which time did not matter. Modern man no longer works at what cannot be abbreviated."

In point of fact, he has succeeded in abbreviating even storytelling. We have witnessed the evolution of the "short story," which has removed itself from oral tradition and no longer permits that slow piling one on top of the other of thin, transparent layers which constitutes the most appropriate picture of the way in which the perfect narrative is revealed through the layers of a variety of retellings.

X

Valéry concludes his observations with this sentence: "It is almost as if the decline of the idea of eternity coincided with the increasing aversion to sustained effort." The idea of eternity has ever had its strongest source in death. If this idea declines, so we reason, the face of death must have changed. It turns out that this change is identical with the one that has diminished the communicability of experience to the same extent as the art of storytelling has declined.

It has been observable for a number of centuries how in the general consciousness the thought of death has declined in omnipresence and vividness. In its last stages this process is accelerated. And in the course of the nineteenth century bourgeois society has, by means of hygienic and social, private and public institutions, realized a secondary effect which may have been its subconscious main purpose: to make it possible for people to avoid the sight of the dying. Dying was once a public process in the life of the individual and a most exemplary one; think of the medieval pictures in which the deathbed has turned into a throne toward which the people press through the wide-open doors of the death house. In the course of modern times dying has been pushed further and further out of the perceptual world of the living. There used to be no house, hardly a room, in which someone had not once died. (The Middle Ages also felt spatially what makes that inscription on a sun dial of Ibiza, *Ultima multis* [the last day for many], significant as the temper of the times.) Today people live in rooms that have never been touched by death, dry dwellers of eternity, and when their end approaches they are stowed away in sanatoria or hospitals by their heirs. It is, however, characteristic that not only a man's knowledge or wisdom, but above all his real life—and this is the stuff that stories are made of—first assumes transmissible form at the moment of his death. Just as a sequence of images is set in motion inside a man as his life comes to an end—unfolding the views of himself under which he has encountered himself without being aware of it—suddenly in his expressions and looks the unforgettable emerges and imparts to everything that concerned him that authority which even the poorest wretch in dying possesses for the living around him. This authority is at the very source of the story.

XI

Death is the sanction of everything that the storyteller can tell. He has borrowed his authority from death. In other words, it is natural history to which his stories refer back. This is expressed in exemplary form in one of the most beautiful stories we have by the incomparable Johann Peter Hebel. It is found in the *Schatzkästlein des rheinischen Hausfreundes*, is entitled "Unexpected Reunion," and begins with the betrothal of a young lad who works in the mines of Falun. On the eve of his wedding he dies a miner's death at the bottom of his tunnel. His bride keeps faith with him after his death, and she lives long enough to become a wizened old woman; one day a body is brought up from the abandoned tunnel which, saturated with iron vitriol, has escaped decay, and she recognizes her betrothed. After this reunion she too is called away by death. When Hebel, in the course of this story, was confronted with the necessity of making this long period of years graphic, he did so in the following sentences: "In the meantime the city of Lisbon was destroyed by an earthquake, and the Seven Years' War came and went, and Emperor Francis I died, and the Jesuit Order was abolished, and Poland was partitioned, and Empress Maria Theresa died, and Struensee was executed. America became independent, and the united French and Spanish forces were unable to capture Gibraltar. The Turks locked up General Stein in the Veteraner Cave in Hungary, and Emperor Joseph died also. King Gustavus of Sweden conquered Russian Finland, and the French Revolution and the long war began, and Emperor Leopold II went to his grave too. Napoleon captured Prussia, and the English bombarded Copenhagen, and the peasants sowed and harvested. The millers ground, the smiths hammered, and the miners dug for veins of ore in their underground workshops. But when in 1809 the miners at Falun..."

Never has a storyteller embedded his report deeper in natural history than Hebel manages to do in this chronology. Read it carefully. Death appears in it with the same regularity as the Reaper does in the processions that pass around the cathedral clock at noon.

XII

Any examination of a given epic form is concerned with the relationship of this form to historiography. In fact, one may go even further and raise the question whether historiography does not constitute the common ground of all forms of the epic. Then written history would be in the same relationship to the epic forms as white light is to the colors of the spectrum. However this may be, among all forms of the epic there is not one whose incidence in the pure, colorless light of written history is more certain than the chronicle. And in the broad spectrum of the chronicle the ways in which a story can be told are graduated like shadings of one and the same color. The chronicler is the history-teller. If we think back to the passage from Hebel, which has the tone of a chronicle throughout, it will take no effort to gauge the difference between the writer of history, the historian, and the teller of it, the chronicler. The historian is bound to explain in one way or another the happenings with which he deals; under no circumstances can he content himself with displaying them as models of the course of the world. But this is precisely what the chronicler does, especially in his classical representatives, the chroniclers of the Middle Ages, the precursors of the historians of today. By basing their historical tales on a divine plan of salvation—an inscrutable one—they have from the very start lifted the burden of demonstrable explanation from their own shoulders. Its place is taken by interpretation, which is not concerned with an accurate concatenation of definite events, but with the way these are embedded in the great inscrutable course of the world.

Whether this course is eschatologically determined or is a natural one makes no difference. In the storyteller the chronicler is preserved in changed form, secularized, as it were. Leskov is among those whose work displays this with particular clarity. Both the chronicler with his eschatological orientation and the storyteller with his profane outlook are so represented in his works that in a number of his stories it can hardly be decided whether the web in which they appear is the golden fabric of a religious view of the course of things, or the multicolored fabric of a worldly view.

Consider the story "The Alexandrite," which transports the reader into "that old time when the stones in the womb of the earth and the planets at celestial heights were still concerned with the fate of men, and not today when both in the heavens and beneath the earth everything has grown indifferent to the fates of the sons of men and no voice speaks to them from anywhere, let alone does their bidding. None of the undiscovered planets play any part in horoscopes any more, and there are a lot of new stones, all measured and weighed and examined for their specific weight and their density, but they no longer proclaim anything to us, nor do they bring us any benefit. Their time for speaking with men is past."

As is evident, it is hardly possible unambiguously to characterize the course of the world that is illustrated in this story of Leskov's. Is it determined eschatologically or naturalistically? The only certain thing is that in its very nature it is by definition outside all real historical categories. Leskov tells us that the epoch in which man could believe himself to be in harmony with nature has expired. Schiller called this epoch in the history of the world the period of naïve poetry. The storyteller keeps faith with it, and his eyes do not stray from that dial in front of which there moves the procession of creatures of which, depending on circumstances, Death is either the leader or the last wretched straggler.

XIII

It has seldom been realized that the listener's naïve relationship to the storyteller is controlled by his interest in retaining what he is told. The cardinal point for the unaffected listener is to assure himself of the possibility of reproducing the story. Memory is the epic faculty *par excellence.* Only by virtue of a comprehensive memory can epic writing absorb the course of events on the one hand and, with the passing of these, make its peace with the power of death on the other. It is not surprising that to a simple man of the people, such as Leskov once invented, the Czar, the head of the sphere in which his stories take place, has the most encyclopedic memory at his command. "Our Emperor," he says, "and his entire family have indeed a most astonishing memory."

Mnemosyne, the rememberer, was the Muse of the epic art among the Greeks. This name takes the observer back to a parting of the ways in world history. For if the record kept by memory—historiography—constitutes the creative matrix of the various epic forms (as great prose is the creative matrix of the various metrical forms), its oldest form, the epic, by virtue of being a kind of common denominator includes the story and the novel. When in the course of centuries the novel began to emerge from the womb of the epic, it turned out that in the novel the element of the epic mind that is derived from the Muse—that is, memory—manifests itself in a form quite different from the way it manifests itself in the story.

Memory creates the chain of tradition which passes a happening on from generation to generation. It is the Muse-derived element of the epic art in a broader sense and encompasses its varieties. In the first place among these is the one practiced by the storyteller. It starts the web which all stories together form in the end. One ties on to the next, as the great storytellers, particularly the Oriental ones, have always readily shown. In each of them there is a Scheherazade who thinks of a fresh story whenever her tale comes to a stop. This is epic remembrance and the Muse-inspired element of the narrative. But this should be set against another principle, also a Muse-derived element in a narrower sense, which as an element of the novel in its earliest form—that is, in the epic—lies concealed, still undifferentiated from the similarly derived element of the story. It can, at any rate, occasionally be divined in the epics, particularly at moments of solemnity in the Homeric epics, as in the invocations to the Muse at their beginning. What announces itself in these passages is the perpetuating remembrance of the novelist as contrasted with the short-lived reminiscences of the storyteller. The first is dedicated to *one* hero, *one* odyssey, *one* battle; the second, to *many* diffuse occurrences. It is, in other words, *remembrance* which, as the Muse-derived element of the novel, is added to reminiscence, the corresponding element of the story, the unity of their origin in memory having disappeared with the decline of the epic.

XIV

"No one," Pascal once said, "dies so poor that he does not leave something behind." Surely it is the same with memories too—although these do not always find an heir. The novelist takes charge of this bequest, and seldom without profound melancholy. For what Arnold Bennett says about a dead woman in one of his novels—that she had had almost nothing in the way of real life—is usually true of the sum total of the estate which the novelist administers. Regarding this aspect of the matter we owe the most important elucidation to Georg Lukács, who sees in the novel "the form of transcendental homelessness." According to Lukàcs, the novel is at the same time the only art form which includes time among its constitutive principles.

"Time," he says in his *Theory of the Novel*, "can become constitutive only when connection with the transcendental home has been lost. Only in the novel are meaning and life, and thus the essential and the temporal, separated; one can almost say that the whole inner action of a novel is nothing else but a struggle against the power of time. . . . And from this . . . arise the genuinely epic experiences of time: hope and memory. . . . Only in the novel . . . does there occur a creative memory which transfixes the object and transforms it. . . .The duality of inwardness and outside world can here be overcome for the subject 'only' when he sees the . . . unity of his entire life . . . out of the past life-stream which is compressed in memory. . . . The insight which grasps this unity . . . becomes the divinatory-intuitive grasping of the unattained and therefore inexpressible meaning of life."

The "meaning of life" is really the center about which the novel moves. But the quest for it is no more than the initial expression of perplexity with which its reader sees himself living this written life. Here "meaning of life"—there "moral of the story": with these slogans novel and story confront each other, and from them the totally different historical co-ordinates of these art forms may be discerned. If *Don Quixote* is the earliest perfect specimen of the novel, its latest exemplar is perhaps the *Éducation sentimentale*.

In the final words of the last-named novel, the meaning which the bourgeois age found in its behavior at the beginning of its decline has settled like sediment in the cup of life. Frédéric and Deslauriers, the boyhood friends, think back to their youthful friendship. This little incident then occurred: one day they showed up in the bordello of their home town, stealthily and timidly, doing nothing but presenting the *patronne* with a bouquet of flowers which they had picked in their own gardens. "This story was still discussed three years later. And now they told it to each other in detail, each supplementing the recollection of the other. 'That may have been,' said Frédéric when they had finished, 'the finest thing in our lives.' 'Yes, you may be right,' said Deslauriers, 'that was perhaps the finest thing in our lives.'"

With such an insight the novel reaches an end which is more proper to it, in a stricter sense, than to any story. Actually there is no story for which the question as to how it continued would not be legitimate. The novelist, on the other hand, cannot hope to take the smallest step beyond that limit at which he invites the reader to a divinatory realization of the meaning of life by writing "Finis."

XV

A man listening to a story is in the company of the storyteller; even a man reading one shares this companionship. The reader of a novel, however, is isolated, more so than any other reader. (For even the reader of a poem is ready to utter the words, for the benefit of the listener.) In this solitude of his, the reader of a novel seizes upon his material more jealously than anyone else. He is ready to make it completely his own, to devour it, as it were. Indeed, he destroys, he swallows up the material as the fire devours logs in the fireplace. The suspense which permeates the novel is very much like the draft which stimulates the flame in the fireplace and enlivens its play.

It is a dry material on which the burning interest of the reader feeds. "A man who dies at the age of thirty-five," said Moritz Heimann once, "is at every point of his life a man who dies at the age of thirty-five." Nothing is more dubious than this sentence—but for the sole reason that the tense is wrong. A man—so says the truth that was meant here—who died at thirty-five will appear to *remembrance* at every point in his life as a man who dies at the age of thirty-five. In other words, the statement that makes no sense for real life becomes indisputable for remembered life. The nature of the character in a novel cannot be presented any better than is done in this statement, which says that the "meaning" of his life is revealed only in his death. But the reader of a novel actually does look for human beings from whom he derives the "meaning of life." Therefore he must, no matter what, know in advance that he will share their experience of death: if need be their figurative death—the end of the novel—but preferably their actual one. How do the characters make him understand that death is already waiting for them—a very definite death and at a very definite place? That is the question which feeds the reader's consuming interest in the events of the novel.

The novel is significant, therefore, not because it presents someone else's fate to us, perhaps didactically, but because this stranger's fate by virtue of the flame which consumes it yields us the warmth which we never draw from our own fate. What draws the reader to the novel is the hope of warming his shivering life with a death he reads about.

XVI

"Leskov," writes Gorky, "is the writer most deeply rooted in the people, and is completely untouched by any foreign influences." A great storyteller will always be rooted in the people, primarily in a milieu of craftsmen. But just as this includes the rural, the maritime, and the urban elements in the many stages of their economic and technical development, there are many gradations in the concepts in which their store of experience comes down to us. (To say nothing of the by no means insignificant share which traders had in the art of storytelling; their task was less to increase its didactic content than to refine the tricks with which the attention of the listener was captured. They have left deep traces in the narrative cycle of *The Arabian Nights.*) In short, despite the primary role which story-telling plays in the household of humanity, the concepts through which the yield of the stories may be garnered are manifold. What may most readily be put in religious terms in Leskov seems almost automatically to fall into place in the pedagogical perspectives of the Enlightenment in Hebel, appears as hermetic tradition in Poe, finds a last refuge in Kipling in the life of British seamen and colonial soldiers. All great storytellers have in common the freedom with which they move up and down the rungs of their experience as on a ladder. A ladder extending downward to the interior of the earth and disappearing into the clouds is the image for a collective experience to which even the deepest shock of every indi-vidual experience, death, constitutes no impediment or barrier.

"And they lived happily ever after," says the fairy tale. The fairy tale, which to this day is the first tutor of children because it was once the first tutor of mankind, secretly lives on in the story. The first true storyteller is, and will continue to be, the teller of fairy tales. Whenever good counsel was at a premium, the fairy tale had it, and where the need was greatest, its aid was nearest. This need was the need created by the myth. The fairy tale tells us of the earliest arrangements that mankind made to shake off the nightmare which the myth had placed upon its chest. In the figure of the fool it shows us how mankind "acts dumb" toward the myth; in the figure of the youngest brother it shows us how one's chances increase as the mythi-cal primitive times are left behind; in the figure of the man who sets out to learn what fear is it shows us that the things we are afraid of can be seen through; in the figure of the wiseacre it shows us that the questions posed by the myth are simple-minded, like the riddle of the Sphinx; in the shape of the animals which come to the aid of the child in the fairy tale it shows that nature not only is subservient to the myth, but much prefers to be aligned with man. The wisest thing—so the fairy tale taught mankind in olden times, and teaches children to this day—is to meet the forces of the mythical world with cunning and with high spirits. (This is how the fairy tale polarizes *Mut*, courage, dividing it dialectically into *Untermut*, that is, cunning, and *Übermut*, high spirits.) The liberating magic which the fairy tale has at its disposal does not bring nature into play in a mythical way, but points to its complicity with liberated man. A mature man feels this complicity only occasionally, that is, when he is happy; but the child first meets it in fairy tales, and it makes him happy.

XVII

Few storytellers have displayed so profound a kinship with the spirit of the fairy tale as did Leskov. This involves tendencies that were promoted by the dogmas of the Greek Orthodox Church. As is well known, Origen's speculation about *apokatastasis*—the entry of all souls into Paradise—which was rejected by the Roman Church plays a significant part in these dogmas. Leskov was very much influenced by Origen and planned to translate his work *On First Principles*. In keeping with Russian folk belief he interpreted the Resurrection less as a transfiguration than as a disenchantment, in a sense akin to the fairy tale. Such an interpretation of Origen is at the bottom of "The Enchanted Pilgrim." In this, as in many other tales by Leskov, a hybrid between fairy tale and legend is involved, not unlike that hybrid which Ernst Bloch mentions in a connection in which he utilizes our distinction between myth and fairy tale in his fashion.

"A hybrid between fairy tale and legend," he says, "contains figuratively mythical elements, mythical elements whose effect is certainly captivating and static, and yet not outside man. In the legend there are Taoist figures, especially very old ones, which are 'mythical' in this sense. For instance, the couple Philemon and Baucis: magically escaped though in natural repose. And surely there is a similar relationship between fairy tale and legend in the Taoist climate of Gotthelf, which, to be sure, is on a much lower level. At certain points it divorces the legend from the locality of the spell, rescues the flame of life, the specifically human flame of life, calmly burning, within as without."

"Magically escaped" are the beings that lead the procession of Leskov's creations: the righteous ones. Pavlin, Figura, the toupee artiste, the bear keeper, the helpful sentry—all of them embodiments of wisdom, kindness, comfort the world, crowd about the storyteller. They are unmistakably suffused with the *imago* of his mother.

This is how Leskov describes her: "She was so thoroughly good that she was not capable of harming any man, nor even an animal. She ate neither meat nor fish, because she had such pity for living creatures. Sometimes my father used to reproach her with this. But she answered: 'I have raised the little animals myself, they are like my children to me. I can't eat my own children, can I?' She would not eat meat at a neighbor's house either. 'I have seen them alive,' she would say; 'they are my acquaintances. I can't eat my acquaintances, can I?'"

The righteous man is the advocate for created things and at the same time he is their highest embodiment. In Leskov he has a maternal touch which is occasionally intensified into the mythical (and thus, to be sure, endangers the purity of the fairy tale). Typical of this is the protagonist of his story "Kotin the Provider and Platonida." This figure, a peasant named Pisonski, is a hermaphrodite. For twelve years his mother raised him as a girl. His male and female organs mature simultaneously, and his bisexuality "becomes the symbol of God incarnate."

In Leskov's view, the pinnacle of creation has been attained with this, and at the same time he presumably sees it as a bridge established between this world and the other. For these earthily powerful, maternal male figures which again and again claim Leskov's skill as a storyteller have been removed from obedience to the sexual drive in the bloom of their strength. They do not, however, really embody an ascetic ideal; rather, the continence of these righteous men has so little privative character that it becomes the elemental counterpoise to uncontrolled lust which the storyteller has personified in *Lady Macbeth of Mzensk.* If the range between a Pavlin and this merchant's wife covers the breadth of the world of created beings, in the hierarchy of his characters Leskov has no less plumbed its depth.

XVIII

The hierarchy of the world of created things, which has its apex in the righteous man, reaches down into the abyss of the inanimate by many gradations. In this connection one particular has to be noted. This whole created world speaks not so much with the human voice as with what could be called "the voice of Nature" in the title of one of Leskov's most significant stories.

This story deals with the petty official Philip Philipovich who leaves no stone unturned to get the chance to have as his house guest a field marshal passing through his little town. He manages to do so. The guest, who is at first surprised at the clerk's urgent invitation, gradually comes to believe that he recognizes in him someone he must have met previously. But who is he? He cannot remember. The strange thing is that the host, for his part, is not willing to reveal his identity. Instead, he puts off the high personage from day to day, saying that the "voice of Nature" will not fail to speak distinctly to him one day. This goes on until finally the guest, shortly before continuing on his journey, must grant the host's public request to let the "voice of Nature" resound. Thereupon the host's wife withdraws. She "returned with a big, brightly polished, copper hunting horn which she gave to her husband. He took the horn, put it to his lips, and was at the same instant as though transformed. Hardly had he inflated his cheeks and produced a tone as powerful as the rolling of thunder when the field marshal cried: 'Stop, I've got it now, brother. This makes me recognize you at once! You are the bugler from the regiment of jaegers, and because you were so honest I sent you to keep an eye on a crooked supplies supervisor.' 'That's it, Your Excellency,' answered the host. 'I didn't want to remind you of this myself, but wanted to let the voice of Nature speak.'"

The way the profundity of this story is hidden beneath its silliness conveys an idea of Leskov's magnificent humor. This humor is confirmed in the same story in an even more cryptic way. We have heard that because of his honesty the official was assigned to watch a crooked supplies supervisor. This is what we are told at the end, in the recognition scene. At the very beginning of the story, however, we learn the following about the host: "All the inhabitants of the town were acquainted with the man, and they knew that he did not hold a high office, for he was neither a state official nor a military man, but a little supervisor at the tiny supply depot, where together with the rats he chewed on the state rusks and boot soles, and in the course of time had chewed himself together a nice little frame house." It is evident that this story reflects the traditional sympathy which storytellers have for rascals and crooks. All the literature of farce bears witness to it. Nor is it denied on the heights of art; of all Hebel's characters, the Brassenheim Miller, Tinder Frieder, and Red Dieter have been his most faithful companions. And yet for Hebel, too, the righteous man has the main role in the *theatrum mundi*. But because no one is actually up to this role, it keeps changing hands. Now it is the tramp, now the haggling Jewish peddler, now the man of limited intelligence who steps in to play this part. In every single case it is a guest performance, a moral improvisation. Hebel is a casuist. He will not for anything take a stand with any principle, but he does not reject it either, for any principle can at some time become the instrument of the righteous man. Compare this with Leskov's attitude. "I realize," he writes in his story "À Propos of the Kreutzer Sonata," "that my thinking is based much more on a practical view of life than on abstract philosophy or lofty morality; but I am nevertheless used to thinking the way I do." To be sure, the moral catastrophes that appear in Leskov's world are to the moral incidents in Hebel's world as the great, silent flowing of the Volga is to the babbling, rushing little millstream. Among Leskov's historical tales there are several in which passions are at work as destructively as the wrath of Achilles or the hatred of Hagen. It is astonishing how fearfully the world can darken for this author and with what majesty evil can raise its scepter. Leskov has evidently known moods—and this is probably one of the few characteristics he shares with Dostoyevsky—in which he was close to antinomian ethics. The elemental natures in his *Tales from Olden Times* go to the limit in their ruthless passion. But it is precisely the mystics who have been inclined to see this limit as the point at which utter depravity turns into saintliness.

XIX

The lower Leskov descends on the scale of created things the more obviously does his way of viewing things approach the mystical. Actually, as

will be shown, there is much evidence that in this, too, a characteristic
is revealed which is inherent in the nature of the storyteller. To be sure,
only a few have ventured into the depths of inanimate nature, and in
modern narrative literature there is not much in which the voice of the
anonymous storyteller, who was prior to all literature, resounds so clearly
as it does in Leskov's story "The Alexandrite." It deals with a semipre-
cious stone, the chrysoberyl. The mineral is the lowest stratum of created
things. For the storyteller, however, it is directly joined to the highest. To
him it is granted to see in this chrysoberyl a natural prophecy of petrified, lifeless nature concerning the historical world in which he himself
lives. This world is the world of Alexander II. The storyteller—or rather,
the man to whom he attributes his own knowledge—is a gem engraver
named Wenzel who has achieved the greatest conceivable skill in his art.
One can juxtapose him with the silversmiths of Tula and say that—in the
spirit of Leskov—the perfect artisan has access to the innermost chamber
of the realm of created things. He is an incarnation of the devout. We are
told of this gem cutter: "He suddenly squeezed my hand on which was
the ring with the alexandrite, which is known to sparkle red in artificial
light, and cried: 'Look, here it is, the prophetic Russian stone! O crafty
Siberian. It was always green as hope and only toward evening was it
suffused with blood. It was that way from the beginning of the world, but
it concealed itself for a long time, lay hidden in the earth, and permitted
itself to be found only on the day when Czar Alexander was declared of
age, when a great sorcerer had come to Siberia to find the stone, a magician. . . .' 'What nonsense are you talking,' I interrupted him; 'this stone
wasn't found by a magician at all, it was a scholar named Nordenskjöld!'
'A magician! I tell you, a magician!' screamed Wenzel in a loud voice. 'Just
look; what a stone! A green morning is in it and a bloody evening . . . This
is fate, the fate of noble Czar Alexander!' With these words old Wenzel
turned to the wall, propped his head on his elbows, and . . . began to sob."

One can hardly come any closer to the meaning of this significant
story than by some words which Paul Valéry wrote in a very remote
context. "Artistic observation," he says in reflections on a woman artist
whose work consisted in the silk embroidery of figures, "can attain an
almost mystical depth. The objects on which it falls lose their names.

Light and shade form very particular systems, present very individual questions which depend upon no knowledge and are derived from no practice, but get their existence and value exclusively from a certain accord of the soul, the eye, and the hand of someone who was born to perceive them and evoke them in his own inner self."

With these words, soul, eye, and hand are brought into connection. Interacting with one another, they determine a practice. We are no longer familiar with this practice. The role of the hand in production has become more modest, and the place it filled in storytelling lies waste. (After all, storytelling, in its sensory aspect, is by no means a job for the voice alone. Rather, in genuine storytelling the hand plays a part which supports what is expressed in a hundred ways with its gestures trained by work.) That old co-ordination of the soul, the eye, and the hand which emerges in Valéry's words is that of the artisan which we encounter wherever the art of storytelling is at home. In fact, one can go on and ask oneself whether the relationship of the storyteller to his material, human life, is not in itself a craftsman's relationship, whether it is not his very task to fashion the raw material of experience, his own and that of others, in a solid, useful, and unique way. It is a kind of procedure which may perhaps most adequately be exemplified by the proverb if one thinks of it as an ideogram of a story. A proverb, one might say, is a ruin which stands on the site of an old story and in which a moral twines about a happening like ivy around a wall.

Seen in this way, the storyteller joins the ranks of the teachers and sages. He has counsel—not for a few situations, as the proverb does, but for many, like the sage. For it is granted to him to reach back to a whole lifetime (a life, incidentally, that comprises not only his own experience but no little of the experience of others; what the storyteller knows from hearsay is added to his own). His gift is the ability to relate his life; his distinction, to be able to tell his entire life. The storyteller: he is the man who could let the wick of his life be consumed completely by the gentle flame of his story. This is the basis of the incomparable aura about the storyteller, in Leskov as in Hauff, in Poe as in Stevenson. The storyteller is the figure in which the righteous man encounters himself.

Defoe, Truthteller

NICHOLSON BAKER

I read Daniel Defoe's *A Journal of the Plague Year* on a train from Boston to New York. That's the truth. It's not a very interesting truth, but it's true. I could say that I read it in sitting on a low green couch in the old smoking room of the Cincinnati Palladium, across from a rather glum-looking Henry Kissinger. Or that I found a beat-up Longman's 1895 edition of Defoe's *Plague Year* in a Dumpster near the Recycle-A-Bicycle shop on Pearl Street when I was high on Guinness and roxies, and I opened it and was drawn into its singular, fearful world, and I sat right down in my own vomit and read the book straight through. It would be easy for me to say these things. But if I did, I would be inventing—and, as John Hersey wrote, the sacred rule for the journalist (or the memoirist, or indeed for any nonfiction writer) is: Never Invent. That's what makes Daniel Defoe, the founder of English journalism, such a thorny shrub. The hoaxers and the embellishers, the fake autobiographers, look on Defoe as a kind of patron saint. Defoe lied a lot. Be he also hated his lying habit, at least sometimes. He said the lying made a hole in the heart. About certain events he wanted truth told. And one event he really cared about was the great plague of 1665, which happened when he was around five years old.

A Journal of the Plague Year begins quietly, without any apparatus of learnedness. It doesn't try to connect this recent plague with past plagues. It draws no historical or classical or literary parallels. It just begins: "It was about the beginning of September, 1664, that I, among the rest of my neighbors, heard in ordinary discourse that the plague was returned again in Holland." The "I" is not Defoe, but an older proxy, somebody mysteriously named H.F., who says he is a saddler. H.F. lives halfway between Aldgate Church and Whitechapel, "on the left hand or north side of the street." That's all we know about him.

H.F. watches the bills of mortality mount—he keeps track—and he debates with himself whether to stay in town or flee. His brother tells him to save himself, get away. But no, H.F. decides to stay. He listens. He walks around. He sees a man race out of an alley, apparently singing and making clownish gestures, pursued by women and children—surgeons had been at work on his plague sores. "By laying strong caustics on them, the surgeons had, it seems, hopes to break them, which caustics were then upon him, burning his flesh as with a hot iron." H.F. hears screams—many different kinds of screams, and screeches, and shrieks. In an empty street in Lothbury, a window opens suddenly just over his head. "A woman gave three frightful screeches, and then cried, 'Oh! death, death, death!'" There was no other movement. The street was still. "For people had no curiosity now in any case."

At the plague's height, H.F. writes, there were no funerals, no wearing of black, no bells tolled, no coffins. "Whole streets seemed to be desolated," he says, "doors were left open, windows stood shattering with the wind in empty houses, for want of people to shut them; in a word, people began to give up themselves to their fears, and to think that all regulations and methods were in vain, and that there was nothing to be hoped for but an universal desolation."

What do we know about Defoe? Very little. He was one of the most prolific men ever to lift a pen, but he wrote almost nothing about himself. Not many letters have survived. Readers have been attributing and de-attributing Defoe's anonymous journalism ever since he died, broke, in Ropemaker's Alley, in 1731. He was almost always writing about someone else—or pretending to be someone else. There are a few engravings of him, and only one surviving prose description. It's unfriendly—in fact it was a sort of warrant for his arrest, printed in a newspaper when Defoe was wanted by the government on a charge of seditious libel. "He is a middle-sized, spare man," said the description, "about forty years old, of a brown complexion, and dark brown-colored hair, but wears a wig; a hooked nose, a sharp chin, grey eyes, and a large mole near his mouth." Anyone who could furnish information leading to his apprehension by her majesty's justices of the peace, said the notice, would receive a reward of fifty pounds.

We know that Defoe, late in life, wrote the first English novels—*Robinson Crusoe* in 1719, about a lonely sailor who sees a man's naked footprint on the beach, and *Moll Flanders* in January 1722, about a woman who was "twelve year a whore." We know that he was born about 1660, the son of a London butcher or candlemaker named James Foe. In his twenties, Daniel went into business as a hosier—that is, as a seller of women's stockings. Trade and speculation went well for a while, then less well, and then he had to hide from his creditors, to whom he owed seventeen thousand pounds. He was rescued by friends on high, and began writing pamphlets and poetry. Soon he was running a large company that made roofing tiles—and the pamphleteering was surprisingly successful. He added a Frenchifying "de" to his name. In 1701 he produced the most-selling poem up to that time, "The True-Born Englishman," which hymned his native land as a motley nation of immigrants: "Thus, from a mixture of all kinds began / That het'rogenous thing, an Englishman." Another pamphlet—in which, several decades before Swift's "Modest Proposal," he pretended to be a rabid high-churchman who advocated the deportation or hanging of nonconformists—got him clamped in a pillory in 1703 and sent to Newgate Prison.

While in prison he started a newspaper, the *Review*, an antecedent to Addison and Steel's *Tatler* and *Spectator*. Besides essays and opinion pieces, the *Review* had an early advice column, and a "weekly history of Nonsense, Impertinence, Vice, and Debauchery." That same year, still in prison, he gathered intelligence on a disaster that had visited parts of England. His book *The Storm*—about what he called "the greatest and the longest storm that ever the world saw"—is one of the earliest extended journalistic narratives in English.

For a faker, Defoe had an enormous appetite for truth and life and bloody specificity. He wanted to know everything knowable about trade, about royalty, about lowlife, about the customs of other countries, about

ships, about folk remedies and quack doctors, about disasters, about scientific advances, and about the shops and streets of London. He listened
to stories people told him. "In this way of Talk I was always upon the
Inquiry," one of his characters says, "asking questions of things done
in Publick, as well as in Private." But his desire to impersonate and
playact kept surging up and getting him into trouble. He wanted to
pass as someone he wasn't—as a Swedish king, as a fallen woman, as a
person who'd seen a ghost, as a pre-Dickensian pickpocket. He was an
especially industrious first-person crime writer. Once he ghost-wrote
the story of a thief and jailbreaker named Jack Sheppard. To promote
its publication, Defoe had Sheppard pause at the gallows and, before
a huge crowd, hand out the freshly printed pamphlet as his last testament—or so the story goes. "The rapidity with which this book sold is
probably unparalleled," writes an early biographer, William Lee.

Robinson Crusoe is Defoe's most famous hoax. We now describe it as
a novel, of course, but it wasn't born that way. On its 1719 title page,
the book was billed as the strange, surprising adventures of a mariner who lived all alone for eight-and-twenty years on an uninhabited
island, "Written by H I M S E L F"—and people at first took this claim
for truth and bought thousands of copies. This prompted an enemy
satirist, Charles Gildon, to rush out a pamphlet, "The Life and Strange
Surprising Adventures of Daniel de Foe, Formerly of London, Hosier,
Who has lived above fifty Years all alone by himself, in the Kingdoms
of North and South Britain."

Addison called Defoe a "false, shuffling, prevaricating rascal."
Another contemporary said he was a master of "forging a story and
imposing it on the world as truth." One of Defoe's nineteenth-century
biographers, William Minto, wrote: "He was a great, a truly great liar,
perhaps the greatest liar that ever lived."

And yet that's not wholly fair. A number of the things that people
later took to be Defoe's dazzlingly colorful tapestries of fabrication,
weren't. In 1718, in *Mist's Journal*, Defoe gave a detailed account of the
volcanic explosion of the island of St. Vincent, relying, he said, on letters he had received about it. A century passed, and doubts crept in. One
Defoe scholar said that the St. Vincent story was imaginary; a second
said it was tomfoolery; a third said it was "make-believe" and "entirely

of Defoe's invention." But the island of St. Vincent had actually blown up, and it had made a lot of noise as it blew. Defoe had done his jour-nalistic best to report this prodigy.

Something similar happened in the case of *A Journal of the Plague Year*. When Defoe published it, he, as usual, left himself off the title page, ascribing the story to H.F. "Written by a Citizen," the title page falsely, sales-boostingly claimed, "Who Continued All the While in London." People believed that for a while, but by 1780, at least, it was generally known that Defoe was the book's author. Then someone did some arithmetic and realized that Defoe had been a young child when the plague struck London—whereupon they began calling the book a historical novel, unequaled in vividness and circumstantiality. Walter Raleigh, in his late-nineteenth-century history of the English novel, called the book "sham history." In a study of "pseudofactual" fiction, Barbara Foley says that the *Plague Year* "creates the majority of its particulars." And John Hollowell, investigating the literary origins of the New Journalism, writes that Defoe's book is "fiction masquerading as fact." Is it?

One night H.F. visits the forty-foot burial trench in Aldgate Churchyard, near where he lives. "A terrible pit it was," he writes, "and I could not resist my curiosity to go and see it." He watches the dead cart dip and the bodies fall "promiscuously" into the pit, while a father stands silently by. Then the father, beside himself with grief, suddenly lets out a cry. Another time, H.F. describes the butchers' market. "People used all possible precaution," he says. "When any one bought a joint of meat in the market, they would not take it out of the butcher's hand, but took it off the hooks themselves. On the other hand, the butcher would not touch the money, but have it put into a pot full of vinegar, which he kept for that purpose."

A Journal of the Plague Year is an astounding performance. It's shocking, it's messy, it's moving, it sobs aloud with its losses, it's got all the urgency and loopingly prolix insistence of a man of sympathy who has lived through an urban catastrophe and wants to tell you what it was like. The fear of death, notes H.F., "took away all Bowels of love, all concern for one another." But not universally: "There were many instances of immovable affection, pity and duty." And Defoe's narrator is at pains to discount some of the stories that he hears. He is told, for example, of nurses smothering plague victims with wet cloths to hasten their end. But the particulars are suspiciously unvarying, and in every version, no matter where he encounters it, the event is said to have happened on the opposite side of town. There is, H.F. judges, "more of tale than of truth" in these accounts.

Still, there's the false frame. The story isn't really being told by H.F., it's being told by Defoe. That's clearly a forgery—although more understandable when you learn that Defoe had an uncle with those initials, Henry Foe. Henry was in fact a saddler, who lived in Aldgate near the burial pit. In order to launch himself into the telling of this overwhelmingly complex story of London's ordeal, Defoe needed to think and write in his uncle's voice. The "I" is more than a bit of commercial-minded artifice. The ventriloquism, the fictional first-person premise, helped Defoe to unspool and make sequential sense of what he knew. He sifted through and used a mass of contemporary published sources, as any journalist would, and he enlivened that printed store with anecdotes that people had told him over the years. (His father could have been a source for the butcher's vinegar pot.) The book feels like something heartfelt, that grew out of decades of accumulated notes and memories—although written with impressive speed. It doesn't feel like an artificial swizzle of falsifications.

In 1919, a young scholar, Watson Nicholson, wrote a book on the sources of Defoe's *Journal of the Plague Year*. He was quite upset by the notion that the *Journal* was now, without qualification, being called a novel. In his book Nicholson claimed to have established "overwhelming evidence of the complete authenticity of Defoe's 'masterpiece of the imagination.'" There was not, Nicholson said, "a single essential statement in the Journal not based on historic fact." True, Defoe had a way of embroidering, but even so, "the employment of the first person in the narrative in no sense interferes with the authenticity of the facts recorded."

Other critics agreed. In 1965, Frank Bastian cross-checked what Defoe said in the *Journal* against Pepys's *Diary*, which Defoe couldn't have seen because it wasn't decoded until a century later. "Characters and incidents once confidently asserted to be the products of Defoe's fertile imagination," wrote Bastian in 1965, "repeatedly prove to have been factual." Introducing the Penguin edition of the *Plague Year* in 1966, Anthony Burgess wrote: "Defoe was our first great novelist because he was our first great journalist."

Six thousand people a month died in London's plague, most of them poor. The locations of many burial pits passed from memory. One was later used, according to Defoe, as a "yard for keeping hogs"; another pit was rediscovered when the foundation of a grand house was being dug: "The women's sculls were quite distinguished by their long hair." Is the author being a reporter here, or a novelist? We don't know. We want to know.

Daniel Defoe seems to have needed a pocketful of passports to get where he was going. But the moral of his story, at least for the nonfictionist, still is: Never Invent. People love hoaxes in theory—from a distance—but they also hate being tricked. If you make sad things up and insist that they're true, nobody afterward will fully trust what you write.

The Wings of Henry James

JAMES THURBER

One night nearly thirty years ago, in a legendary New York *boîte de nuit et des arts* called Tony's, I was taking part in a running literary gun fight that had begun with a derogatory or complimentary remark somebody made about something, when one of the participants, former Pinkerton man Dashiell Hammett, whose *The Maltese Falcon* had come out a couple of years before, suddenly startled us all by announcing that his writing had been influenced by Henry James's novel *The Wings of the Dove*. Nothing surprises me any more, but I couldn't have been more surprised then if Humphrey Bogart, another frequenter of that old salon of wassail and debate, had proclaimed that his acting bore the deep impress of the histrionic art of Maude Adams.

I was unable, in a recent reinvestigation, to find many feathers of *The Dove* in the claws of *The Falcon*, but there are a few "faint, far" (as James used to say) resemblances. In both novels, a fabulous fortune—jewels in *The Falcon*, inherited millions in *The Dove*—shapes the destinies of the disenchanted central characters; James's designing woman Kate Croy, like Hammett's pistol-packing babe Brigid O'Shaughnessy, loses her lover, although James's Renunciation Scene is managed, as who should say, rather more exquisitely than Hammett's, in which Sam Spade speaks these sweetly sorrowful parting words: "You angel! Well, if you get a good break you'll be out of San Quentin in twenty years and you can come back to me then." Whereupon he turns her over to the cops for the murder of his partner, Miles Archer (a good old Henry James name, that). Some strong young literary excavator may one day dig up other parallels, but I suggest that he avoid trying to relate the character in *The Falcon* called Cairo to James's early intention to use Cairo, instead of Venice, as the major setting of his novel. That is simply, as who should not say, one of those rococo coincidences.

The Wings of the Dove is now fifty-eight years old, but it still flies on, outward bound for the troubled future. Since 1902, it has become a kind of *femme fatale* of literature, exerting a curiously compelling effect upon authors, critics, playwrights, producers, and publishers. Seemingly, almost every playwright, from hack to first-rate talent, has been burned by the drama that glows within the novel's celebrated triangle, and has taken a swing at adapting it for stage or screen, usually with less than no success. It was James's own original intention to present his plot and characters in play form, but guardian angel or artist's insight caused him wisely to refrain from diverting into the theatre his delicately flowering, slowly proliferating history of fine consciences, which belongs so clearly between covers and not between curtains.

This doesn't keep people from adapting it, though. In 1956, Guy Bolton made a play out of it, *Child of Fortune*, which was produced on Broadway by the usually canny Jed Harris, who had earlier touched with art ("art schmart," he himself once disdainfully called it) his directing of *The Heiress*, based on Henry James's novel *Washington Square*. The Bolton *Dove* died miserably after twenty-three performances. That debacle did not deter television's *Playhouse 90* from having a go at dramatizing the novel just last year. This adaptation, made by a young man named Meade Roberts, seemed to me closer to the James tone and mood, closer to perfection of total production, than any other dramatization I have seen, and I have seen plenty. (The first one I ever encountered was shown to me by a young professor of English in Ohio forty-one years ago.) The success of *The Dove* on television lay in a discipline that gave it Henry James's key and pitch, if not his depth and range. Because my sight has failed, I could not see Inga Swenson, who played Milly, and this was probably fortunate, since I was told she looked as healthy as one of Thomas Hardy's milkmaids. But her words fell persuasively upon the ear, and she was the dying Milly to me. The direction gave the play a proper unhurried pace ("sluggish," wrote one restless newspaper critic), and there were moving offstage effects—the sound of distant bells in one scene, the haunting cry of gondoliers in another.

In my own college years, 1913–17, the literature courses in the modern English novel that were offered west of the Alleghenies included Hardy and Meredith, and sometimes Trollope, Samuel Butler, and Conrad, but rarely James. My own professor in this field, the late Joseph Russell Taylor, of Ohio State, rated James higher than the rest, and assigned *The Wings of the Dove* as required class reading, with this admonition: "If you can't make anything at all out of the first hundred pages, don't let it worry you." It was James's method to introduce his principal characters late, or, as John McNulty once put it, "to creep up on them in his stocking feet." Since only about one student in every thirty could stand, or understand, Henry James's writing, there were few persons with whom you could discuss the Old Master in those years. It was in 1930 that the Modern Library first introduced Henry James to its readers, with its edition of *The Turn of the Screw*, which has sold to date ninety thousand copies. The so-called Henry James Revival did not take place until the nineteen-forties, and centered on the hundredth anniversary of his birth. In 1946, the Modern Library brought out *The Wings of the Dove*, which has sold more than forty-one thousand copies. In 1958, *The Dove* lost its American copyright and fell into the public domain, and in January, 1959, Dell's Laurel edition of paperbacks printed seventy-five thousand copies of the novel, a little more than two-thirds of which either were sold or are out on the newsstands or in the bookstores.

The James Revival deserves the capital "R," because the increased sales of his books and the rapidly expanding literature on the man and his life and his work began crowding library shelves all over the country. In 1932, I bought the complete 1922 edition of James, issued by Macmillan of London, but it had not been easy to find. It was available in no New York bookstore then, and I finally got my set through a collector. It came from a private library on Park Avenue, which was then being sold, and not a single page of any of the more than thirty volumes had been cut. It was as if the owner of this particular edition had said, "I want to buy about two and a half or three feet of the works of Henry James." Interest in the Revival spread from Broadway to Hollywood. For years, David O. Selznick held the movie rights to *The Dove*, but he never produced an adaptation of the novel, unquestionably because of the difficulty of casting the three principal roles and of finding an adapter who could satisfactorily cope with the dramatization.

This seems the right place to describe briefly the "game," as James called it, that is afoot in his masterpiece.

Kate Croy, then, an ambitious young Englishwoman, emotionally intense and deeply amorous (James dresses her in such words as "ardor," "desire," and "passion"), is eager to marry a struggling young writer and journalist, Merton Densher in the novel but, mercifully, Miles Enshaw in the television play. Having developed, because of a penniless life with a wastrel father, what would now be called a neurosis or psychosis, Kate, with her "talent for life," is determined to enjoy money and marriage, and neither without the other. Into her predicament and preoccupation drifts the American girl Milly Theale, attractive, enormously wealthy, naïve, and genuine, but perceptive ("mobile of mind"), in the best Henry James tradition, and dying. She falls in love with Densher, and the possessed, designing Kate perceives how she can use Milly's situation for her own selfish ends. She deliberately throws Milly and Densher together in Venice, and then reveals her scheme to him. He shall marry Milly, thus killing, you might say, two doves with one stone—Milly's final months on earth will be made happy ones, after which Kate and Densher will live happily ever after on the dead bride's millions. But Milly, again true to the James tradition of innocent American girls entangled in European society intrigue, discovers the true situation—that Kate is in love with and secretly engaged to Densher and that Densher is in love with Kate. Milly dies and, in her "copious will," leaves much of her wealth to the lovers, but they can never be happy with it, or without it. They are shadowed and separated forever by the wings of the dead dove, by the presence of a girl who is gone but everlastingly there.

Lest my oversimplification in this summary cause the ghost of Henry James to pace and mutter, I shall let him insert here a typical elucidation of the "conspiracy" of Kate and Merton: "The picture constituted, so far as may be, is that of a pair of natures well-nigh consumed by a sense of their intimate affinity and congruity, the reciprocity of their desire, and thus passionately impatient of barriers and delays, yet with qualities of intelligence and character that they are meanwhile extraordinarily able to draw upon for the enrichment of their relation, the extension of their prospect and the support of their 'game.'"

There has probably been no other major novelist whose work has been so often criticized not so much for what it is but for what certain critics think it should have been. One critic, whose name I do not know, becoming impatient of the carpers, once said that they criticized Henry James as they might criticize a cat for not being a dog. These carpers are given to attacking, at the same time, the involved James style and his viewpoint on love, sex, women, affairs, and marriage. One reviewer of the *Playhouse 90* production insisted that no woman as passionately in love as Kate would hand her lover over to another woman, even temporarily, however great the promised compensation. The sensitive novelist never got used to the assaults upon him—understandably enough, for many of them were brutal. He was accused of "bombinating in a vacuum" and, by H. G. Wells, of laboring like a hippopotamus trying to pick up a pea. It was not a pea but a pearl, a James defender pointed out, and the hippopotamus had unbelievably skillful fingers.

As James's novels everywhere show, and his prefaces repeatedly declaim, he was caught unceasingly between the urge to "dramatize!" and his passion for indirection—an ambivalence that must present both challenge and handicap to the adapter, however ingenious, of his work. In the last chapter of *The Dove*, James observes that walks taken by Kate and Densher were "more remarkable for what they didn't say than for what they did." The book ends with a hopeless headshake by Kate and then the final speech "We shall never be again as we were!," which is scarcely the way a born dramatist would bring down his third-act curtain. And what can the helpless adapter do when confronted, as he frequently is, by such lines as this: "The need to bury in the dark blindness of each other's arms the knowledge of each other that they couldn't undo." Incidentally, few artists with the physical ability to see appreciate the truth known to all those without sight, that there is a dark blindness and a lighted blindness. Henry James was at home in the dark and in the light and in the shadows that lie between.

The theme of *The Dove* had germinated in what Edmund Wilson has called James's "marvelous intelligence" (and Wells his "immensely abundant brain") upon the death of a first cousin extremely dear to him, Minny Temple, who departed his world and our world (they are in many ways distinctly different) at the age of twenty-four. He became so absorbed in his theme that he was moved to prefigure Milly's death as dragging everybody and everything down with it, like a great ship sinking or a big business collapsing. This massive contemplation of effect belongs to the mind and scheme of the novelist, but it can't very well be encompassed in a dramatization, because one can't get stream of consciousness into a three-act play. It is a commonplace of the ordeal of Henry James that the presentation of his work on the stage, to which he devoted many years, has been invariably better managed in the theatre by other hands than his own. A few years ago, *The Turn of the Screw* was turned into *The Innocents*, and much earlier the unfinished novel *The Sense of the Past* shone upon the stage as *Berkeley Square*. Among the failures on Broadway ("It didn't just close, it flew closed," said Richard Maney) was an adaptation, nearly four years ago, of James's *The Europeans*, called *Eugenia* and starring Tallulah Bankhead, of whom Louis Kronenberger wrote, in a preface to his *Best Plays of 1956–57*, "only Mae West as Snow White could have seemed more unsuited to a part." Finding an actress, however gifted, who can play a Henry James woman convincingly must be a nightmare to any producer. One such rare lady is Flora Robson, who starred in London as Tina in Sir Michael Redgrave's recent dramatization of *The Aspern Papers*, a substantial hit and, I am told by a man who has seen them all, the finest presentation of a James work ever brought to the stage.

It had always seemed a wonder to me, until I got involved myself, that practically everybody wanted to write about *The Dove*. In the preface to the new paperback edition, R. P. Blackmur says, "By great luck I had been introduced simply and directly, and had responded in the same way, to what a vast number of people have thought an impossible novel by an impossible author and a vast number of other people have submitted to the stupefying idolatry of both gross and fine over-interpretation." Recently, Dr. Saul Rosenzweig, a psychologist and student of Henry James, dug up the opinion of the novelist-psychiatrist Dr. S. Weir

Mitchell: "I have read his [H. J.'s] last book with bewildered amazement. Since I played cat's cradle as a child, I have seen no tangle like it. To get the threads of his thought off his mind onto mine with the intermediation of his too exasperating style has been too much for me. A friend of mine says his 'Wings of a Dove' [*sic*] are unlike any dove she ever saw; for it has neither head nor tail. However, I am too old to learn a new language and still struggle to write my own with clearness."

Dr. Rosenzweig discovered a reply to the Mitchell objections in the correspondence of Owen Wister, creator of *The Virginian* and of the sundown gun duel on the deserted Western main street. "Henry James is in essence inscrutable," Wister wrote to Mitchell, "but one thing of him I know: our language has no artist more serious or austere at this moment. I explain to myself his bewildering style thus: he is attempting the impossible with it—a certain very particular form of the impossible; namely, to produce upon the reader, as a painting produces upon the gazer, a number of superimposed, simultaneous impressions. He would like to put several sentences on top of each other so that you could read them all at once, and get all at once the various shadings and complexities, instead of getting them consecutively as the mechanical nature of his medium compels. This I am sure is the secret of his involved parentheses, his strangely injected adverbs, the whole structure, in short, of his twisted syntax. One grows used to it by persisting. I read *The Ambassadors* twice, and like it amazingly as a prodigy of skill. One other thing of signal importance is a key to his later books. He does not undertake to tell a story but to deal with a situation, a single situation. Beginning (in his scheme) at the center of this situation, he works outward, intricately and exhaustively, spinning his web around every part of the situation, every little necessary part no matter how slight, until he gradually presents to you the organic whole, worked out. You don't get the organic whole until he wishes you to and that is at the very end. But he never lets the situation go, never digresses for a single instant; and no matter how slow or long his pages may seem as you first read them, when you have at the end grasped the total thing, if you then look back you find that the voluminous texture is woven closely and that every touch bears upon the main issue. I don't say that if I could I would work like this, or that the situations he chooses to weave into such verbal labyrinth are such as I should care to deal with so minutely and laboriously, even if I had the art to do so; but I do say that judged as only any works of art can ever be judged; viz., by *themselves*, by what they undertake to do and how thoroughly they do it, Henry James's later books are the work of a master. . . ."

Wolcott Gibbs, to get back to the Guy Bolton adaptation of *The Dove*, found *Child of Fortune* ineffably tedious and dull, and Louis Kronenberger concluded that *The Dove* on the stage "can only succeed as something quite trashy or as something truly tremendous." It can, that is to say, succeed only on the scale of soap opera—*Milly Faces Life, Death Can Be Bountiful, The First Mrs. Densher, Wings of Riches*—or on that of grand opera, with such arias as "O gentle dove!," "This heart to thy swift flight," "Fold now thy tender wings," "Ah, passion but an hour!"

Thus, Meade Robert's *Playhouse 90* dramatization was a unique achievement. I sat before my television set that night last year hoping for the passable, fearing the worst.

The worst is a perverse tendency, exhibited by at least one adapter in the past, to twist the plot into low, ironic comedy by saving the life of Milly Theale. Densher, that is, marries the rich girl only to find, to his dismay, and that of Kate, that Milly becomes a rose, no longer choked in the grass but fresh-sprung in the June of salutary happiness. We are a sentimental, soft-hearted nation, prone to lay violent hands upon death in art by calling in play doctors and heroine specialists of the kind that "saved" the doomed Lena, of Joseph Conrad's *Victory*, forty years ago, when it was made into a silent movie that was a combination of Pollyanna and Jack Holt. This saving of heroines, for a more recent instance in another sphere, was rudely accomplished by the Andrews Sisters in the case of the old Irish ballad "Molly Malone." The ballad has it that "She died of a fever and no one could save her," but the sympathetic Andrews Sisters did save her by cutting out that line, fitting her up with an artificial husband, and removing "Now a ghost wheels her barrow" and inserting "Now they both wheel her barrow," to the sorrow of millions who love Molly Malone not only alive, alive O, but dying and dead. When the resurrected Molly was crying her cockles and mussels over the airwaves a few years ago, I began fearing that the heroine specialists would go on to resurrect Shakespeare's Juliet, Verdi's

Violetta, Wordsworth's Lucy, Browning's Evelyn Hope, Tennyson's Elaine, Poe's Annabel Lee, and Hemingway's Catherine Barkley. My fears gave rise to a terrifying nightmare in which I picked up a copy of *A Farewell to Arms* to discover that its title had been changed to *Over the Fever and through the Crise*. It was during this period of apprehension that I went about muttering "I am mending, Egypt, mending." But *Playhouse 90*, bless its young heart, let Milly Theale die in the beauty of the Henry James lilies.

The profound and lasting effect upon Henry James of Minny Temple's untimely death shows up in many ways and places in his novels and stories. The simple, faintly comic name Minny Temple is reflected not only in Milly Theale but, in varying degrees, in the names of such other James heroines as Maggie Verver; Maisie, of *What Maisie Knew*; Mamie Pocock; Daisy Miller; May Bartram; Maria Gostrey; and Mary Antrim. Even Madame la Comtesse de Vionnet was named Marie. More than one of the girls in this "M" category die in the novels and novellas. I have set down the foregoing names from memory, and I am sure a research through the books would turn up many more. Probably dozens of seniors in English literature courses—like one I met at Yale a few years ago—have devoted their theses to a study of the proper names in Henry James. He had something more than a gift, almost an impish perversity, for the invention of plain, even homely feminine names, and by no means all of them were for his American women. The weediest of all is, I think, Fleda Vetch, of *The Spoils of Poynton*. As for his best-known American females, only a few, such as Isabel Archer and Carolina Spencer, do not grate upon the ear. This is partly because the voices of American women, from coast to coast, as he once said, were a torture to his own ear. Some fifty years ago, in *Harper's Bazar* (this was before it became *Harper's Bazaar*), he wrote half a dozen pieces about the speech and manners of the American Woman, which have never been brought together in any book. They might conceivably throw some light upon the James names for women, and upon his complicated, ambivalent attitude toward the ladies themselves. In any case, he usually took them up tenderly, fashioned so slenderly, young and so rich. What feminine reader has not wept over the death of poor dear Daisy Miller? And what sensitive gentleman can read the closing pages of *The Beast in the Jungle* and ever forget the anguish of John Marcher, to whom nothing whatever had happened, who through life had love forgone, quit of scars and tears but bearing the deep, incurable wound of emptiness? This story tells the tale of its author's loss of "the wings of experience," the burden and beauty and blessing of the love of a woman—something that was denied to Henry James for a complex of reasons, upon which the Freudians, especially during the nineteen-thirties, liked to get their eager fingers. Basically, he deliberately chose a loveless life because of his transfiguring conviction that the high art he practiced was not consonant with marriage but demanded the monastic disciplines of celibacy. He loved vicariously, though, and no man more intensely and sensitively.

It has always seemed to me that Henry James plunged into the theatre to escape, perhaps without conscious intention, from the lifelessness of the silent study and the stuffy ivory tower. But no one can simply, or romantically, account for any novelist's taking on the theatre at intervals. There is always the lure of contact with an audience and the immediate response of appreciation, and there is also always what James called "the lust of a little possible gold." He supported himself by his writings, and he had the hope of making a killing on the stage for the sake of his budget and coffers. What resulted was an unequal struggle—his "tussle with the Black Devil of the theatre." He wrote a dozen plays in all, but only four were produced, and none were outstanding, and none made any money to speak of. And around him, all the time, bloomed, to his envy and usually to his disdain, such successes by his colleagues as *The Second Mrs. Tanqueray*, *An Ideal Husband*, and *The Passing of the Third Floor Back*. James's theatre pieces have been collected by Leon Edel, one of the most eminent living Jamesians, in *The Complete Plays of Henry James*.

Edel's swift and fascinating account of what was probably James's most hideous hour, the first night of his play *Guy Domville*, at the St. James's Theatre, in London, one January night in 1895, is itself worth the price of the volume. What happened that terrifying night would take too long to tell, and could not be done by anyone as well as Edel has done it. The evening might have grown out of the conjoined imaginations of Agatha Christie, Ed Wynn, and Robert Benchley. It began with the receipt of a mysterious telegram of bad wishes, and, after a compelling first act, abruptly changed gear and color in the second, with the entrance of an actress wearing a strange and comical hat. If James had, up to that night, still toyed with the idea of dramatizing the story of Milly Theale, he must have given up all thought of such a venture the moment he was dragged out upon the stage, at the end of the play, to the boos and catcalls that dominated the applause of an audience containing, among its host of celebrities, three comparatively unknown literary men—Arnold Bennett, H. G. Wells, and George Bernard Shaw. Incidentally, there have been few literary feuds so fascinating, and few so voluminously documented, as that between James and Wells, the introvert against the extrovert, the self-conscious artist versus the social-conscious novelist. The history of this long bicker and battle has been done by Edel and Gordon N. Ray in their *Henry James and H. G. Wells*, published, in 1958, by the University of Illinois Press.

Admirers of literature's hippopotamus with the skillful fingers and the sensitive soul must always mourn his having missed *The Heiress* and *The Innocents* and *Berkeley Square*, but their sorrow is compensated for by a sense of relief that he didn't have to experience the rigors and rigidities of Broadway. Anybody can survive editors and publishers, one way or another, but it takes the constitution of a Marine sergeant major to stand up under the bombardment of producers and directors, not to mention actors and actresses. Ellen Terry once promised to appear in a Henry James play in America, but never did, with the result that he called her "perfidious." He did manage to get the great Forbes-Robertson to appear in a play of his, but it is a now forgotten *succès d'estime*, a dim footnote to the record of that actor's achievements in the theatre. Once, James decided to turn a long one-act play of his into three acts by "curtain drops," dividing it into what he called stanzas or cantos. I can see now the faces of Jed Harris, Herman Shumlin, and Kermit Bloomgarden listening to the Old Master's "polysyllabic ponderosities" about *that*.

I think it is safe to say that television's voracious gobbling up of the literature of the past, which it regurgitates as Westerns, will leave Henry James's works uneaten, and even unbitten. There are now so many Westerns on television that their writers may soon be forced to adapt even the more famous Bible stories, and we may expect before long a bang-bang based on this distorted text: "Whither thou goest, I will go, God and the Cheyennes willing."

Until his untimely death, John Lardner, head of *The New Yorker*'s department of television investigation, viewed with sound alarm and insight the Westernizing, among other things, of de Maupassant's sardonic classic "Boule de Suif," in which the fat French prostitute of the original was transmutilated into a slender and virtuous Apache princess, while quotations from Shakespeare flowered all over the desert till Hell wouldn't have it. That distortion of an indestructible piece of literature alarmed me, too, coming, as it did, only nine days after my happily groundless fears about the debauching of Henry James's *Dove*. When de Maupassant's famous coach was diverted from its journey between Rouen and Le Havre and rerouted across the Indian country, I began fretting about what might happen to other celebrated coaches of literature—the one in *Vanity Fair*, all those that rumble through Dickens, and even the one that carries Cinderella to the ball. Then I began worrying about Lewis Carroll's coachless Alice. I could see her being driven, behind four horses, from a ladies' finishing school in Boston to California in order to be joined in unholy matrimony with a disturbed ex-haberdasher, one Mat Hadder, now a deranged U.S. marshal. Down from the hills, at the head of his howling tribe, sweeps Big Chief White Rabbit, but out of the West, the Far-fetched West, to the blare of bugle music, rides Captain Marston ("March") Hare, who falls in love with Alice through the gun smoke, and—Ah, the hell with it. (For the sake of the record, it should be noted, in passing, that "Boule de Suif" was once dramatized for Broadway, with reasonable reverence, in a play called *The Channel Road*.)

I keep thinking of other possible—nay, probable—television corruptions: *Trelawny of the Wells Fargo*, *Lady Windermere's Gun*, *She Shoots to Conquer*, *Fanny's First Gunplay*, and even *The Sheriff Misses Tanqueray*. This Tanqueray is the fastest draw in English literature, and can outshoot the notorious desperado Long Gun Silver (and a high-ho to you, Long Gun, says I). To get all this frightening phantasmagoria off my mind, I have begun rereading, and hiding in, Henry James's *The Sacred Fount*, a story that will, I feel sure, forever foil the bang-bang transmutilators. For such small and negative blessings let us thank with brief thanksgiving whatever gods may be.

One thing that I can't yet dismiss from my waking thoughts and dawn dreams is the impish, tongue-in-cheek compulsion of the Western televisionaries to commingle the Bard and the bang-bangs. The other morning, I woke up with this line, from *Have Gun, Will Shakespeare*, chasing through my head: "How sweet the moonlight sleeps upon this—*bang!*"

Thataway, stranger, lies madness, so let us iris out on a quieter and safer area.

H. G. Wells, long-time friend and finally enemy of Henry James, once wrote, "For generations to come a select type of reader will brighten appreciatively to 'The Spoils of Poynton,' 'The Ambassadors,' 'The Tragic Muse,' 'The Golden Bowl' and many other stories." His prophecy was right, if you change "type" to "types," but his list of the stories he apparently liked best himself is unconvincing to me. I doubt, for instance, whether he ever got through *The Golden Bowl*, but if he did he left me somewhere in the middle of it. It is hard to understand how he could have left out the most controversial of all James's creations, *The Turn of the Screw*.

The undiminished power of the great "ghost story," after more than sixty years, was proved again, this time on television, when Ingrid Bergman starred in a dramatization by James Costigan, put on by the Ford *Startime* series just last year. I put "ghost story" in quotes because of the controversy that still rages, as rage goes in literary and psychological circles, about the true meaning of the narrative. Critical minds, in practically all known areas of research and analysis, have got answers, dusty and otherwise, when hot for certainties in this, one of the greatest of all literary mysteries. Even with a merely competent cast, it would be hard to mar, or even dilute, the effectiveness of any dramatization, but Miss Bergman brought a memorable performance to a well-written, well-directed *Turn of the Screw*. She was equaled in every way by the performances of Alexandra Wager and Hayward Morse, as the two children of the eerie household.

One New York critic called it an "honest to God ghost story," and most viewers must indeed have been haunted and chilled by the

strange goings-on in the great house of the wide circular staircase and
the gloomy corridors. Dramatic and theatrical effectiveness aside, the
question that has fascinated literary critics and psychoanalysts for six
decades is this: Were the apparitions of the dead ex-governess, Miss
Jessel, and of the violently dead ex-valet, Peter Quint, actual visitations
from beyond the grave, or were they figments of the inflamed psyche of
the new governess? The literature on the subject is extensive. Watchers
of the television show who want to pursue the mystery into the library
could turn to Edmund Wilson's "The Ambiguity of Henry James" in
his *The Triple Thinkers*, James's own preface, and the narrative itself.
Mr. Wilson pays tribute to Edna Kenton, one of the first psychogra-
phers to put forward the theory of hallucination instead of apparition.
The James preface, in the manner of the Master, weaves a glittery web
around his intention, at once brightening and obscuring it. He speaks
of fairy tale and witchcraft, touches lightly on psychic research, and, of
course, jumps over Freud completely. He can set so many metaphors and
implications dancing at the same time on the point of his pen that it is
hard to make out the pattern in the fluttering of all the winged words. I
myself have never had the slightest doubt that he was completely aware
of almost every latent meaning that has been read into the famous
story. Henry James was not a student of Freud; he was a sophomore in
psychology compared to his distinguished brother William, and I once
read a letter of Henry's in which he somewhat pettishly dismissed the
assumptions of Freud as akin to those of spiritualism. But when it came
to pondering his plots, turning over his characters and incidents the
way a squirrel turns over a nut, he was the pure artist, less susceptible
than almost any other to unreasoned impulse.

Some years ago, in a little town in Connecticut, I had the pleasure
of meeting, at a party, a gracious lady whose mother was the sister of
Minny Temple. She told me a wonderful tale of something that happened at twilight in England many, many years ago, when she was a
young girl. I like to think that the incident took place at the very time
Henry James was working out, in his conscious mind, the tricks and
devices of *The Turn of the Screw*. At any rate, the venerable figure of
the distinguished novelist, wearing opera hat and cape, stood outside a
house, in the fading light, and peered through a window at the young

lady and one or two other girls, to give them what he might have called "the tiniest of thrills." And so to me, if to no one else, it is clear that this gave him the idea of the apparition, at a window, of the ghostly figure of Peter Quint.

Alas, I am now told that the gracious lady not only has forgotten the incident but does not believe it happened, and cannot recall telling me about it. And so this rambling flight into the past ends, as perhaps it should properly end, on a faint, far note of mystery.

Billy Budd

ELIZABETH HARDWICK

Billy Budd, Foretopman,[1] left at death in an unfinished or unedited state and preserved by his wife. A return to prose fiction, a last will and testament, a going back to the spirit of his earlier work, before the diversion into poetry. He is ailing, plagued, as he has been forever, by trouble with his eyes, and yet the luminous imagination remains with this strange man as if reluctant to be blotted out by darkness. In *Billy Budd* he writes a lyrical tragedy on the extremes in human character, a contemplation of goodness appearing as naturally as a sunrise and of midnight evil also inhabiting a human soul naturally, without necessity or even clear advantage.

Into this deeply affecting reflection on the human condition, he has imagined details of a challenging singularity; and as a storyteller there is a magical plot, a dramatic series of actions, without which the tale would be a philosophical daydream. Billy Budd, a young sailor of preternatural beauty, good nature, and loyalty, is accused by the master-at-arms, a sort of naval MP, of intention to mutiny. The young sailor,

---

1 Scholars, deciphering the messy manuscript, have decided that Melville's final title was *Billy Budd, Sailor*. I have kept *Foretopman* out of a sentimental affection for the old title under which most of us first read the story. The name of the ship, formerly the *Indomitable*, was changed by Melville to the *Bellipotent*, and I have reluctantly honored that. Still, it's hard to imagine that the ribald old sailors would have wished to sign on the "Belly-potent."

who, under stress, suffers from a stutter or speech pause, is unable to express his innocence and outrage and strikes out at the accuser, killing him by a blow. According to maritime law, the sailor, Billy Budd, must be hanged and his body consigned to the sea.

But who is Billy Budd? He is a curiosity indeed, almost defying credible description. He is the Handsome Sailor, he is Apollo with a portmanteau, he is Baby Budd, he is Beauty—all of these things as he comes swinging onto the English ship the *Bellipotent*. He is twenty-one, an able-bodied seaman, fit to climb the great sails, as if ready to fly. Billy is also from the first a creature of inborn moral sweetness. He is free and innocent, a beautiful changeling from nowhere. In fact, he is an orphan, an illiterate, reminding one of a freshly hatched, brilliantly colored bird. His only flaw is the one mentioned, the stutter under stress. Peaceful himself, he brings peace to those around him "like a Catholic priest striking peace in an Irish shindy."

Melville gives evidence of a compositional strain to bring credibility to the beloved youth, to the demands of his perfection, united with the purest naturalness. The pictorial Billy: "A lingering adolescent expression in the as yet smooth face, all but feminine in purity of natural complexion." And then a leap: "Cast in a mold peculiar to the finest physical examples of those Englishmen in whom the Saxon strain would seem not at all to partake of any Norman or other admixture, he showed in his face that humane look of reposeful good nature which the Greek sculptor in some instances gave to the heroic strong man, Hercules." The pretty boy as Hercules is a preparation for the development of the story. The captain of the ship from which Billy was taken, impressed, by the *Bellipotent* told of an altercation on his ship in which Billy had been insulted by a sailor named Red Whiskers. "Quick as lightning Billy let fly his arm. I dare say he never meant to do as much as he did, but anyhow he gave the burly fool a terrible drubbing." Billy's previous ship was named *Rights-of-Man*.

John Claggart, the Master-at-Arms, is a mirror opposite of Billy Budd. His unaccountable but concentrated hostility to the universally loved Billy is a conundrum, an exceptional circumstance. Claggart exhibits the floating, "motiveless malignity" Coleridge in a kind of psychological resignation falls back on as the explanation for Shakespeare's Iago. Like Billy, Claggart has no known past, no baggage of previous circumstance to carry about with him. He has entered the naval ship at thirty-five, causing his shipmates to imagine some cloud of disrepute driving him.

He is carefully described by Melville, the lover of verbal portraiture. Claggart does not cut an ill figure, being spare and tall, with clean-cut features, except that something about his chin recalls the Titus Oates of the Popish plot. It is noted that Claggart's hands do not give evidence of hard toil, and his complexion is interestingly pale for a seaman. He is educated, and there is something in his speech not quite that of a native-born Englishman. However he entered the man-of-war's crew, Claggart soon made his mark due to "the superior capacity he immediately evinced, his constitutional sobriety, and ingratiating deference to superiors, together with a peculiar ferreting genius manifested on a singular occasion; all this, capped by a certain austere patriotism, abruptly advanced him to the position of master-at-arms."

Claggart will take a bold dislike for Billy Budd that will infect his spirit with an inflammatory passion, outwardly controlled by the "uncommon prudence" habitual with "the subtler depravity." And, as such natures can, Claggart enlists the help of a corrupt, sniveling crewman called Squeak, who tries to enlist Billy Budd, an impressed seaman, into thoughts of mutiny but is violently rejected by the Hercules in Billy's nature.

And yet another coil in Claggart's twisted nature:

> When Claggart's unobserved glance happened to light on belted Billy rolling along the upper gun deck in the leisure of the second dogwatch . . . that glance would follow the cheerful sea Hyperion with a settled meditative and melancholy expression, his eyes strangely suffused with incipient feverish tears. Then would Claggart look like a man of sorrows. Yes, and sometimes the melancholy expression would have in it a touch of soft yearning, as if Claggart could even have loved Billy but for fate and ban.

Thinking about the dense stabs in the thicket of Claggart's character, the great American critic F. O. Matthiesen writes: " . . . a writer today would be fully aware of what may have been only latent for Melville, the sexual element in Claggart's ambivalence. Even if Melville did not have this consciously in mind, it emerges for the reader now with intense psychological accuracy."

The story is set on British ships in 1797 after the fleet mutiny at Nore. Crews seized a ship previously at Spithead, sent the officers ashore, in protest against the brutal conditions prevailing in the British navy. The mutiny at Nore was a more serious outbreak, a threat to Britain's sea power, and also felt connected to the tide of revolutionary feeling spreading from France and from Napoleon's conquests. The *Bellipotent* has been called to shift from merchant service to a man-of-war. For this purpose, men were dragged off the street and impressed into service, and thus Billy is taken from his ship, *Rights-of-Man*. He is willing to serve, and as he boards his new berth, he cheerfully waves to the departing vessel and calls out, "And good-bye to you, too, old *Rights-of-Man*." This, interpreted, or in pretended interpretation, will figure in the claim by Claggart that Billy is inciting the *Bellipotent* to mutiny.

The accusation is brought to Captain Vere, who summons Billy to a confrontation with Claggart in his quarters. In the cabin, the captain instructs Claggart to "tell this man to his face what you told of him to me." Billy stood like one "impaled and gagged" while the captain calls out, "Speak, man! Speak! Defend yourself!" The terrible speech impediment overcomes him, and "the next instant, quick as the flame from a discharged cannon at night, his right arm shot out, and Claggart dropped to the deck." Struck down by the Angel of God!

Captain Vere, sometimes called Starry Vere, is a rare being but not one of extreme definition, like Billy and Claggart. At the cabin hearing, Billy proclaims his lack of intention to kill Claggart, and some of the officers speak for a mitigation of the penalty, but Captain Vere will insist that intent is not to the issue. With his admirable qualities as a gentleman, Captain Vere was also known to be somewhat pedantic. He believes Billy's account of his state of mind; he is half in love with the Angel of God himself, and it is clear in the end that the death by hanging, ordained by marine law, will bring a greater grief to him than to the officers pointing to some mitigation, although, as officers, not insisting with vehemence.

At the moment of execution, Billy will call out the justly famous, resounding "God bless Captain Vere!" He expires in a sacramental mist:

At the moment it chanced that the vapoury fleece hanging low in the East, was shot through with a soft glory as of the fleece of the Lamb of God seen in a mystical vision; and simultaneously therewith, watched by the wedged mass of upturned faces, Billy ascending, took the full rose of the dawn.

And Captain Vere will die from the wounds inflicted by a musket ball, die with the words "Billy Budd, Billy Budd" on his lips.

Garden of Eden before the Fall, sunlit, happy-go-lucky, blissful ignorance; there lies the brute human temptation to bewilder confidence, to test, like Claggart, the defensive powers of the beguiling, androgynous athlete. And there in the end is Melville voicing the name of the Angel of God in his last creative work before dying. The reader, too, ascends, like Billy, into the vapory fleece of language to honor this beautiful vision.

Certainly the End of *Something* or Other, One Would Sort of Have to Think (Re John Updike's *Toward the End of Time*)

DAVID FOSTER WALLACE

> *Of nothing but me... I sing, lacking another song.*
> —J. Updike, *Midpoint*, Canto I, 1969

Mailer, Updike, Roth—the Great Male Narcissists[1] who've dominated postwar American fiction are now in their senescence, and it must seem to them no coincidence that the prospect of their own deaths appears backlit by the approaching millennium and online predictions of the death of the novel as we know it. When a solipsist dies, after all, everything goes with him. And no U.S. novelist has mapped the inner terrain of the solipsist better than John Updike, whose rise in the 1960s and '70s established him as both chronicler and voice of probably the single most self-absorbed generation since Louis XIV. As were Freud's, Updike's big preoccupations have always been with death and sex (not necessarily in that order), and the fact that his books' mood has gotten more wintry in recent years is understandable—Updike has always written mainly about himself, and since the surprisingly moving *Rabbit at Rest* he's been exploring, more and more overtly, the apocalyptic prospect of his own death.

---

1 Hereafter, GMNs.

Toward the End of Time concerns an extremely erudite, successful, narcissistic, and sex-obsessed retired guy who's keeping a one-year journal in which he explores the apocalyptic prospect of his own death. *Toward the End of Time* is also, of the let's say two dozen Updike books I've read, far and away the worst, a novel so clunky and self-indulgent that it's hard to believe the author let it be published in this kind of shape.

I'm afraid the preceding sentence is this review's upshot, and most of the remainder here will consist simply of presenting evidence/justification for such a disrespectful assessment. First, though, if I may poke the critical head into the frame for just one moment, I'd like to offer assurances that your reviewer is not one of these spleen-venting spittle-spattering Updike haters one often encounters among literary readers under forty. The fact is that I am probably classifiable as one of the very few actual subforty Updike *fans*. Not as rabid a fan as, say, Nicholson Baker, but I do believe that *The Poorhouse Fair*, *Of the Farm*, and *The Centaur* are all great books, maybe classics. And even since '81's *Rabbit Is Rich*—as his characters seemed to become more and more repellent, and without any corresponding sign that the author understood that they were repellent—I've continued to read Updike's novels and to admire the sheer gorgeousness of his descriptive prose.

Most of the literary readers I know personally are under forty, and a fair number are female, and none of them are big admirers of the postwar GMNs. But it's John Updike in particular that a lot of them seem to hate. And not merely his books, for some reason—mention the poor man *himself* and you have to jump back:

"Just a penis with a thesaurus."

"Has the son of a bitch ever had one unpublished thought?"

"Makes misogyny seem literary the same way Rush makes fascism seem funny."

And trust me: these are actual quotations, and I've heard even worse ones, and they're all usually accompanied by the sort of facial expression where you can tell there's not going to be any profit in appealing to the intentional fallacy or talking about the sheer aesthetic pleasure of Updike's prose. None of the other famous phallocrats of Updike's generation—not Mailer, not Exley or Roth or even Bukowski—excites such violent dislike.

There are, of course, some obvious explanations for part of this dis-like—jealousy, iconoclasm, PC backlash, and the fact that many of our parents revere Updike and it's easy to revile what your parents revere. But I think the deep reason so many of my generation dislike Updike and the other GMNs has to do with these writers' radical self-absorption, and with their uncritical celebration of this self-absorption both in themselves and in their characters.

John Updike, for example, has for decades been constructing pro-tagonists who are basically all the same guy (see for instance Rabbit Angstrom, Dick Maple, Piet Hanema, Henry Bech, Rev. Tom Marshfield, *Roger's Version*'s "Uncle Nunc") and who are all clearly stand-ins for Updike himself. They always live in either Pennsylvania or New England, are either unhappily married or divorced, are roughly Updike's age. Always either the narrator or the point-of-view charac-ter, they tend all to have the author's astounding perceptual gifts; they think and speak in the same effortlessly lush, synesthetic way that Updike does. They are also always incorrigibly narcissistic, philander-ing, self-contemptuous, self-pitying . . . and deeply alone, alone the way only an emotional solipsist can be alone. They never seem to belong to any sort of larger unit or community or cause. Though usually family men, they never really love anybody—and, though always heterosexual to the point of satyriasis, they especially don't love women.[2] The very world around them, as gorgeously as they see and describe it, tends to exist for them only insofar as it evokes impressions and associations and emotions and desires inside the great self.

I'm guessing that for the young educated adults of the sixties and seventies, for whom the ultimate horror was the hypocritical confor-mity and repression of their own parents' generation, Updike's evection of the libidinous self appeared refreshing and even heroic. But young adults of the nineties—many of whom are, of course, the children of all the impassioned infidelities and divorces Updike wrote about so

---

2 Unless, of course, you consider delivering long encomiums to a woman's "sacred several-lipped gateway" or saying things like "It is true, the sight of her plump lips obediently distended around my swollen member, her eyelids lowered demurely, afflicts me with a religious peace" to be the same as loving her.

beautifully, and who got to watch all this brave new individualism and sexual freedom deteriorate into the joyless and anomic self-indulgence of the Me Generation—today's subforties have very different horrors, prominent among which are anomie and solipsism and a peculiarly American loneliness: the prospect of dying without even once having loved something more than yourself. Ben Turnbull, the narrator of Updike's latest novel, is sixty-six years old and heading for just such a death, and he's shitlessly scared. Like so many of Updike's protagonists, though, Turnbull seems scared of all the wrong things.

Toward the End of Time is being marketed by its publisher as an ambitious departure for Updike, his foray into the futuristic-dystopic tradition of Huxley and Ballard and soft sci-fi. The year is AD 2020, and time has as they say not been kind. A Sino-American nuclear war has killed millions and ended centralized government as we know it. The dollar's gone; Massachusetts now uses scrip named for Bill Weld. There are no more taxes; local toughs now charge fees to protect the well-to-do from other local toughs. AIDS has been cured, the Midwest is depopulated, and parts of Boston are bombed out and (presumably?) irradiated. An abandoned low-orbit space station hangs in the night sky like a junior moon. There are tiny but rapacious "metallobioforms" that have somehow mutated from toxic waste and go around eating electricity and the occasional human. Mexico has reappropriated the U.S. Southwest and is threatening wholesale invasion even as thousands of young Americans are sneaking south across the Rio Grande in search of a better life. America, in short, is getting ready to die.

The novel's futuristic elements are sometimes cool, and verily they would represent an ambitious departure for Updike if they weren't all so sketchy and tangential, mostly tossed off as subordinate clauses in the narrator's endless descriptions of every tree, plant, flower, and shrub around his home. What 95 percent of *Toward the End of Time* actually consists in is Ben Turnbull describing the prenominate flora (over and over again as each season passes) and his brittle, castrating wife Gloria, and remembering the ex-wife who divorced him for adultery, and rhapsodizing about a young prostitute he moves into the house when Gloria's away on a trip. It's also got a lot of pages of Turnbull brooding about senescence, mortality, and the tragedy of the human condition,

and even more pages of Turnbull talking about sex and the imperi-
ousness of the sexual urge, and detailing how he lusts after assorted
prostitutes and secretaries and neighbors and bridge partners and
daughters-in-law and a girl who's part of the group of young toughs he
pays for protection, a thirteen-year-old whose breasts—"shallow taut
cones tipped with honeysuckle-berry nipples"—Turnbull finally gets
to fondle in the woods behind his house when his wife's not looking.

In case that summary sounds too harsh, here is some hard statistical
evidence of just how much a "departure" from Updike's regular MO
this novel really is:

Total # of pages about Sino-American war—causes, duration,
casualties: 0.75
Total # of pages about deadly mutant metallobioforms: 1.5
Total # of pages about flora around Turnbull's New England
home, plus fauna, weather, and how his ocean view looks in
different seasons: 86
Total # of pages about Mexican repossession of U.S. Southwest: 0.1
Total # of pages about Ben Turnbull's penis and his various
thoughts and feelings about it: 10.5
Total # of pages about what life's like in Boston proper without
municipal services or police, plus whether the war's nuclear
exchanges have caused fallout or radiation sickness: 0.0
Total # of pages about prostitute's body, w/particular attention
to sexual loci: 8.5
Total # of pages about golf: 15
Total # of pages of Ben Turnbull saying things like "I want
women to be dirty" and "She was a choice cut of meat and I
hoped she held out for a fair price" and the quoted stuff at the
bottom of [p. 217] and "The sexual parts are fiends, sacrificing
everything to that aching point of contact" and "ferocious
female nagging is the price men pay for our much-lamented
prerogatives, the power and the mobility and the penis": 36.5

Toward the End of Time's best parts are a half-dozen little set pieces
where Turnbull imagines himself inhabiting different historical

figures—a tomb robber in ancient Egypt, Saint Mark, a guard at a Nazi death camp, etc. They're gems, and the reader wishes there were more of them. The problem is that they don't have much of a function other than to remind us that Updike can write really great little imaginative set pieces when he's in the mood. Their plot justification stems from the fact that the narrator is a science fan (the novel has minilectures on astrophysics and quantum mechanics, nicely written but evincing a roughly *Newsweek*-level comprehension). Turnbull is particularly keen on subatomic physics and something he calls the "Theory of Many Worlds"—a real theory, by the way, which was proposed in the fifties as a solution to certain quantum paradoxes entailed by the Principles of Indeterminacy and Complementarity, and which in truth is wildly complex and technical, but which Turnbull seems to believe is basically the same as the Theory of Past-Life Channeling, thereby explaining the set pieces where Turnbull is somebody else. The whole quantum setup ends up being embarrassing in the special way something pretentious is embarrassing when it's also wrong.

Better, and more convincingly futuristic, are the narrator's soliloquies on the blue-to-red shift and the eventual implosion of the known universe near the book's end; and these would be among the novel's highlights, too, if it weren't for the fact that Ben Turnbull is interested in cosmic apocalypse all and only because it serves as a grand metaphor for his own personal death. Likewise all the Housmanesque descriptions of the Beautiful But Achingly Transient flowers in his yard, and the optometrically significant year 2020, and the book's final, heavy description of "small pale moths [that] have mistakenly hatched" on a late-autumn day and "flip and flutter a foot or two above the asphalt as if trapped in a narrow wedge of space-time beneath the obliterating imminence of winter."

The clunky bathos of this novel seems to have infected even the line-by-line prose, Updike's great strength for almost forty years. *Toward the End of Time* does have flashes of beautiful writing—deer described as "tender-faced ruminants," leaves as "chewed to lace by Japanese beetles," a car's tight turn as a "slur" and its departure as a "dismissive acceleration down the driveway." But a horrific percentage of the book consists of stuff like "Why indeed do women weep? They weep, it seemed to my wandering mind, for the world itself, in its beauty and waste, its min- gled cruelty and tenderness" and "How much of summer is over before it begins! Its beginning marks its end, as our birth entails our death" and "This development seems remote, however, among the many more urgent issues of survival on our blasted, depopulated planet." Not to mention whole reams of sentences with so many modifiers—"The insou- ciance and innocence of our independence twinkled like a kind of sweat from their bare and freckled or honey-colored or mahogany limbs"— and so much subordination—"As our species, having given itself a hard hit, staggers, the others, all but counted out, move in"—and such heavy alliteration—"the broad sea blares a blue I would not have believed obtainable without a tinted filter"—that they seem less like John Updike than like somebody doing a mean parody of John Updike.

Besides distracting us with worries about whether Updike might be injured or ill, the turgidity of the prose here also ups our dislike of the novel's narrator. (It's hard to like somebody whose way of saying that his wife doesn't like going to bed before him is "She hated it when I crept into bed and disturbed in her the fragile chain of steps whereby consciousness dissolves" or who refers to his grandchildren as "this evidence that my pending oblivion had been hedged, my seed had taken root.") And this dislike pretty much torpedoes *Toward the End of Time*, a novel whose tragic climax is a prostate operation that leaves Turnbull impotent and extremely bummed. It is made clear that the author expects us to sympa- thize with or even share Turnbull's grief at "the pathetic shrunken wreck the procedures [have] made of my beloved genitals." These demands on our compassion echo the major crisis of the book's first half, described in a flashback, where we are supposed to empathize not only with the rather textbookish existential dread that hits Turnbull at thirty as he's in his basement building a dollhouse for his daughter—"I would die, but also the little girl I was making this for would die. . . . There was no God, each detail of the rusting, moldering cellar made clear, just Nature, which would consume my life as carelessly and relentlessly as it would a dung-beetle corpse in a compost pile"—but also with Turnbull's relief at discovering a remedy for this dread—"an affair, my first. Its colorful weave of carnal revelation and intoxicating risk and craven guilt eclipsed the devouring gray sensation of time."

Maybe the one thing that the reader ends up appreciating about Ben Turnbull is that he's such a broad caricature of an Updike protagonist that he helps clarify what's been so unpleasant and frustrating about this author's recent characters. It's not that Turnbull is stupid: he can quote Pascal and Kierkegaard on angst, discourse on the death of Schubert, distinguish between a sinistrorse and a dextrorse *Polygonum* vine, etc. It's that he persists in the bizarre, adolescent belief that getting to have sex with whomever one wants whenever one wants to is a cure for human despair. And *Toward the End of Time*'s author, so far as I can figure out, believes it too. Updike makes it plain that he views the narrator's final impotence as catastrophic, as the ultimate symbol of death itself, and he clearly wants us to mourn it as much as Turnbull does. I am not shocked or offended by this attitude; I mostly just don't get it. Rampant or flaccid, Ben Turnbull's unhappiness is obvious right from the novel's first page. It never once occurs to him, though, that the reason he's so unhappy is that he's an asshole.

Lincoln the Writer

JACQUES BARZUN

A great man of the past is hard to know, because his legend, which is a sort of friendly caricature, hides him like a disguise. He is one thing to the man in the street and another to those who study him closely—and who seldom agree. And when a man is so great that not one but half a dozen legends are familiar to all who recognize his name, he becomes once more a mystery, almost as if he were an unknown.

This is the situation that Lincoln occupies in the United States on the 150th anniversary of his birth. Everybody knows who he was and what he did. But what was he like? For most people, Lincoln remains the rail splitter, the shrewd country lawyer, the cracker-barrel philosopher and humorist, the statesman who saved the Union, and the compassionate leader who saved many a soldier from death by court-martial, only to meet his own end as a martyr.

Not being a Lincoln scholar, I have no wish to deal with any of these images of Lincoln. I want only to help celebrate his sesquicentennial year by bringing out a Lincoln who I am sure is real though unseen. The Lincoln I know and revere is a historical figure who should stand— I will not say, instead of, but by the side of all the others. No one need forget the golden legends, yet anyone may find it rewarding to move them aside a little so as to get a glimpse of the unsuspected Lincoln I have so vividly in mind.

I refer to Lincoln the artist, the maker of a style that is unique in English prose and doubly astonishing in the history of American literature, for nothing led up to it. The Lincoln who speaks to me through the written word is a figure no longer to be described wholly or mainly by the old adjectives, shrewd, humorous, or saintly, but rather as one combining the traits that biography reports in certain artists among the greatest— passionate, gloomy, seeming-cold, and conscious of superiority.

These elements in Lincoln's makeup have been noticed before, but they take on a new meaning in the light of the new motive I detect in his prose. For his style, the plain, undecorated language in which he addresses posterity, is no mere knack with words. It is the manifestation of a mode of thought, of an outlook which colors every act of the writer's and tells us how he rated life. Only let his choice of words, the rhythm and shape of his utterances, linger in the ear, and you begin to feel as he did—hence to discern unplumbed depths in the quiet intent of a conscious artist.

But before taking this path of discovery, it is necessary to dispose of a few too familiar ideas. The first is that we already know all there is to know about Lincoln's prose. Does not every schoolchild learn that the Gettysburg Address is beautiful, hearing this said so often that he ends by believing it? The belief is general, of course, but come by in this way, it is not worth much. One proof of its little meaning is that most Americans also believe that for fifty years Lincoln's connection with the literary art was to tell racy stories. Then, suddenly, on a train journey to Gettysburg he wrote a masterpiece. This is not the way great artists go to work—so obviously not, that to speak of Lincoln as an *artist* will probably strike some readers as a paradox or a joke. Even so, the puzzle remains: How did this strange man from Illinois produce, not a few happy phrases, but an unmistakable style?

On this point the books by experts do no better than the public. The latest collective attempt to write a literary history of the United States does indeed speak of Lincoln's styles, in the plural: but this reference is really to Lincoln's various tones, ranging from the familiar to the elevated. Like all other books that I have searched through, this authoritative work always talks of the subject or the occasion of Lincoln's words when attempting to explain the power of his best-known pieces. It is as if a painter's genius were explained by the landscapes he depicted.

Lincoln has indeed had praise as a writer, but nearly all of it has been conventional and absentminded. The few authors of serious studies have fallen into sentimentality and incoherence. Thus, in the Hay and Nicolay edition of Lincoln's works, a famous editor of the nineties writes: "Of style, in the ordinary use of the word, Lincoln may be said to have had little. There was nothing ambitiously elaborate or self-consciously simple in Lincoln's way of writing. He had not the scholar's range of words. He was not always grammatically accurate. He would doubtless have been very much surprised if anyone had told him that he 'had' a style at all."

Here one feels like asking: Then why discuss "Lincoln as a writer"? The answer is unconvincing: "And yet, because he was determined to be understood, because he was honest, because he had a warm and true heart, because he read good books eagerly and not coldly, and because there was in him a native good taste, as well as a strain of imagination, he achieved a singularly clear and forcible style, which took color from his own noble character and became a thing individual and distinguished. . . ."

So the man who had no style had a style—clear, forcible, individual and distinguished. This is as odd a piece of reasoning as that offered by the late Senator Beveridge: "The cold fact is that not one faint glimmer appears in his whole life, at least before his Cooper Union speech, which so much as suggests the radiance of the last two years." Perhaps a senator is never a good judge of what a president writes: this one asks us to believe in a miracle. One would think the "serious" critics had simply failed to read their author.

Yet they must have read him, to be so obviously bothered. "How did he do it?" they wonder. They think of the momentous issues of the Civil War, of the grueling four years in Washington, of the man beset by politicians who were too aggressive and by generals who were not enough so, and the solution flashes upon them: "It was the strain that turned homespun into great literature." This is again to confuse a literary occasion with the literary power which rises to it. The famous documents—the two inaugurals, the Gettysburg Address, the letter to Mrs. Bixby—marvelous as they are, do not solve the riddle. On the contrary, the subjects have such a grip on our emotions that we begin to think almost anybody could have moved us. For all these reasons—inadequate criticism, overfamiliarity with a few masterpieces, ignorance of Lincoln's early work and the consequent suppression of one whole side of his character—we must go back to the source and begin at the beginning.

Pick up any early volume of Lincoln's works and start reading as if you were approaching a new author. Pretend you know none of the anecdotes, nothing of the way the story embedded in these pages comes out. Your aim is to see a life unfold and to descry the character of the man from his own words, written, most of them, not to be published, but to be felt.

Here is Lincoln at twenty-three telling the people of his district by means of a handbill that they should send him to the state legislature: "Upon the subjects of which I have treated, I have spoken as I thought. I may be wrong in regard to any or all of them; but holding it a sound maxim that it is better to be only sometimes right than at all times wrong, so soon as I discover my opinions to be erroneous, I shall be ready to renounce them." And he closes his appeal for votes on an unpolitical note suggestive of melancholy thoughts: "But if the good people in their wisdom shall see fit to keep me in the background, I have been too familiar with disappointments to be very much chagrined."

One does not need to be a literary man to see that Lincoln was a born writer, nor a psychologist to guess that here is a youth of uncommon mold—strangely self-assertive, yet detached, and also laboring under a sense of misfortune.

For his handbill Lincoln may have had to seek help with his spelling, which was always uncertain, but the rhythm of those sentences was never taught by a grammar book. Lincoln, as he himself said, went to school "by littles," which did not in the aggregate amount to a year. Everybody remembers the story of his reading the Bible in the light of the fire and scribbling with charcoal on the back of the shovel. But millions have read the Bible and not become even passable writers. The neglected truth is that not one but several persons who remembered his childhood remarked on the boy's singular determination to express his thoughts in the best way.

His stepmother gave an account of the boy which prefigures the literary artist much more than the rail splitter: "He didn't like physical labor.

He read all the books he could lay his hands on. . . . When he came across
a passage that struck him, he would write it down on boards if he had
no paper and keep it there till he did get paper, then he would rewrite it,
look at it, repeat it." Later, Lincoln's law partner, William H. Herndon,
recorded the persistence of this obsessive habit with words: "He used to
bore me terribly by his methods. . . . Mr. Lincoln would doubly explain
things to me that needed no explanation. . . . Mr. Lincoln was a very
patient man generally, but . . . just go at Lincoln with abstractions, glittering generalities, indefiniteness, mistiness of idea or expression. Here
he flew up and became vexed, and sometimes foolishly so."

In youth, Lincoln had tried to be a poet, but found he lacked the
gift. What he could do was think with complete clarity in words and
imagine the workings of others' minds at the same time. One does not
read far in his works before discovering that as a writer he toiled above
all to find the true order for his thoughts—order first, and then a light-
ninglike brevity. Here is how he writes in 1846, a young politician far
from the limelight, and of whom no one expected a lapidary style: "If
I falsify in this you can convict me. The witnesses live, and can tell."
There is a fire in this, and a control of it, which shows the master.

That control of words implied a corresponding control of the emotions. Herndon described several times in his lectures and papers the
eccentric temperament of his lifelong partner. This portrait the kindly
sentimental people have not been willing to accept. But Herndon's
sense of greatness was finer than that of the admirers from afar, who
worship rather storybook heroes than the mysterious, difficult, unsatisfactory sort of great man—the only sort that history provides.

What did Herndon say? He said that Lincoln was a man of sudden
and violent moods, often plunged in deathly melancholy for hours, then
suddenly lively and ready to joke; that Lincoln was self-centered and
cold, not given to revealing his plans or opinions, and ruthless in using
others' help and influence; that Lincoln was idle for long stretches of
time, during which he read newspapers or simply brooded; that Lincoln
had a disconcerting power to see into questions, events, and persons,
never deceived by their incidental features or conventional garb, but
extracting the central matter as one cores an apple; that Lincoln was
a man of strong passions and mystical longings, which he repressed

because his mind showed him their futility, and that this made him cold-blooded and a fatalist.

In addition, as we know from other sources, Lincoln was subject to vague fears and dark superstitions. Strange episodes, though few, marked his relations with women, including his wife-to-be, Mary Todd. He was subject, as some of his verses show, to obsessional gloom about separation, insanity, and death. We should bear in mind that Lincoln was orphaned, reared by a stepmother, and early cast adrift to make his own way. His strangely detached attitude toward himself, his premonitions and depressions, his morbid regard for truth and abnormal suppression of aggressive impulses, suggest that he hugged a secret wound which ultimately made out of an apparent common man the unique figure of an artist-saint.

Lincoln moreover believed that his mother was the illegitimate daughter of a Virginia planter, and like others who have known or fancied themselves of irregular descent, he had a powerful, unreasoned faith in his own destiny—a destiny he felt would combine greatness and disaster.

Whatever psychiatry might say to this, criticism recognizes the traits of a type of artist one might call "the dark outcast." Michelangelo and Byron come to mind as examples. In such men the sense of isolation from others is in the emotions alone. The mind remains a clear and fine instrument of common sense—Michelangelo built buildings, and Byron brilliantly organized the Greeks in their revolt against Turkey. In Lincoln there is no incompatibility between the lawyer-statesman, whom we all know, and the artist, whose physiognomy I have been trying to sketch.

Lincoln's detachment was what produced his mastery over men. Had he not, as president, towered in mind and will over his cabinet, they would have crushed or used him without remorse. Chase, Seward, Stanton, the Blairs, McClellan had among them enough egotism and ability to wreck several administrations. Each thought Lincoln would be an easy victim. It was not until he was removed from their midst that any of them conceived of him as an apparition greater than themselves. During his life their dominant feeling was exasperation with him for making them feel baffled. They could not bring him down to their reach. John Hay, who saw the long struggle, confirms Herndon's judgments: "It is absurd to call him a modest man. No great man was ever modest. It was his intellectual arrogance and unconscious assumption of superiority that men like Chase and Sumner could never forgive."

This is a different Lincoln from the clumsy country lawyer who makes no great pretensions, but has a trick or two up his sleeve and wins the day for righteousness because his heart is pure. Lincoln's purity was that of a supremely conscious genius, not of an innocent. And if we ask what kind of genius enables a man to master a new and sophisticated scene as Lincoln did, without the aid of what are called personal advantages, with little experience in affairs of state and no established following, the answer is: military genius or its close kin, artistic genius.

The artist contrives means and marshals forces that the beholder takes for granted and that the bungler never discovers for himself. The artist is always scheming to conquer his material and his audience. When we speak of his craft, we mean quite literally that he is crafty.

Lincoln acquired his power over words in the only two ways known to man—by reading and by writing. His reading was small in range and much of a kind: the Bible, Bunyan, Byron, Burns, Defoe, Shakespeare, and a then-current edition of Aesop's Fables. These are books from which a genius would extract the lesson of terseness and strength. The Bible and Shakespeare's poetry would be less influential than Shakespeare's prose, whose rapid twists and turns Lincoln often rivals, though without imagery. The four other British writers are all devotees of the telling phrase, rather than the suggestive. As for Aesop, the similarity of his stories with the anecdotes Lincoln liked to tell—always in the same words—is obvious. But another parallel occurs, that between the shortness of a fable and the mania Lincoln had for condensing any matter into the fewest words:

"John Fitzgerald, eighteen years of age, able-bodied, but without pecuniary means, came directly from Ireland to Springfield, Illinois, and there stopped, and sought employment, with no present intention of returning to Ireland or going elsewhere. After remaining in the city some three weeks, part of the time employed, and part not, he fell sick, and became a public charge. It has been submitted to me, whether the City of Springfield, or the County of Sangamon is, by law, to bear the charge."

As Lincoln himself wrote on another occasion, "This is not a long letter, but it contains the whole story." And the paragraph would prove, if it were necessary, that style is independent of attractive subject matter. The pleasure it gives is that of lucidity and motion, the motion of Lincoln's mind.

In his own day, Lincoln's prose was found flat, dull, lacking in taste. It differed radically in form and tone from the accepted models—Webster's or Channing's for speeches, Bryant's or Greeley's for journalism. Once or twice, Lincoln did imitate their genteel circumlocutions or resonant abstractions. But these were exercises he never repeated. His style, well in hand by his thirtieth year and richly developed by his fiftieth, has the eloquence which comes of the contrast between transparency of medium and density of thought. Consider this episode from a lyceum lecture written when Lincoln was twenty-nine:

"Turn, then, to that horror-striking scene at St. Louis. A single victim was only sacrificed there. His story is very short; and is, perhaps, the most highly tragic of anything of its length that has ever been witnessed in real life. A mulatto man by the name of McIntosh was seized in the street, dragged to the suburbs of the city, chained to a tree, and actually burned to death; and all within a single hour from the time he had been a freeman, attending to his own business, and at peace with the world."

Notice the contrasting rhythm of the two sentences: "A single victim was only sacrificed there. His story is very short." The sentences are very short, too, but let anyone try imitating their continuous flow or subdued emotion on the characteristic Lincolnian theme of the swift passage from the business of life to death.

Lincoln's prose works fall into three categories: speeches, letters, and proclamations. The speeches range from legal briefs and arguments to political debates. The proclamations begin with his first offer of his services as a public servant and end with his presidential statements of policy or calls to Thanksgiving between 1861 and 1865. The letters naturally cover his life span and a great diversity of subjects. They are, I surmise, the crucible in which Lincoln cast his style. By the time he was in the White House, he could frame, impromptu, hundreds of messages such as this telegram to General McClellan: "I have just read your despatch about sore-tongued and fatigued horses. Will you pardon me for asking what the horses of your army have done since the battle of Antietam that fatigues anything?"

Something of Lincoln's tone obviously comes from the practice of legal thought. It would be surprising if the effort of mind that Lincoln put into his profession had not come out again in his prose. After all, he made his name and rose to the presidency over a question of constitutional law. Legal thought encourages precision through the imagining and the denial of alternatives. The language of the law foresees doubt, ambiguity, confusion, stupid or fraudulent error, and one by one it excludes them. Most lawyers succeed at least in avoiding misunderstanding, and this obviously is the foundation of any prose that aims at clear expression.

As a lawyer Lincoln knew that the courtroom vocabulary would achieve this purpose if handled with a little care. But it would remain jargon, obscure to the common understanding. As an artist, therefore, he undertook to frame his ideas invariably in one idiom, that of daily life. He had to use, of course, the technical names of the actions and documents he dealt with. But all the rest was in the vernacular. His first achievement, then, was to translate the minute accuracy of the advocate and the judge into the words of common men.

To say this is to suggest a measure of Lincoln's struggle as an artist. He started with very little confidence in his stock of knowledge, and having to face audiences far more demanding than ours, he toiled to improve his vocabulary, grammar, and logic. In the first year of his term in Congress he labored through six books of Euclid in hopes of developing the coherence of thought he felt he needed in order to demonstrate his views. Demonstration was to him the one proper goal of argument; he never seems to have considered it within his power to convince by disturbing the judgment through the emotions. In the few passages where he resorts to platform tricks, he uses only irony or satire, never the rain-barrel booming of the Fourth-of-July orator.

One superior gift he possessed from the start and developed to a supreme degree, the gift of rhythm. Take this fragment, not from a finished speech, but from a jotting for a lecture on the law:

"There is a vague popular belief that lawyers are necessarily dishonest. I say vague, because when we consider to what extent confidence and honors are reposed in and conferred upon lawyers by the people, it appears improbable that their impression of dishonesty is very distinct and vivid. Yet the impression is common, almost universal. Let no young man choosing the law for a calling for a moment yield to the popular belief—resolve to be honest at all events; and if in your own judgment you cannot be an honest lawyer, resolve to be honest without being a lawyer."

Observe the ease with which the theme is announced: "There is a vague popular belief that lawyers are necessarily dishonest." It is short without crackling like an epigram, the word "necessarily" retarding the rhythm just enough. The thought is picked up with hardly a pause: "I say vague, because, when we consider . . ." and so on through the unfolding of reasons, which winds up in a kind of calm: "it appears improbable that their impression of dishonesty is very distinct and vivid." Now a change of pace to refresh interest: "Yet the impression is common, almost universal." And a second change, almost immediately, to usher in the second long sentence, which carries the conclusion: "Let no young man choosing the law . . ."

The paragraph moves without a false step, neither hurried nor drowsy; and by its movement, like one who leads another in the dance, it catches up our thought and swings it into willing compliance. The ear notes at the same time that none of the sounds grate or clash: the piece is sayable like a speech in a great play; the music is manly, the alliterations are few and natural. Indeed, the paragraph seems to have come into being spontaneously as the readiest incarnation of Lincoln's thoughts.

From hints here and there, one gathers that Lincoln wrote slowly—meaning, by writing, the physical act of forming letters on paper. This would augment the desirability of being brief. Lincoln wrote before the typewriter and the dictating machine, and wanting to put all his meaning into one or two lucid sentences, he thought before he wrote. The great compression came after he had, lawyerlike, excluded alternatives and hit upon right order and emphasis.

Obviously this style would make use of skips and connections unsuited to speechmaking. The member of the cabinet who received a terse memorandum had it before him to make out at leisure. But an audience requires a looser texture, just as it requires a more measured delivery. This difference between the written and the spoken word lends color to the cliché that if Lincoln had a style, he developed it in his presidential years. Actually, Lincoln, like an artist, adapted his means to the occasion. There was no pathos in him before pathos was due. When he supposed his audience intellectually alert—as was the famous gathering at Cooper Union in 1860—he gave them his concentrated prose. We may take as a sample a part of the passage where he addresses the South:

"Again, you say we have made the slavery question more prominent than it formerly was. We deny it. We admit that it is more prominent, but we deny that we made it so. It was not we, but you, who discarded the old policy of the fathers. We resisted, and still resist, your innovation; and thence comes the greater prominence of the question. Would you have that question reduced to its former proportions? Go back to that old policy. What has been, will be again, under the same conditions. If you would have the peace of the old times, readopt the precepts and policy of the old times."

This is wonderfully clear and precise and demonstrative, but two hours of equally succinct argument would tax any but the most athletic audience. Lincoln gambled on the New Yorkers' agility of mind, and won. But we should not be surprised that in the debates with Stephen A. Douglas, a year and a half before, we find the manner different. Those wrangles lasted three hours, and the necessity for each speaker to interweave prepared statements of policy with improvised rebuttals of charges and "points" gives these productions a coarser grain. Yet on Lincoln's side, the same artist mind is plainly at work:

"Senator Douglas is of world-wide renown. All the anxious politicians of his party, or who have been of his party for years past, have been looking upon him as certainly, at no distant day, to be the President of the United States. They have seen in his round, jolly, fruitful face, post offices, land offices, marshalships, and cabinet appointments, chargéships and foreign missions, bursting and sprouting out in wonderful exuberance ready to be laid hold of by their greedy hands."

The man who could lay the ground for a splendid yet catchy metaphor about political plums by describing Douglas's face as round, jolly and *fruitful* is not a man to be thought merely lucky in the handling of words.

The debates abound in happy turns, but read less well than Lincoln's more compact productions. Often, Douglas's words are more polished:

"We have existed and prospered from that day to this thus divided and have increased with a rapidity never before equaled in wealth, the extension of territory, and all the elements of power and greatness, until we have become the first nation on the face of the globe. Why can we not thus continue to prosper?"

It is a mistake to underrate Douglas's skill, which was that of a professional. Lincoln's genius needs no heightening through lowering others. Douglas was smooth and adroit, and his arguments were effective, since Lincoln was defeated. But Douglas—not so Lincoln—sounds like anybody else.

Lincoln's extraordinary power was to make his spirit felt, a power I attribute to his peculiar relation to himself. He regarded his face and physique with amusement and dismay, his mind and destiny with wonder. Seeming clumsy and diffident, he also showed a calm superiority which he expressed as if one half of a double man were talking about the other.

In conduct, this detachment was the source of his saintlike forebearance; in his art, it yielded the rare quality of elegance. Nowhere is this link between style and emotional distance clearer than in the farewell Lincoln spoke to his friends in Springfield before leaving for Washington. A single magical word, easy to pass over carelessly, holds the clue:

"My friends: No one, not in my situation, can appreciate my feeling of sadness at this parting. To this place, and the kindness of these people, I owe everything. . . ." If we stop to think, we ask: "This place"?—yes. But why "*these* people"? Why not "you people," whom he was addressing from the train platform, or "this place and the kindness of *its* people"? It is not, certainly, the mere parallel of *this* and *these* that commanded the choice. "These" is a stroke of genius, which betrays Lincoln's isolation from the action itself—Lincoln talking to himself about the place and the people whom he was leaving, foreboding the possibility of his never returning, and closing the fifteen lines with one of the greatest cadences in English speech: "To His care commending you, as I hope in your prayers you will commend me, I bid you an affectionate farewell."

The four main qualities of Lincoln's literary art—precision, vernacular ease, rhythmical virtuosity, and elegance—may at a century's remove seem alien to our tastes. Yet it seems no less odd to question their use and interest to the present when one considers one continuing strain in our literature. Lincoln's example, plainly, helped to break the monopoly of the dealers in literary plush. After Lincoln comes Mark Twain, and out of Mark Twain come contemporaries of ours as diverse as Sherwood Anderson, H. L. Mencken, and Ernest Hemingway. Lincoln's use of his style for the intimate genre and for the sublime was his alone; but his workaday style is the American style par excellence.

Grace Paley

VIVIAN GORNICK

I remember the first time I laid eyes on a Paley sentence. The year was 1960, the place a Berkeley bookstore, and I a depressed graduate student, leafing restlessly. I picked up a book of stories by a writer I'd never heard of and read: "I was popular in certain circles, says Aunt Rose. I wasn't no thinner then, only more stationary in the flesh. In time to come, Lillie, don't be surprised—change is a fact of God. From this no one is excused. Only a person like your mama stands on one foot, she don't notice how big her behind is getting and sings in the canary's ear for thirty years." The next time I looked up it was dark outside, the store was closing, and I had completed four stories, among them the incomparable "An Interest in Life" and "The Pale Pink Roast." I saw that the restlessness in me had abated. I felt warm and solid. More than warm: safe. I was feeling safe. Glad to be alive again.

There have been three story collections in thirty-five years. They have made Paley internationally famous. All over the world, in languages you never heard of, she is read as a master storyteller in the great tradition: people love life more because of her writing. In her own country Paley is beloved as well, but it's complicated. Familiarity is a corrective. Limitations are noted as well as virtues. The euphoria is harder earned. For many American readers, the third collection is weaker by far than the first. Scope, vision, and delivery in a Paley story seem never to vary or to advance: the wisdom does not increase: the cheerful irony grows wearisome, begins to seem folksy. Oh Grace! the critically minded reader berates a page of Paley prose, as though it were a relative. You've done this *before*. And besides, this, what you have written here, is not a story at all, this is a mere fragment, a little song and dance you have performed times without number. Then suddenly, right there, in the middle of this same page refusing to get on with it, is a Paley sentence that arrests the eye and amazes the heart. The impatient reader quiets down, becomes calm, even wordless. She stares into the sentence. She feels its power. Everything Paley knows went into the making of that sentence. The way the sentence was made *is* what she knows: just as the right image is what the poet knows. The reader is reminded then of why—even though the stories don't "develop," and the collections don't get stronger—Paley goes on being read in languages you never heard of.

※

No matter how old Paley characters get they remain susceptible to the promise that someone or something is about to round the corner and make them feel again the crazy, wild, sexy excitement of life. Ordinary time in a Paley story passes like a dream, embracing the vividness of remembered feeling. Age, loss of appetite, growing children, economic despair, all mount up: the "normalcy" that surrounds the never-forgotten man, moment, Sunday morning when ah! one felt intensely.

Strictly speaking, women and men in Paley stories do not fall in love with each other, they fall in love with the desire to feel alive. They are, for each other, projections and provocations. Sooner or later, of course (mostly sooner), from such alliances human difficulty is bound to emerge, and when it does (more often than not), the sensation of love evaporates. The response to the evaporation is what interests Paley. She sees that people are made either melancholy by the loss of love, or agitated by it. When agitated they generally take a hike, when melancholy they seem to get paralyzed. Historically speaking, it is the man who becomes agitated and the woman who becomes melancholy. In short, although each is trapped in behavior neither can resist and both will regret, men fly the coop and women stand bolted to the kitchen floor.

This sense of things is Paley's wisdom. The instrumental nature of sexual relations is mother's milk to the Paley narrator. She knows it so well it puts her beyond sentiment or anger, sends her into a Zen trance. From that trance has come writer's gold: the single insight made penetrating in those extraordinary sentences. Sentences brimming with the consequence of desire once tasted, now lost, and endlessly paid for. Two examples will do.

Faith Darwin—of "Faith in the Afternoon"—is swimming in misery over the defection of her husband, Ricardo. When her mother tells her that Anita Franklin, a high-school classmate, has been left by *her* husband, Faith loses it:

> Anita Franklin, she said to herself. . . . How is it these days, now you are never getting laid anymore by clever Arthur Mazzano, the brilliant Sephardic Scholar and Lecturer? Now it is time that leans across you and not handsome, fair Arthur's mouth on yours, or his intelligent Boy Scouty conflagrating fingers.
>
> At this very moment, the thumb of Ricardo's hovering shadow jabbed her in her left eye, revealing for all the world the shallowness of her water table. Rice could have been planted at that instant on the terraces of her flesh and sprouted in strength and beauty in the floods that overwhelmed her from that moment on through all the afternoon. For herself and Anita Franklin, Faith bowed her head and wept.

Now, the obverse. In "Wants" the Paley narrator runs into her ex-husband and has an exchange with him that reminds her "he had had a habit throughout the twenty-seven years of making a narrow remark which, like a plumber's snake, could work its way through the ear down the throat, halfway to my heart. He would then disappear, leaving me choking with equipment."

These sentences are born of a concentration in the writer that runs so deep, is turned so far inward, it achieves the lucidity of the poet. The material is transformed in the sound of the sentence: the sound of the sentence *becomes* the material; the material is at one with the voice that is speaking. What Paley knows—that women and men remain longing, passive creatures most of their lives: always acted upon, rarely acting—is now inextricable from the way her sentences "talk" to us.

She is famous for coming down against the fiction of plot and character because "everyone, real or invented, deserves the open destiny of life," but her women and her men, so far from having an open destiny, seem hopelessly mired in their unknowing, middle-aged selves. It is the narrating Paley voice that is the open destiny. That voice is an unblinking stare; it is modern art; it fills the canvas. Its sentences are the equivalent of color in a Rothko painting. In Rothko, color *is* the painting; in Paley, voice *is* the story.

Like that of her friend Donald Barthelme, Grace Paley's voice has become an influential sound in contemporary American literature because it reminds us that although the story can no longer be told as it once was, it still needs to go on being told. The idiosyncratic intelligence hanging out in space is now the story: and indeed it is story enough. I felt safe in its presence in a Berkeley bookstore thirty years ago, it makes me feel safe today. As long as this voice is coming off the page I need not fear the loss of the narrative impulse. I need not, as Frank O'Hara says, regret life.

Theodore Dreiser

H. L. MENCKEN

Out of the desert of American fictioneering, so populous and yet
so dreary, Dreiser stands up—a phenomenon inescapably visible,
but disconcertingly hard to explain. What forces combined to produce
him in the first place, and how has he managed to hold out so long
against the prevailing blasts—of disheartening misunderstanding
and misrepresentation, of Puritan suspicion and opposition, of artistic isolation, of commercial seduction? There is something downright
heroic in the way the man has held his narrow and perilous ground,
disdaining all compromise, unmoved by the cheap success that lies so
inviting around the corner. He has faced, in his day, almost every form
of attack that a serious artist can conceivably encounter, and yet all of
them together have scarcely budged him an inch. He still plods along in
the laborious, cheerless way he first marked out for himself; he is quite
as undaunted by baited praise as by bludgeoning, malignant abuse; his
later novels are, if anything, more unyieldingly dreiserian than his earliest. As one who has long sought to entice him in this direction or that,
fatuously presuming to instruct him in what would improve and profit
him, I may well bear a reluctant and resigned sort of testimony to his
gigantic steadfastness. It is almost as if any change in his manner, any
concession to what is usual and esteemed, any amelioration of his blind,
relentless exercises of *force majeure,* were a physical impossibility. One
feels him at last to be authentically no more than a helpless instrument

(or victim) of that inchoate flow of forces which he himself is so fond of depicting as at once the answer to the riddle of life, and a riddle ten times more vexing and accursed.

And his origins, as I say, are quite as mysterious as his motive power. To fit him into the unrolling chart of American, or even of English fiction is extremely difficult. Save one thinks of H. B. Fuller (whose "With the Procession" and "The Cliff-Dwellers" are still remembered by Huneker, but by whom else?[1]), he seems to have had no fore-runner among us, and for all the discussion of him that goes on, he has few avowed disciples, and none of them gets within miles of him. One catches echoes of him, perhaps, in Willa Sibert Cather, in Mary S. Watts, in David Graham Phillips, in Sherwood Anderson and in Joseph Medill Patterson, but, after all, they are no more than echoes. In Robert Herrick the thing descends to a feeble parody; in imitators further removed to sheer burlesque. All the latter-day American novelists of consideration are vastly more facile than Dreiser in their philosophy, as they are in their style. In the fact, perhaps, lies the measure of their difference. What they lack, great and small, is the gesture of pity, the note of awe, the profound sense of wonder—in a phrase, that "soberness of mind" which William Lyon Phelps sees as the hallmark of Conrad and Hardy, and which even the most stupid cannot escape in Dreiser. The normal American novel, even in its most serious forms, takes colour from the national cocksureness and superficiality. It runs monotonously to ready explanations, a somewhat infantile smugness and hopefulness, a habit of reducing the unknowable to terms of the not worth knowing. What it cannot explain away with ready formulae, as in the later Winston Churchill,[2] it snickers over as scarcely worth explaining at all, as in the later Howells. Such a brave and tragic book as "Ethan Frome" is so rare as to be almost singular, even with Mrs. Wharton. There is, I daresay, not much market for that sort of thing. In the arts, as in the concerns of everyday, the American seeks escape from the insoluble

---

1 Fuller's disappearance is one of the strangest phenomena of American letters. I was astonished some time ago to discover that he was still alive. Back in 1899 he was already so far forgotten that William Archer mistook his name, calling him Henry Y. Puller. "Vide" Archer's pamphlet, The American Language; New York, 1899.

2 The American novelist, not Sir Winston. A.C.

by pretending that it is solved. A comfortable phrase is what he craves beyond all things—and comfortable phrases are surely not to be sought in Dreiser's stock.

I have heard argument that he is a follower of Frank Norris, and two or three facts lend it a specious probability. "McTeague" was printed in 1899; "Sister Carrie" a year later. Moreover, Norris was the first to see the merit of the latter book, and he fought a gallant fight, as literary advisor to Doubleday, Page & Co., against its suppression after it was in type. But this theory runs aground upon two circumstances, the first being that Dreiser did not actually read "McTeague," nor, indeed, grow aware of Norris, until after "Sister Carrie" was completed, and the other being that his development, once he began to write other books, was along paths far distant from those pursued by Norris himself. Dreiser, in truth, was a bigger man than Norris from the start; it is to the latter's unending honour that he recognized the fact instanter, and yet did all he could to help his rival. It is imaginable, of course, that Norris, living fifteen years longer, might have overtaken Dreiser, and even surpassed him; one finds an arrow pointing that way in "Vandover and the Brute" (not printed until 1914). But it swings sharply around in "The Epic of the Wheat." In the second volume of that incomplete trilogy, "The Pit," there is an obvious concession to the popular taste in romance; the thing is so frankly written down, indeed, that a play has been made of it, and Broadway has applauded it. And in "The Octopus," despite some excellent writing, there is a descent to a mysticism so fantastic and preposterous that it quickly passes beyond serious consideration. Norris, in his day, swung even lower—for example, in "A Man's Woman" and in some of his short stories. He was a pioneer, perhaps only half sure of the way he wanted to go, and the evil lures of popular success lay all about him. It is no wonder that he sometimes seemed to lose his direction.

Émile Zola is another literary father whose paternity grows dubious on examination. I once printed an article exposing what seemed to me to be a Zolaesque attitude of mind, and even some trace of the actual Zola manner, in "Jennie Gerhardt"; there came from Dreiser the news that he had never read a line of Zola, and knew nothing about his novels. Not a complete answer, of course; the influence might have been exerted at second hand. But through whom? I confess that I am unable to name a likely medium. The effects of Zola upon Anglo-Saxon fiction have been almost *nil*; his only avowed disciple, George Moore, has long since recanted and reformed; he has scarcely rippled the prevailing romanticism. . . . Thomas Hardy? Here, I daresay, we strike a better scent. There are many obvious likenesses between "Tess of the D'Urbervilles" and "Jennie Gerhardt" and again between "Jude the Obscure" and "Sister Carrie." All four stories deal penetratingly and poignantly with the essential tragedy of women; all disdain the petty, specious explanations of popular fiction; in each one finds a poetical and melancholy beauty. Moreover, Dreiser himself confesses to an enchanted discovery of Hardy in 1896, three years before "Sister Carrie" was begun. But it is easy to push such a fact too hard, and to search for likenesses and parallels that are really not there. The truth is that Dreiser's points of contact with Hardy might be easily matched by many striking points of difference, and that the fundamental ideas in their novels, despite a common sympathy, are anything but identical. Nor does one apprehend any ponderable result of Dreiser's youthful enthusiasm for Balzac, which antedated his discovery of Hardy by two years. He got from both men a sense of the scope and dignity of the novel; they taught him that a story might be a good one, and yet considerably more than a story; they showed him the essential drama of the commonplace. But that they had more influence in forming his point of view, or even in shaping his technique, than any one of half a dozen other gods of those young days—this I scarcely find. In the structure of his novels, and in their manner of approach to life no less, they call up the work of Dostoyevsky and Turgenev far more than the work of either of these men—but of all the Russians save Tolstoi (as of Flaubert) Dreiser himself tells us that he was ignorant until ten years after "Sister Carrie." In his days of preparation, indeed, his reading was so copious and disorderly that antagonistic influences must have well-nigh neutralized one another, and so left the curious youngster to work out his own method and his own philosophy. Stevenson went down with Balzac, Poe with Hardy, Dumas *fils* with Tolstoi. There were even months of delight in Sienkiewicz, Lew Wallace and E. P. Roe! The whole repertory of the pedagogues had been fought through in school and college: Dickens, Thackeray, Hawthorne, Washington Irving, Kingsley, Scott. Only Irving and Hawthorne seem to have made deep impressions.

"I used to lie under a tree," says Dreiser, "and read 'Twice Told Tales' by the hour. I thought 'The Alhambra' was a perfect creation, and I still have a lingering affection for it." Add Bret Harte, George Ebers, William Dean Howells, Oliver Wendell Holmes, and you have a literary stew indeed! . . . But for all its bubbling I see a far more potent influence in the chance discovery of Spencer and Huxley at twenty-three—the year of choosing! Who, indeed, will ever measure the effect of those two giants upon the young men of that era—Spencer with his inordinate meticulousness, his relentless pursuit of facts, his overpowering syllogisms, and Huxley with his devastating agnosticism, his insatiable questionings of the old axioms, above all, his brilliant style? Huxley, it would appear, has been condemned to the scientific hulks, along with bores innumerable and unspeakable; one looks in vain for any appreciation of him in treatises on beautiful letters.[3] And yet the man was a superb artist in works, a master-writer even more than a master-biologist, one of the few truly great stylists that England has produced since the time of Anne. One can easily imagine the effect of two such vigorous and intriguing minds upon a youth groping about for self-understanding and self-expression. They swept him clean, he tells us, of the lingering faith of his boyhood—a mediaeval Rhenish Catholicism—more, they filled him with a new and eager curiosity, an intense interest in the life that lay about him, a desire to seek out its hidden workings and underlying causes. A young man set afire by Huxley might perhaps make a very bad novelist, but it is a certainty that he could never make a sentimental and superficial one. There is no need to go further than this single moving adventure to find the genesis of Dreiser's disdain of the current platitudes, his sense of life as a complex biological phenomenon, only dimly comprehended, and his tenacious way of thinking things out, and of holding to what he finds good. Ah, that he had learned from Huxley, not only how to inquire, but also how to report! That he had picked up a talent for that dazzling style, so sweet to the ear, so damnably persuasive, so crystal-clear!

---

3 For example, in *The Cambridge History of English Literature*, which runs to fourteen large volumes and a total of nearly 10,000 pages, Huxley receives but a page and a quarter of notice, and his remarkable mastery of English is barely mentioned in passing. His two debates with Gladstone, in which he did some of the best writing of the century, are not noticed at all.

But the more one examines Dreiser, either as writer or as theorist of man, the more his essential isolation becomes apparent. He got a habit of mind from Huxley, but he completely missed Huxley's habit of writing. He got a view of woman from Hardy, but he soon changed it out of all resemblance. He got a certain fine ambition and gusto out of Balzac, but all that was French and characteristic he left behind. So with Zola, Howells, Tolstoi and the rest. The tracing of likenesses quickly becomes rabbinism, almost cabalism. The differences are huge and sprout up in all directions. Nor do I see anything save a flaming up of colonial passion in the current efforts to fit him into a German frame, and make him an agent of Prussian frightfulness in letters. Such bosh one looks for in the *Nation* and the Boston *Transcript*, and there is where one actually finds it. Even the *New Republic* has stood clear of it; it is important only as material for that treatise upon the patrio-teer and his bawling which remains to be written. The name of the man, true enough, is obviously Germanic, and he has told us himself, in "A Traveler at Forty," how he sought out and found the tombs of his ancestors in some little town of the Rhine country. There are more of these genealogical revelations in "A Hoosier Holiday," but they show a Rhenish strain that was already running thin in boyhood. No one, indeed, who reads a Dreiser novel can fail to see the gap separating the author from these half-forgotten forebears. He shows even less of German influence than of English influence.

There is, as a matter of fact, little in modern German fiction that is intelligibly comparable to "Jennie Gerhardt" and "The Titan," either as a study of man or as a work of art. The naturalistic movement of the eighties was launched by men whose eyes were upon the theatre, and it is in that field that nine-tenths of its force has been spent.

<hr>

In his manner, as opposed to his matter, he is more the Teuton, for he shows all of the racial patience and pertinacity and all of the racial lack of humour. Writing a novel is as solemn a business to him as trimming a beard is to a German barber. He blasts his way through his interminable stories by something not unlike main strength; his writing, one feels, often takes on the character of an actual siege operation, with tunnellings, drum fire, assaults in close order and hand-to-hand fighting. Once, seeking an analogy, I called him the Hindenburg of the novel. If it holds, then "The 'Genius'" is his Poland. The field of action bears the aspect, at the end, of a hostile province meticulously brought under the yoke, with every road and lane explored to its beginning, and every crossroads village laboriously taken, inventoried and policed. Here is the very negation of Gallic lightness and intuition, and of all forms of impressionism as well. Here is no series of illuminating flashes, but a gradual bathing of the whole scene with white light, so that every detail stands out.

And many of those details, of course, are trivial; even irritating. They do not help the picture; they muddle and obscure it; one wonders impatiently what their meaning is, and what the purpose may be of revealing them with such a precise, portentous air. . . . Turn to page 703 of "The 'Genius.'" By the time one gets there, one has hewn and hacked one's way through 702 large pages of fine print—97 long chapters, more than 250,000 words. And yet, at this hurried and impatient point, with the *coda* already begun, Dreiser halts the whole narrative to explain the origin, nature and inner meaning of Christian Science, and to make us privy to a lot of chatty stuff about Mrs. Althea Jones, a professional healer, and to supply us with detailed plans and specifications of the apartment house in which she lives, works her tawdry miracles, and has her being. Here, in sober summary, are the particulars:

1. That the house is "of conventional design."
2. That there is "a spacious areaway" between its two wings.
3. That these wings are "of cream-coloured pressed brick."
4. That the entrance between them is "protected by a handsome wrought-iron door."
5. That to either side of this door is "an electric lamp support of handsome design."
6. That in each of these lamp supports there are "lovely cream-coloured globes, shedding a soft luster."
7. That inside is "the usual lobby."
8. That in the lobby is "the usual elevator."
9. That in the elevator is the usual "uniformed negro elevator man."

10. That this negro elevator man (name not given) is "indifferent and impertinent."

11. That a telephone switchboard is also in the lobby.

12. That the building is seven stories in height.

In "The Financier" there is the same exasperating rolling up of irrelevant facts. The court proceedings in the trial of Cowperwood are given with all the exactness of a parliamentary report in the London *Times*. The speeches of the opposing counsel are set down nearly in full, and with them the remarks of the judge, and after that the opinion of the Appellate Court on appeal, with the dissenting opinions as a sort of appendix. In "Sister Carrie" the thing is less savagely carried out, but that is not Dreiser's fault, for the manuscript was revised by some anonymous hand, and the printed version is but little more than half the length of the original. In "The Titan" and "Jennie Gerhardt" no such brake upon exuberance is visible; both books are crammed with details that serve no purpose, and are as flat as ditch-water. Even in the two volumes of personal record, "A Traveler at Forty" and "A Hoosier Holiday," there is the same furious accumulation of trivialities. Consider the former. It is without structure, without selection, without reticence. One arises from it as from a great babbling, half drunken. On the one hand the author fills a long and gloomy chapter with the story of the Borgias, apparently under the impression that it is news, and on the other hand he enters into intimate and inconsequential confidences about all the persons he meets en route, sparing neither the innocent nor the obscure. The children of his English host at Bridgely Level strike him as fantastic little creatures, even as a bit uncanny—and he duly sets it down. He meets an Englishman on a French train who pleases him much, and the two become good friends and see Rome together, but the fellow's wife is "obstreperous" and "haughty in her manner" and so "loud-spoken in her opinions" that she is "really offensive"—and down it goes. He makes an impression on a Mlle. Marcelle in Paris, and she accompanies him from Monte Carlo to Ventimiglia, and there gives him a parting kiss and whispers, "*Avril-Fontainebleau*"—and lo, this sweet one is duly spread upon the minutes. He permits himself to be arrested by a fair privateer in Piccadilly, and goes with her to one of the dens of sin that suffragettes see in their nightmares, and cross-examines her at length regarding her ancestry, her professional ethics and ideals, and her earnings at her dismal craft—and into the book goes a full report of the proceedings. He is entertained by an eminent Dutch jurist in Amsterdam—and upon the pages of the chronicle it appears that the gentleman is "waxy" and "a little pedantic," and that he is probably the sort of "thin, delicate, well barbered" professor that Ibsen had in mind when he cast about for a husband for the daughter of General Gabler.

Such is the art of writing as Dreiser understands it and practices it—an endless piling up of minutiae, an almost ferocious tracking down of ions, electrons and molecules, an unshakable determination to tell it all. One is amazed by the mole-like diligence of the man, and no less by his exasperating disregard for the ease of his readers. A Dreiser novel, at least of the later canon, cannot be read as other novels are read—on a winter evening or summer afternoon, between meal and meal, travelling from New York to Boston. It demands the attention for almost a week, and uses up the faculties for a month. If, reading "The 'Genius,'" one were to become engrossed in the fabulous manner described in the publishers' advertisement, and so find oneself unable to put it down and go to bed before the end, one would get no sleep for three days and three nights.

Worse, there are no charms of style to mitigate the rigours of these vast steppes and pampas of narration. Joseph Joubert's saying that "words should stand out well from the paper" is quite incomprehensible to Dreiser; he never imitates Flaubert by writing for "*la respiration et l'oreille.*" There is no painful groping for the inevitable word, or for what Walter Pater called "the gipsy phrase"; the common, even the commonplace, coin of speech is good enough. On the first page of "Jennie Gerhardt" one encounters "frank, open countenance," "diffident manner," "helpless poor," "untutored mind," "honest necessity," and half a dozen other stand-bys of the second-rate newspaper reporter. In "Sister Carrie" one finds "high noon," "hurrying throng," "unassuming restaurant," "dainty slippers," "high-strung nature," and "cool, calculating world"—all on a few pages. Carrie's sister, Minnie Hanson, "gets" the supper. Hanson himself is "wrapped up" in his child. Carrie decides to enter Storm and King's office, "no matter what." In "The Titan" the word "trig" is worked to death; it takes on, toward the end, the character of a banal and preposterous refrain. In the other books one encounters mates for it—words made to do duty in as many senses as the American verb "to fix" or the journalistic "to secure."

I often wonder if Dreiser gets anything properly describable as plea-sure out of this dogged accumulation of threadbare, undistinguished, uninspiring nouns, adjectives, verbs, adverbs, pronouns, participles and conjunctions. To the man with an ear for verbal delicacies—the man who searches painfully for the perfect word, and puts the way of saying a thing above the thing said—there is in writing the constant joy of sudden discovery, of happy accident. A phrase springs up full blown, sweet and caressing. But what joy can there be in rolling up sentences that have no more life and beauty in them, intrinsically, than so many election bulletins? Where is the thrill in the manufacture of such a paragraph as that in which Mrs. Althea Jones' sordid habitat is described with such inexorable particularity? Or in the laborious confection of such stuff as this, from Book I, Chapter IV, of "The 'Genius'"?:

> The city of Chicago—who shall portray it! This vast ruck of life that had sprung suddenly into existence upon the dank marshes of a lake shore!

Or this from the epilogue to "The Financier":

> There is a certain fish whose scientific name is *Mycteroperca Bonaci,* and whose common name is Black Grouper, which is of considerable value as an afterthought in this connection, and which deserves much to be better known. It is a healthy creature, growing quite regularly to a weight of two hundred and fifty pounds, and living a comfortable, lengthy existence because of its very remarkable ability to adapt itself to conditions. . . .

Or this from his pamphlet, "Life, Art and America":[4]

> Alas, alas! for art in America. It has a hard stubby row to hoe.

---

4 New York, 1917; reprinted from *The Seven Arts* for Feb. 1917.

But I offer no more examples. Every reader of the Dreiser novels must cherish astounding specimens—of awkward, platitudinous marginalia, of whole scenes spoiled by bad writing, of phrases as brackish as so many lumps of sodium hyposulphite. Here and there, as in parts of "The Titan" and again in parts of "A Hoosier Holiday," an evil conscience seems to haunt him and he gives hard striving to his manner, and more than once there emerges something that is almost graceful. But a backsliding always follows this phosphorescence of reform. "The 'Genius,'" coming after "The Titan," marks the high tide of his bad writing. There are passages in it so clumsy, so inept, so irritating that they seem almost unbelievable; nothing worse is to be found in the newspapers. Nor is there any compensatory deftness in structure, or solidity of design, to make up for this carelessness in detail. The well-made novel, of course, can be as hollow as the well-made play of Scribe—but let us at least have a beginning, a middle and an end! Such a story as "The 'Genius'" is as gross and shapeless as Brünnhilde. It billows and bulges out like a cloud of smoke, and its internal organization is almost as vague. There are episodes that, with a few chapters added, would make very respectable novels. There are chapters that need but a touch or two to be excellent short stories. The thing rambles, staggers, trips, heaves, pitches, struggles, totters, wavers, halts, turns aside, trembles on the edge of collapse. More than once it seems to be foundering, both in the equine and in the maritime senses. The tale has been heard of a tree so tall that it took two men to see to the top of it. Here is a novel so brobdingnagian that a single reader can scarcely read his way through it. . . .

Of the general ideas which lie at the bottom of all of Dreiser's work it is impossible to be in ignorance, for he has exposed them at length in "A Hoosier Holiday" and summarized them in "Life, Art and America." In their main outlines they are not unlike the fundamental assumptions of Joseph Conrad. Both novelists see human existence as a seeking without a finding; both reject the prevailing interpretations of its meaning and mechanism; both take refuge in "I do not know." Put "A Hoosier Holiday" beside Conrad's "A Personal Record," and you will come upon parallels from end to end. Or better still, put it beside Hugh Walpole's

"Joseph Conrad," in which the Conradean metaphysic is condensed from the novels even better than Conrad has done it himself: at once you will see how the two novelists, each a worker in the elemental emotions, each a rebel against the current assurance and superficiality, each an alien to his place and time, touch each other in a hundred ways.

"Conrad," says Walpole, "is of the firm and resolute conviction that life is too strong, too clever and too remorseless for the sons of men." And then, in amplification, "It is as though, from some high window, looking down, he were able to watch some shore, from whose security men were forever launching little cockleshell boats upon a limitless and angry sea. . . . From his height he can follow their fortunes, their brave struggles, their fortitude to the very end. He admires their courage, the simplicity of their faith, but his irony springs from his knowledge of the inevitable end. . . ."

Substitute the name of Dreiser for that of Conrad, and you will have to change scarcely a word. Perhaps one, to wit, "clever." I suspect that Dreiser, writing so of his own creed, would be tempted to make it "stupid," or, at all events, "unintelligible." The struggle of man, as he sees it, is more than impotent; it is gratuitous and purposeless. There is, to his eye, no grand ingenuity, no skillful adaptation of means to end, no moral (or even dramatic) plan in the order of the universe. He can get out of it only a sense of profound and inexplicable *dis*order. The waves which batter the cockleshells change their direction at every instant. Their navigation is a vast adventure, but intolerably fortuitous and inept—a voyage without chart, compass, sun or stars. . . .

So at bottom. But to look into the blackness steadily, of course, is almost beyond the endurance of man. In the very moment that its impenetrability is grasped the imagination begins attacking it with pale beams of false light. All religions, I daresay, are thus projected from the questioning soul of man, and not only all religions, but also all great agnosticisms. Nietzsche, shrinking from the horror of that abyss of negation, revived the Pythagorean concept of *der ewigen Wiederkunft*—a vain and blood-curdling sort of comfort. To it, after a while, he added explanations almost Christian—a whole repertoire of whys and wherefores, aims and goals, aspirations and significances. The late Mark Twain, in an unpublished work, toyed with an equally daring idea; that men are to some unimaginably vast and incomprehensible Being what the unicellular organisms of his body are to man, and so on *ad infinitum*. Dreiser occasionally inclines to much the same hypothesis; he likens the endless reactions going on in the world we know, the myriadal creation, collision and destruction of entities, to the slow accumulation and organization of cells *in utero*. He would make us specks in the insentient embryo of some gigantic Presence whose form is still unimaginable and whose birth must wait for Eons and Eons. Again, he turns to something not easily distinguishable from philosophical idealism, whether out of Berkeley or Fichte it is hard to make out—that is, he would interpret the whole phenomenon of life as no more than an appearance, a nightmare of some unseen sleeper or of men themselves, an "uncanny blur of nothingness"—in Euripides' phrase, "a song sung by an idiot, dancing down the wind." Yet again, he talks vaguely of the intricate polyphony of a cosmic orchestra, cacophonous to our dull ears. Finally, he puts the observed into the ordered, reading a purpose in the displayed event: "life was intended to sting and hurt. . . ." But these are only gropings, and not to be read too critically. From speculations and explanations he always returns, Conrad-like, to the bald fact: to "the spectacle and stress of life." All he can make out clearly is "a vast compulsion which has nothing to do with the individual desires or tastes or impulses of individuals." That compulsion springs "from the settling processes of forces which we do not in the least understand, over which we have no control, and in whose grip we are as grains of dust or sand, blown hither and thither, for what purpose we cannot even suspect."[5] Man is not only doomed to defeat, but denied any glimpse or understanding of his antagonist. Here we come upon an agnosticism that has almost got beyond curiosity. What good would it do us, asks Dreiser, to know? In our ignorance and helplessness, we may at least get a slave's consolation out of cursing the unknown gods. Suppose we saw them striving blindly, too, and pitied them? . . .

But, as I say, this scepticism is often tempered by guesses at a possibly hidden truth, and the confession that this truth may exist reveals the practical unworkableness of the unconditioned system, at least

5 "Life, Art and America," p. 5.

for Dreiser. Conrad is far more resolute, and it is easy to see why. He is, by birth and training, an aristocrat. He has the gift of emotional detachment. The lures of facile doctrine do not move him. In his irony there is a disdain which plays about even the ironist himself. Dreiser is a product of far different forces and traditions, and is capable of no such escapement. Struggle as he may, and fume and protest as he may, he can no more shake off the chains of his intellectual and cultural heritage than he can change the shape of his nose. What that heritage is you may find out in detail by reading "A Hoosier Holiday," or in summary by glancing at the first few pages of "Life, Art and America." Briefly described, it is the burden of a believing mind, a moral attitude, a lingering superstition. One-half of the man's brain, so to speak, wars with the other half. He is intelligent, he is thoughtful, he is a sound artist—but there come moments when a dead hand falls upon him, and he is once more the Indiana peasant, snuffing absurdly over imbecile sentimentalities, giving a grave ear to quackeries, snorting and eye-rolling with the best of them. One generation spans too short a time to free the soul of man. Nietzsche, to the end of his days, remained a Prussian pastor's son, and hence two-thirds a Puritan; he erected his war upon holiness, toward the end, into a sort of holy war. Kipling, the grandson of a Methodist preacher, reveals the tin-pot evangelist with increasing clarity as youth and its ribaldries pass away and he falls back upon his fundamentals. And that other English novelist who springs from the servants' hall—let us not be surprised or blame him if he sometimes writes like a bounder.

The truth about Dreiser is that he is still in the transition stage between Christian Endeavour and civilization, between Warsaw, Indiana and the Socratic grove, between being a good American and being a free man, and so he sometimes vacillates perilously between a moral sentimentalism and a somewhat extravagant revolt. "The 'Genius,'" on the one hand, is almost a tract for rectitude, a Warning to the Young; its motto might be *Scheut die Dirnen*! And on the other hand, it is full of a laborious truculence that can only be explained by imagining the author as heroically determined to prove that he is a plain-spoken fellow and his own man, let the chips fall where they may. So, in spots, in "The Financier" and "The Titan," both of them far better books. There is an almost moral frenzy to expose and riddle what passes for morality among the stupid. The isolation of irony is never reached; the man is still evangelical; his ideas are still novelties to him; he is as solemnly absurd in some of his floutings of the Code Américain as he is in his respect for Bouguereau, or in his flirtings with the New Thought, or in his naif belief in the importance of novel-writing. Somewhere or other I have called all this the Greenwich Village complex. It is not genuine artists, serving beauty reverently and proudly, who herd in those cockroached cellars and bawl for art; it is a mob of half-educated yokels and cockneys to whom the very idea of art is still novel, and intoxicating—and more than a little bawdy.

Not that Dreiser actually belongs to this ragamuffin company. Far from it, indeed. There is in him, hidden deep-down, a great instinctive artist, and hence the makings of an aristocrat. In his muddled way, held back by the manacles of his race and time, and his steps made uncertain by a guiding theory which too often eludes his own comprehension, he yet manages to produce works of art of unquestionable beauty and authority, and to interpret life in a manner that is poignant and illuminating. There is vastly more intuition in him than intellectualism; his talent is essentially feminine, as Conrad's is masculine; his ideas always seem to be deduced from his feelings. The view of life that got into "Sister Carrie," his first book, was not the product of a conscious thinking out of Carrie's problems. It simply got itself there by the force of the artistic passion behind it; its coherent statement had to wait for other and more reflective days. The thing began as a vision, not as a syllogism. Here the name of Franz Schubert inevitably comes up. Schubert was an ignoramus, even in music; he knew less about polyphony, which is the mother of harmony, which is the mother of music, than the average conservatory professor. But nevertheless he had such a vast instinctive sensitiveness to musical values, such a profound and accurate feeling for beauty in tone, that he not only arrived at the truth in tonal relations, but even went beyond what, in his day, was known to be the truth, and so led an advance. Likewise, Giorgione de Castelfranco and Masaccio come to mind: painters of the first rank, but untutored, unsophisticated, uncouth. Dreiser, within his limits, belongs to this sabot-shod company of the elect. One thinks of Conrad, not as artist first, but as savant. There is something of the icy aloofness of the laboratory in him, even when the images he conjures up pulsate with the very glow of life. He is almost as self-conscious as the Beethoven of the last quartets. In Dreiser the thing is more intimate, more disorderly, more a matter of pure feeling. He gets his effects, one might almost say, not by designing them, but by living them.

But whatever the process, the power of the image evoked is not to be gainsaid. It is not only brilliant on the surface, but mysterious and appealing in its depths. One swiftly forgets his intolerable writing, his mirthless, sedulous, repellent manner, in the face of the Athenian tragedy he instils into his seduced and soul-sick servant girls, his barbaric pirates of finances, his conquered and hamstrung supermen, his wives who sit and wait. He has, like Conrad, a sure talent for depicting the spirit in disintegration. Old Gerhardt, in "Jennie Gerhardt," is alone worth all the *dramatis personae* of popular American fiction since the days of "Rob o' the Bowl"; Howells could no more have created him, in his Rodinesque impudence of outline, than he could have created Tartuffe or Gargantua. Such a novel as "Sister Carrie" stands quite outside the brief traffic of the customary stage. It leaves behind it an unescapable impression of bigness, of epic sweep and dignity. It is not a mere story, not a novel in the customary American meaning of the word; it is at once a psalm of life and a criticism of life—and that criticism loses nothing by the fact that its burden is despair. Here, precisely, is the point of Dreiser's departure from his fellows. He puts into his novels a touch of the eternal *Weltschmerz*. They get below the drama that is of the moment and reveal the greater drama that is without end. They arouse those deep and lasting emotions which grow out of the recognition of elemental and universal tragedy. His aim is not merely to tell a tale; his aim is to show the vast ebb and flow of forces which sway and condition human destiny. One cannot imagine him consenting to Conan Doyle's statement of the purpose of fiction, quoted with characteristic approval by the New York *Times*: "to amuse mankind, to help the sick and the dull and the weary." Nor is his purpose to instruct; if he is a pedagogue it is only incidentally and as a weakness. The thing he seeks to do is to stir, to awaken, to move. One does not arise from such a book as "Sister Carrie" with a smirk of satisfaction; one leaves it infinitely touched.

Dreiser, like Mark Twain and Emerson before him, has been far more hospitably greeted in his first stage, now drawing to a close, in England than in his own country. The cause of this, I daresay, lies partly in the fact that "Sister Carrie" was in general circulation over there during the seven years that it remained suppressed on this side. It was during these years that such men as Arnold Bennett, Theodore Watts-Dunton, Frank Harris and H. G. Wells, and such critical journals as the *Spectator*, the *Saturday Review* and the *Athenaeum* became aware of him, and so laid the foundations of a sound appreciation of his subsequent work. Since the beginning of the war, certain English newspapers have echoed the alarmed American discovery that he is a literary agent of the Wilhelmstrasse, but it is to the honour of the English that this imbecility has got no countenance from reputable authority and has not injured his position.

At home, as I have shown, he is less fortunate. When criticism is not merely an absurd effort to chase him out of court because his ideas are not orthodox, as the Victorians tried to chase out Darwin and Swinburne, and their predecessors pursued Shelley and Byron, it is too often designed to identify him with some branch or other of "radical" poppycock, and so credit him with purposes he has never imagined. Thus Chautauqua pulls and Greenwich Village pushes. In the middle ground there proceeds the pedantic effort to dispose of him by labelling him. One faction maintains that he is a realist; another calls him a naturalist; a third argues that he is really a disguised romanticist. This debate is all sound and fury, signifying nothing, but out of it has come a valuation by Lawrence Gilman,[6] which perhaps strikes very close to the truth. He is, says Mr. Gilman, "a sentimental mystic who employs the mimetic gestures of the realist." This judgment is apt in particular and sound in general. No such thing as a pure method is possible in the novel. Plain realism, as in Gorky's "Nachtasyl" and the war stories of Ambrose Bierce, simply wearies us by its vacuity; plain romance,

---

6 The *North American Review*, February 1916.

if we ever get beyond our nonage, makes us laugh. It is their artistic combination, as in life itself, that fetches us—the subtle projection of the concrete muddle that is living against the ideal orderliness that we reach out for—the eternal war of experience and aspiration—the contrast between the world as it is and the world as it might be or ought to be. Dreiser describes the thing that he sees, laboriously and relentlessly, but he never forgets the dream that is behind it. "He gives you," continues Mr. Gilman, "a sense of actuality; but he gives you more than that: out of the vast welter and surge, the plethoric irrelevancies . . . emerges a sense of the infinite sadness and mystery of human life. . . ."[7]

"To see truly," said Renan, "is to see dimly." Dimness or mystery, call it what you will: it is in all these overgrown and formless, but profoundly moving books. Just what do they mean? Just what is Dreiser driving at? That such questions should be asked is only a proof of the straits to which pedagogy has brought criticism. The answer is simple: he is driving at nothing, he is merely trying to represent what he sees and feels. His moving impulse is no flabby yearning to teach, to expound, to make simple; it is that "obscure inner necessity" of which Conrad tells us, the irresistible creative passion of a genuine artist, standing spell-bound before the impenetrable enigma that is life, enamoured by the strange beauty that plays over its sordidness, challenged to a wondering and half-terrified sort of representation of what passes understanding. And *jenseits von Gut und Böse.* "For myself," says Dreiser, "I do not know what truth is, what beauty is, what love is, what hope is. I do not believe anyone absolutely and I do not doubt anyone absolutely. I think people are both evil and well-intentioned." The hatching of the Dreiser bugaboo is here; it is the flat rejection of the rubber-stamp formulae that outrages petty minds; not being "good," he must be "evil"—as William Blake said of Milton, a true poet is always "of the devil's party." But in that very groping toward a light but dimly seen there is a measure, it seems to me, of Dreiser's rank and consideration as an artist. "Now comes the public," says Hermann Bahr, "and demands that we explain what the poet is trying to say. The answer is this: If we knew exactly he would not be a poet. . . ."

---

7 Another competent valuation, by Randolph Bourne, is in *The Dial,* June 14, 1917.

Little Women

SUSAN CHEEVER

Louisa May Alcott was a reluctant, rebellious thirty-six-year-old on the May morning in 1868 when she sat down to write *Little Women*. She worked at a small desk built in between two windows in her second-floor bedroom at Orchard House. A woolen shawl, worn over her usual brown muslin, warmed her against the drafts and the chill of New England. "Mr. Niles wants a girls' story, and I begin *Little Women*," she wrote in her journal about her publisher's wish and the way in which it had become her command. "Marmee, Anna and May all approve my plan. So I plod away although I don't enjoy this sort of thing. Never liked girls or knew many, except my sisters, but our queer plays and experiences may prove interesting, though I doubt it."

In spite of her doubts, *Little Women*, which was to become one of the best-selling books of all time and end the Alcott family's decades of debilitating poverty, seemed to take hold of Louisa as she wrote. True, the writing of *Moods* had also taken hold of her in a similar way. She quickly realized that she had already written some pieces about her family among the dozens of magazine pieces she had published, and she wrote fast, without revision.

When she looked up during the day, past the rustic board fence her father had built at the edge of the property, she saw people and carriages passing on the Lexington Road and, beyond the road, pastures sparkling with wildflowers. When she wrote at night, by candlelight, she communed with a family of barred owls that lived in broad branches of the huge elm tree outside her windows.

As she wrote during the day, she could sometimes look down from the window and see her father, not working in the gardens behind the house, but sitting on the bench with a pile of his finest Red Pippin apples waiting for the occasional traveler who might be ready for a dose of his own brand of high philosophical discourse. Sometimes Emerson dropped by. Sometimes, Alcott would entertain a special visitor from Boston like Henry Wadsworth Longfellow, or Franklin Sanborn would wander up the Lexington Road to talk pedagogy, or one of the Hawthorne children would come over from next door. Beyond the meadows lay the shimmering water of Walden Pond, and the fields and marshes where Louisa had taken so many passionate walks so long ago with her teacher and friend Thoreau.

The little half-moon-shaped desk her father had built for her sat at the foot of Louisa's bed, surrounded by her books in a crowded cabinet bookcase, her sewing basket, family portraits, flower paintings by her older sister Anna, and a bust of the poet Schiller on the mantle. Although Orchard House was unheated except by fireplaces, and the Alcotts in later years often closed it up for the winter and moved to Boston, Louisa's room had a fireplace and windows facing south and west toward Concord. Her parents slept in the bedroom across the hall.

When she began writing *Little Women*, Louisa herself was still battling nervous exhaustion and arthritis brought on by the mercury poisoning as well as pains in her legs and back. Sometimes she was too weak to write. Sometimes she seemed to lose touch with who she was and what she was doing. Her right hand was beginning to cramp so painfully as she bore down on the metal pen nib and moved it over the paper that she would soon have to write with her left hand. Eventually, the mercury poisoning would kill her.

That spring, there were many other reasons for her to be discouraged. Her first serious novel had failed. As the culmination of decades of writing to order, editing others' work, teaching, and turning out the novelistic melodramas she called "rubbish" in order to alleviate the Alcotts' habitual poverty, it had held all her hopes for a literary career, and those hopes were once again dashed.

As she wrote at her second-floor windows, the last lilacs faded and the rhododendron bloomed. By June, after a month of writing day and night, she sent in twelve chapters of the book to Thomas Niles of Roberts Brothers, who was also her father's publisher. "He thought it dull," she wrote in her journal; "so do I." Nevertheless, she continued to work and by July 15 had completed the four-hundred-page manuscript that was the first part of *Little Women*. (The second part of the book was written later that year in another marathon writing session from October to January.)

By the time the hydrangeas bloomed in August, she was at her desk reading proofs. "It reads better than I expected," she wrote. "Not a bit sensational but simple and true, for we really lived most of it." Later, when the book began its extraordinary success, she expanded on this idea in a letter to another neighbor, Mary the wife of Colonel Thomas Wentworth Higginson—Emily Dickinson's editor and correspondent and one of John Brown's Secret Six. "The book was very hastily written to order & I had many doubts about the success of my first attempt at a girl's book," she wrote. "The characters were drawn from life, which gives them whatever merit they possess, for I find it impossible to invent anything half so true or touching as the simple facts with which everyday life supplies me."

But were they the facts? The difficulties, the debilitating poverty and claustrophobia of the Alcotts' life in Concord, become opportunities and closeness in the pages of *Little Women*. Sister Beth's horrifying and dreadful death from scarlet fever becomes a sweet and peaceful letting go. Louisa's furious jealousy at age thirty when her sister Anna married the penniless John Pratt becomes Jo's more normal teenage snit when her sister marries the adorable John Brooke. The family's grinding poverty, which had caused twenty moves in as many years, was transformed into friendly penny-pinching. The burden of running the household that fell largely on Louisa was shared in the fictional March household with a fictional loyal household retainer named Hannah. There was no Hannah in real life. The loss of Louisa's hair from disease in wartime became the noble sacrifice of Jo's hair to provide money to help her father when he was a soldier stricken with disease. (Jo's hair would quickly grow back. Louisa's would not.)

Most of all, Jo's rebelliousness in the book never keeps anyone from loving her, and in the end it serves her well. Jo is that rare thing, a rebel who somehow manages to be adored by the very people she's rebelling against. They understand her good intentions and love her for them. In real life, Louisa's rebelliousness made her a family outcast. Her father openly preferred her more conventional sisters. Her rebellion—her intelligence and her contrary nature—seems to have kept her from ever marrying or having her own family as Jo does. The book's energy comes from a fierce yearning, a longing to have had the fictional experience instead of the real one. *Little Women*, as many great books do, hovers in the gap between art and life—just alive enough so that we can recognize ourselves in its pages, just artistic enough so that we can find the lives we read about completely satisfying.

The huge success of *Little Women* changed the direction of Alcott's career, and for the remaining twenty years of her life she churned out best-selling sequels to the brilliant novel she wrote, almost by accident, in the spring of 1868. Although the money enabled her family to live comfortably, Alcott was never really resigned to her role as the beloved and celebrated author of her books for girls. She worried that she had become "a literary nursemaid providing moral pap for the young."

I first read *Little Women* when I was about ten. Like many women, I always wanted to be Jo. I was also the family rebel, the one who could never mind her manners, the one who was often angry, the one who was always pretending to be a horse when the time came to put on a dress and curtsy to Mrs. Frothingham. Most of the girls in the books I read—and in the life I led—were ladylike and pretty. Successful girls were thin and loved to wear nice clothes that always looked wonderful on them. On me, clothes always looked as if they belonged to someone else, and they often got torn and dirty on my excursions through the fields and woods around our house.

Jo March offered me a different kind of image, a new definition of what it meant to be a girl. Instead of a graceful young lady who always minded her manners and knew that her future lay in loving the right man, she was an outspoken, clumsy girl who turned down the right man even though he loved her.

Reading *Little Women* again, now, I can see how profoundly the book influenced me—as a woman, but even more than that as a writer. Without intending to, Louisa May Alcott invented a new way to write about the ordinary lives of women, and to tell stories that are usually heard in kitchens or bedrooms. She made literature out of the kind of conversations women have while doing the dishes together or taking care of their children. It was in *Little Women* that I learned that domestic details can be the subject of art, that small things in a woman's life—cooking, the trimming of a dress or hat, quiet talk—can be just as important a subject as a great whale or a scarlet letter. *Little Women* gave my generation of women permission to write about our daily lives; in many ways, even though it's a novel, in tone and voice it is the precursor of the modern memoir—the book that gives voice to people who have traditionally kept quiet. In fact, the foundation of the American memoir can be found in Alcott's masterpiece and in that of her friend Henry David Thoreau. Alcott's greatest work was so powerful because it was about ordinary things—I think that's why it felt ordinary even as she wrote it. She transformed the lives of women into something worthy of literature. Without even meaning to, Alcott exalted the everyday in women's lives and gave it greatness.

Stephen Crane and the Mainstream of American Fiction

RALPH ELLISON

Of all our nineteenth-century masters of fiction—Hawthorne, Melville, Henry James, Mark Twain and Stephen Crane—it was Crane, the youngest, arrived most distantly from the Civil War in point of time, who was the most war-haunted. Born in Newark, New Jersey, six years after the firing ceased, Crane was the youngest of fourteen offspring of parents whose marriage marked the union of two lines of hard-preaching, fundamentalist Methodist ministers. The time and place of his birth and his parents' concern with conduct, morality and eloquence were, when joined with his self-dedication to precise feeling and writing, perhaps as portentous and as difficult a gift to bear as any seer's obligation to peer through walls and into the secret places of the heart, or around windy corners and into the enigmatic future. Indeed, such words as "clairvoyant," "occult" and "uncanny" have been used to describe his style, and while these tell us little, there was nonetheless an inescapable aura of the marvelous about Stephen Crane. For although there is no record of his eyes having been covered at birth with that caul which is said to grant one second sight, he revealed a unique vision of the human condition and an unusual talent for projecting it. His was a costly vision, won through personal suffering, hard living and harsh artistic discipline, and by the time of his death, at twenty-nine, he was recognized as one of the important innovators of American fictional prose and master of a powerful and original style.

Fortunately it was the style and not the myth which was important. Thus today, after sixty years during which there was little interest in the meaning and sources of Crane's art, the best of the work remains not only alive but capable of speaking to us with a new resonance of meaning. While recent criticism holds that the pioneer style, which leads directly to Ernest Hemingway, sprang from a dedication to the moral and aesthetic possibilities of literary form similar to that of Henry James, Crane's dedication to art was no less disciplined or deadly serious than that which characterized his preaching forefathers' concern with religion. Indeed, John Berryman and Robert Wooster Stallman, the most perceptive of Crane's recent critics, see much of the tension in the work as arising from his desperate struggle with the rejected angel of his parents' Methodism—an insight which we find highly suggestive.

Surely if fundamentalist Christianity could get so authoritatively into national politics (especially in the Bible Belt), so ambiguously into our system of education (as in the Scopes trial issue), into our style of crime (through Prohibition's spawn of bootleggers, gangsters, jellybeans and flappers), and so powerfully into jazz, it is about time we recognized its deeper relationship to the art of our twentieth-century literature. And not simply as subject matter, but as a major source of its technique, its form and rhetoric. For while much has been made of the role of the high church in the development of modern poetry, and with Kierkegaard become a household god for many contemporary novelists, Crane's example suggests that for the writer a youthful contact with the emotional intensity and harsh authority of American fundamentalism can be as important an experience as contact with those churches which possess a ritual containing elements of high art and a theology spun subtle and fine through intellectualization. Undoubtedly the Methodist Church provided Crane an early schooling in the seriousness of spiritual questions—of the individual's ultimate relationship to his fellow men, to the universe and to God—and was one source of the youthful revolt which taught him to look upon life with his own eyes. Just as important, perhaps, is the discipline which the church provided him in keeping great emotion under the control of the intellect, as during the exciting services (which the boy learned to question quite early), along with an awareness of the disparity between the individual's public testimony (a rite common to evangelical churches) and his private deeds—a matter intensified by the fact that the celebrant of this rite of public confession was his own father. In brief, Crane was concerned very early with private emotions publicly displayed as an act of purification and self-definition, an excellent beginning for a writer interested in the ordeals of the private individual struggling to define himself as against the claims of society. Crane, who might well have become a minister, turned from religion but transferred its forms to his art.

For his contemporaries much of the meaning of Crane's art was obscured by a personal myth compounded of elements ever fascinating to the American mind: his youth and his early mastery of a difficult and highly technical skill (like a precocious juvenile delinquent possessed of an uncanny knowledge not of pocket pool, craps or tap dancing, but of advanced literary technique), coupled with that highly individual way of feeling and thinking which is the basis of all significant innovation in art; his wild bohemian way of life; his maverick attitude toward respectability; his gallantry toward prostitutes no less than toward their respectable sisters; his friendship with Bowery outcasts ("What Must I Do to Be Saved?" was the title of a tract by his mother's uncle, the Methodist Bishop of Syracuse and a founder of the university there); his gambler's prodigality with fame and money; his search for wars to observe and report; and finally the fatality of "genius" which followed the fair, slight, gifted youth from obscurity to association with the wealthy and gifted in England (Joseph Conrad, H. G. Wells, Ford Madox Ford and Henry James were among his friends), to his death from tuberculosis, one of the period's most feared and romanticized scourges, in the far Black Forest of Germany.

Blind to the cost of his knowledge, many of his contemporaries regarded Crane's adventures as undertaken merely to provide them with entertainment: Crane chasing bandits in Mexico; Crane shipwrecked while running guns to Cuba; Crane reporting the Greco-Turkish War; Crane taking on the New York police force and being obliged to abandon the city; Crane marrying a woman said to have been an ex-madam; Crane on a spree. And there was, in fact, some truth to their assumption. Crane was as gifted at acting out good newspaper copy as Hemingway or F. Scott Fitzgerald were to be, and no less a delight to the reporters.

Yet despite the headlines and malicious gossip concerning his wife's past (which motivated their taking up residence in England), the fiction presented here testifies that whatever else Crane might have been seeking, the playboy author was engaged in a most desperate moral struggle. At a time when the capacity for moral seriousness appeared to have disappeared from American society, Crane was attempting to live his own life as cleanly, as imaginatively, and with as much immediacy and realistic poetry as he aspired to convey in his writing. If there was something of the entertainer in his public role (and this was still the time of that great popular entertainer, Mark Twain), there was also an element of the self-sacrificial, and the sensational features of the public adventures hint at the cost of the art. There was in Crane something of Emerson and Thoreau as well as the fundamentalist moralist-designate, and the quiet, desperate, unthinking life was to be avoided at the cost of life itself.

At the center of Crane's myth there lay, of course, the mystery of the creative talent with which a youth of twenty-one was able to write what is considered one of the world's foremost war novels when he had neither observed nor participated in combat. And, indeed, with this second book, *The Red Badge of Courage*, Crane burst upon the American public with the effect of a Civil War projectile lain dormant beneath a city square for thirty years. Two years before he had appeared with *Maggie: A Girl of the Streets*, a stripped little novel of social protest written in a strange new idiom. But although Hamlin Garland and William Dean Howells had recognized the work's importance, the reading public was prepared neither for such a close look at the devastating effect of the Bowery upon the individual's sense of life, nor for the narrow choice between the sweatshop and prostitution which Crane saw as the fate of such girls as Maggie. Besides, with its ear attuned to the languid accents of genteel fiction, it was unprepared for the harsh, although offbeat, poetic realism of Crane's idiom.

In a famous inscription in which he exhorted a reader to have the "courage" to read his book to the end, Crane explained that he had tried to show that

environment is a tremendous thing in the world, and frequently shapes lives regardless. If one proves that theory, one makes room in heaven for all sorts of souls, notably an occasional street girl, who are not confidently expected to be there by many excellent people. . . .

Crane's statement reveals that the young author knew the mood of his prospective audience much better than it was prepared to know him. For although Crane published *Maggie* at his own expense (significantly, under a pseudonym) and paid four men to read it conspicuously while traveling up and down Manhattan on the El, it failed.

This was for American literature a most significant failure indeed; afterward, following *Maggie*, Crane developed the strategy of understatement and the technique of impressionism which was to point the way for Hemingway and our fiction of the twenties. Crane was not to return to an explicit projection of his social criticism until "The Monster," a work written much later in his career; he turned, instead, to exploring the psychology of the individual under extreme pressure. *Maggie*, which is omitted here in favor of the neglected and more mature "The Monster," stands with *The Adventures of Huckleberry Finn* as one of the parents of the modern American novel, but it is *The Red Badge of Courage* which claims our attention with all the authority of a masterpiece.

One cannot help but feel, however, that the romantic mystery made of the fact that Crane had no direct experience of war before writing *The Red Badge* has served to obscure much of its true importance. For even while rejecting the assumption that the creative act is completely accountable, it is evident that Crane was the type of writer upon whom, to use Henry James's phrase, "nothing was lost," and the possessor of an imagination for which minor experiences ever revealed their more universal implications. It is not necessary for even the most unimaginative of us to be consumed by flame in order to envision hellfire—the hot head of a match against the fingernail suffices—and the embers of the Civil War, let us recall, had far from ceased their burning in the American mind.

We know that one of Crane's brothers was an expert on the Civil War; that while attending the Hudson River Institute at Claverack, N.Y., Crane had listened to the exciting war experiences of Lieutenant John

Van Petten, a hero of the old 34th New York, then teaching elocution and drill at the little military academy; that he possessed an excellent memory for detail and a marvelous ear for speech accents, rhythms and idioms; and that as a college athlete he had gained some notion of the psychology of men engaged in mass action while on the football field. As for his concern with the ambiguities of fear and of courage, coward-ice and heroism, and the problem of the relation of the individual to the group and to God, these were a part of his religious and family back-ground, while the deeper insights were available to him (as they are to each of us) through a ruthless plunging into the dark depths of his own heart and mind. More than this, we know truly that although the fight-ing had ceased six years before Crane's birth, the moral climate which it created formed the only climate Crane was ever to know. Having been born in the world which the war had brought into being, much of his activity was a search for ways of living within it with meaningful intensity. Historically wars and revolutions form the background for the high periods of the novel, and civil wars, Hemingway has written, are the best wars for the writer. To which we would add, yes, because they have a way of continuing long after wars between nations are resolved; because, with the combatants being the same people, civil wars are never really won; and because their most devastating engagements are fought within the individual human heart.

For all our efforts to forget it, the Civil War was the great shap-ing event not only of our political and economic life, but following Crane, of our twentieth-century fiction. It was the agency through which many of the conflicting elements within the old republic were brought to maximum tension, leaving us a nation fully aware of the continental character of our destiny, preparing the emergence of our predominantly industrial economy and our increasingly urban way of life, and transforming us from a nation consisting of two major regions which could pretend to a unity of values despite their basic split over fundamental issues, to one which was now consciously divided. To put it drastically, if war, as Clausewitz insisted, is the continuation of politics by other means, it requires little imagination to see American life since the abandonment of the Reconstruction as an abrupt reversal of that formula: the continuation of the Civil War by means other than arms.

In this sense the conflict has not only gone unresolved, but the line between civil war and civil peace has become so blurred as to require of the sensitive man a questioning attitude toward every aspect of the nation's self-image. Stephen Crane, in his time, was such a man.

The America into which Crane was born was one of mirrorlike reversals in which the victors were the defeated and the defeated the victors; with the South, its memory frozen at the fixed moment of its surrender, carrying its aggression to the North in the form of guerrilla politics, and with the North, compromising as it went, retreating swiftly into the vast expanse of its new industrial development, eager to lose any memory traces of those values for which it had gone to war. Mark Twain had attacked this postwar society, infamous for its carpetbaggers, its Hayes-Tilden Compromise, its looting of the nation's resources during the Grant administrations, in "The Man That Corrupted Hadleyburg," and Henry James depicted the inversion of its moral values in *The Bostonians* and was stimulated by it to those subtleties of moral perception which inform his major fiction.

For all of this, however, Twain's bitter satire was taken for comedy and the best of James was left unread. Despite the prosperity and apparent openness and freedom of the society, it was as though a rigid national censorship had been imposed—and not by an apparatus set up in Washington, but within the center of the American mind. Now there was much of which Americans were morally aware but little which they wished to confront in literature, and the compelling of such confrontation was the challenge flung down to Crane by history.

Let us not forget, then, that while the setting of *The Red Badge* is the Civil War, its issues are drawn from the lax society of the eighteen-eighties and nineties, a society which Crane viewed as hostile to those who would achieve manhood and moral identity, whose tendency toward moral evasion he set out to overcome with his technique of understatement, and whose capacity for reality and moral responsibility he sought to ensnare through the realistic poetry of his diction.

Thus, in *The Red Badge* social reality is filtered through the sensibility of a young Northern soldier who is only vaguely aware of the larger issues of the war, and we note that for all the complex use of the symbolic connotations of blackness, only one Negro, a dancing teamster, appears throughout the novel. The reader is left to fill in the understated background, to re-create those matters of which the hero, Henry Fleming, is too young, too self-centered and too concerned with the more immediate problems of courage, honor and self-preservation to be aware. This leaves the real test of moral courage as much a challenge to the reader as to the hero; he must decide for himself whether or not to confront the public issues evoked by Henry's private ordeal. *The Red Badge* is a novel about a lonely individual's struggle for self-definition, written for lonely individualists, and its style, which no longer speaks in terms of the traditional American rhetoric, implies a deep skepticism as to the possibility of the old American ideals being revived by a people who had failed to live up to them after having paid so much to defend them in hardship and blood. Here in place of the conventional plot—which implies the public validity of private experiences—we find a series of vividly impressionistic episodes that convey the discontinuity of feeling and perception of one caught up in a vast impersonal action, and a concentration upon the psychology of one who seeks first to secede from society and then to live in it with honor and courage.

Indeed, for a novel supposedly about the war, *The Red Badge* is intensely concerned with invasion of the private life, a theme announced when the men encounter the body of their first dead soldier, whose shoe soles, "worn to the thinness of writing paper," strike Henry as evidence of a betrayal by fate which in death had exposed to the dead Confederate's enemies "that poverty which in life he had perhaps concealed from his friends." But war is nothing if not an invasion of privacy, and so is death (the "invulnerable" dead man forces his way between the men as they open ranks to avoid him), and society more so. For society, even when reduced to a few companions, invades personality and demands of the individual an almost impossible consistency while guaranteeing the individual hardly anything. Or so it seems to the naïve Henry, much of whose anguish springs from the fear that his friends will discover that the wound which he received from the rifle butt of another frightened soldier is not the red badge of courage they assume but a badge of shame. Thus the Tattered Soldier's questions as to the circumstance of his injury (really questions as to his moral identity) fill Henry with fear and hostility, and he regards them as

> the assertion of a society that probed pitilessly at secrets until all is apparent. . . . His late companion's chance persistency made him feel that he could not keep his crime [of malingering] concealed in his bosom. It was sure to be brought plain by one of those arrows which cloud the air and are constantly pricking, discovering, proclaiming those things which are willed to be forever hidden. He admitted that he could not defend himself against this agency. It was not within the power of vigilance. . . .

In time Henry learns to act with honor and courage and to perceive something of what it means to be a man, but this perception depends upon the individual fates of those who make up his immediate group, upon the death of Jim Conklin, the most mature and responsible of the men, and upon the Loud Soldier's attainment of maturity and inner self-confidence. But the cost of perception is primarily personal, and for Henry it depends upon the experience of the moral discomfort which follows the crimes of malingering and assuming a phony identity, and the further crime of allowing the voice of conscience, here symbolized by the Tattered Soldier, to wander off and die. Later he acquits himself bravely and comes to feel that he has attained

> a quiet manhood, non-assertive but of sturdy and strong blood. He knew that he would no more quail before his guides wherever they should point. He had been to touch the great death, and found that, after all, it was but the great death. He was a man.

Obviously although Henry has been initiated into the battle of life, he has by no means finished with illusion—but that, too, is part of the human condition.

That *The Red Badge* was widely read during Crane's own time was a triumph of his art, but the real mystery lay not in his re-creation of the simpler aspects of battle: the corpses, the wounds, the sound of rifle fire, the panic and high elation of combat; the real mystery lay in the courage out of which one so young could face up to the truth which so many Americans were resisting with a noisy clamor of optimism and with frantic gestures of materialistic denial. War, the jungle and hostile Nature became Crane's underlying metaphors for the human drama and the basic situations in which the individual's capacity for moral and physical courage were put to their most meaningful testing.

And so with "The Open Boat." In January 1897, Crane was one of four men who spent thirty hours in a ten-foot dinghy after their ship, bound on a gun-running expedition to Cuba, developed a leak and sank. It was from this experience that Crane shaped what is considered his most perfect short story. When "The Open Boat" is compared with the report which Crane wrote for the New York *Press*, we can see that it keeps to the order of events as they actually occurred, but such is the power of Crane's shaping vision that the reader is made to *experience* the events as a complete, dynamic, symbolic action. We become one with the men in the boat, who pit their skill and courage against the raging sea, living in their hope and despair and sharing the companion-ship won within the capricious hand of fate. Under the shaping grace of Crane's imagination the actual event is reduced to significant form, with each wave and gust of wind, each intonation of voice and gesture of limb combining toward a single effect of meaning.

And as with most of Crane's fiction, the point at issue is the cost of moral perception, of achieving an informed sense of life, in a universe which is essentially hostile to man and in which skill and courage and loyalty are virtues which help in the struggle but by no means exempt us from the necessary plunge into the storm-sea-war of experience. For it is thus and thus only that humanity is won, and often the best are destroyed in the trial—as with Higgins, the oiler, whose skill and gener-osity have helped save the men from the sea but who in the end lies dead upon the shore. Through their immersion into the raging sea of life, and through Higgins's sacrificial death, the survivors are initiated into a personal knowledge of the human condition—and "when the wind brought the sound of the great sea's voice to the men on the shore . . . they felt that they could be interpreters."

In his essay on storytelling, Mark Twain informs us that the humor-ous story is especially American and that it depends for its effect upon the manner of its telling . . . [it] is told gravely; the teller doing his best to conceal the fact that he even dimly suspects that there is anything funny about it. . . .

It is this same noncommittal manner which Stephen Crane brings to the depiction of events which are far from humorous, and while he is seldom comic in the manner of Twain, the method gives his fiction an endless complexity of meaning, and among those matters of which his style pretends unawareness are the social and historical references of his stories. Here, too, the effect depends upon a collaboration between the teller, who conceals the range of his intention, and the listener, who must pit his sense of reality against the enigmatic order of the narrated events—as in "The Bride Comes to Yellow Sky," a story which dances over its apparent terrain with such a tight choreography of ironic reversals that the reader must be extremely light-footed lest he fall out of the pattern of the dance.

Scratchy Wilson, the drunken badman of deadly marksmanship, terrorizes the town and appears to have Jack Potter at his mercy—until the unarmed marshal's announcement of his marriage unnerves him. For Scratchy, who is the last of a local gang, the news is like a "glimpse of another world," and he sees the bride as foreshadowing the end of his way of life. The point, it would seem, is that history has played a joke on Scratchy; the man with the gun is defeated by the unarmed man who has embraced those civilized values symbolized by marriage. But is this all? Doesn't the story pivot at this point and return to the westward-moving train of its beginning?

When the marshal faces the badman's pistol it is clear that despite being unarmed he reacts out of an old habit of courage; he has fought Scratchy many times and even shot him once—in the leg (the red-topped boots with gilded imprints "of the kind beloved in winter by little sledding boys on the hillsides of New England" rob Scratchy of much of his menace for the contemporary reader). But the marshal is also sustained by a vision of the Pullman car from which he and his bride have just departed. He sees in its sea-green velvet, its glass and its gleaming surfaces of silver, brass and darkly brilliant wood "all the glory of marriage, the environment of [his] new estate," and it is this vision, when conveyed to Scratchy, which defeats the badman.

But here we have a double reversal. Because for all of Scratchy's simplemindedness, his moment of defeat is also one of perception; he has learned where he is. While in his moment of unarmed triumph the marshal is even more unarmed than he knows; for he is unaware that his new estate has its own complications—even though he has already been subjected to them. In the actual Pullman car the Negro porter has played with him and his bride much as the gunman has played with the town (and as Crane plays with the reader's susceptibilities), and they have been bullied

> with skill in ways that did not make it exactly plain to them that they were bullied. He [the porter] subtly used all the manners of the most unconquerable kinds of snobbery. He oppressed them; but of his oppression they had small knowledge, and they speedily forgot that infrequently a number of travelers covered them with stares of derisive enjoyment.

And again, in the dining car the waiter's patronage had been so entwined with deference that when they returned to their coach their faces revealed "a sense of escape."

"Historically," we are told, "there was supposed to be something infinitely humorous in their situation…" And there is indeed something humorous in their situation which is limited neither to the circumstances of their middle-aged wedlock nor to their provincial discomfort in the Pullman car; there is the humor arising from their *historical* situation. For in face of the complexities of American civilization represented by the bullying yet patronizing Negro servants, the marshal is no less a "child of the earlier plains" than Scratchy Wilson. The Stephen Crane who wrote "The Bride" was essentially the same moral man who wrote the social protest of *Maggie*, only he has learned to hide his perceptions behind a sardonic smile. Still, the form of the story is at one with its meaning: the necessity for vigilance in confronting historical change is unending, and living with American change is much like Crane's description of keeping a small boat afloat in an angry sea, where "after successfully surmounting one wave you discover that there is another behind it just as important and just as nervously anxious to do something effective in the way of swamping boats." A similar vigilance is required when reading his fiction.

Perhaps at the root of our American fascination with the humorous story lies the awareness that if we don't know *where* we are, we have little chance of knowing *who* we are, that if we confuse the *time* we confuse the *place*; and that when we confuse these we endanger our humanity, both physically and morally. "Any room," writes Crane in "The Blue Hotel," "can present a tragic front; any room be comic." Thus men determine their own social weather, and human fate is a creation of human confusion.

The background of "The Blue Hotel" is that same confusion of time and place underlying "The Bride," and the Swede's failure to understand the rapidity of American historical change and its effect upon social relationships and personality is his undoing. Frightened and believing himself to be in a West that has long since passed, he evokes the violence which he associates with it out of the very intensity of his illusion. Arriving at a place where he believes he is to be killed, he forces a fight from men who are usually peaceful, wins it, then goes, full of his victory, to a peaceful barroom and there, confused perhaps by his ten years of hiding the reality of the human form (he is a tailor), as well as by drinking, he picks on the man who appears least likely to defend himself and is killed. No other Crane fiction—except, perhaps, "The Monster"—expresses such a violence of disgust with man and his condition, and one feels behind the noncommittal mask of the prose a conviction that man exists in the universe ever at the mercy of a capricious fate, a hostile nature, an indifferent and unjust god—*and* his own misconceptions.

And yet, for all the self-destructive actions of the Swede, the Easterner sees his death as the corporate sin of society. Society is responsible to itself *for* itself; the death is thus a failure of social charity. It is the same failure of social charity which characterizes "The Monster." Here Crane presents the cost of two acts of human loyalty and courage when they occur in a small, smug Northern town. Henry Johnson's self-sacrificial act, which destroys his face and his mind, is repaid first with applause and then with demands for his death or banishment. Dr. Trescott's loyalty to his oath as physician and to the man who has saved his son's life costs him his practice, his friends and ultimately his social

276 | The Story About the Story II

identity. In short, "The Monster" places us in an atmosphere like that of post–Civil War America, and there is no question as to the Negro's part in it, nor to the fact that the issues go much deeper than the question of race. Indeed, the work is so fresh that the daily papers tell us all we need to know of its background and the timeliness of its implications.

As for Crane, the conscious artist, "The Monster" reminds us that he not only anticipated many of the techniques and themes of Hemingway, but that he also stands as the link between the Twain of *Pudd'nhead Wilson* and *Huckleberry Finn* and the Faulkner of *The Sound and the Fury*. The point is not simply that in *The Sound and the Fury*, as in Crane's work, a young boy is warned against "projecking" with flowers, or that Benjy is as much a "monster" as Henry Johnson, or Henry as much an idiot as Benjy, or that their communities are more monstrous than either, or that to touch either is considered a test of courage by the small fry, or even that both suffer when young white girls are frightened by them. The important point is that between Twain and the emergence of the driving honesty and social responsibility of Faulkner, no artist of Crane's caliber looked so steadily at the wholeness of American life and discovered such far-reaching symbolic equivalents for its unceasing state of civil war. Crane's work remains fresh today because he was a great artist, but perhaps he became a great artist because under conditions of pressure and panic he stuck to his guns.

Essay on Stephen Crane and *The Red Badge of Courage*

JOSEPH CONRAD

One of the most enduring memories of my literary life is the sensation produced by the appearance in 1895 of Crane's "Red Badge of Courage" in a small volume belonging to Mr. Heinemann's Pioneer Series of Modern Fiction—very modern fiction of that time, and upon the whole not devoid of merit. I have an idea the series was meant to give us shocks, and as far as my recollection goes there were, to use a term made familiar to all by another war, no "duds" in that small and lively bombardment. But Crane's work detonated on the mild din of that attack on our literary sensibilities with the impact and force of a twelve-inch shell charged with a very high explosive. Unexpected it fell amongst us; and its fall was followed by a great outcry.

Not of consternation, however. The energy of that projectile hurt nothing and no one (such was its good fortune), and delighted a good many. It delighted soldiers, men of letters, men in the street; it was welcomed by all lovers of personal expression as a genuine revelation, satisfying the curiosity of a world in which war and love have been subjects of song and story ever since the beginning of articulate speech.

Here we had an artist, a man not of experience but a man inspired, a seer with a gift for rendering the significant on the surface of things and with an incomparable insight into primitive emotions, who, in order to give us the image of war, had looked profoundly into his own breast. We welcomed him. As if the whole vocabulary of praise had been blown up sky-high by this missile from across the Atlantic, a rain of words descended on our heads, words well or ill chosen, chunks of pedantic praise and warm appreciation, clever words, and words of real understanding, platitudes, and felicities of criticism, but all as sincere in their response as the striking piece of work which set so many critical pens scurrying over the paper.

One of the most interesting, if not the most valuable, of printed criticisms was perhaps that of Mr. George Wyndham, soldier, man of the world, and in a sense a man of letters. He went into the whole question of war literature, at any rate during the nineteenth century, evoking comparisons with the *Mémoires* of General Marbot and the famous *Diary of a Cavalry Officer* as records of a personal experience. He rendered justice to the interest of what soldiers themselves could tell us, but confessed that to gratify the curiosity of the potential combatant who lurks in most men as to the picturesque aspects and emotional reactions of a battle we must go to the artist with his Heaven-given faculty of words at the service of his divination as to what the truth of things is and must be. He comes to the conclusion that:

"Mr. Crane has contrived a masterpiece."

"Contrived"—that word of disparaging sound is the last word I would have used in connection with any piece of work by Stephen Crane, who in his art (as indeed in his private life) was the least "contriving" of men. But as to "masterpiece," there is no doubt that "The Red Badge of Courage" is that, if only because of the marvellous accord of the vivid impressionistic description of action on that woodland battlefield, and the imaged style of the analysis of the emotions in the inward moral struggle going on in the breast of one individual—the Young Soldier of the book, the protagonist of the monodrama presented to us in an effortless succession of graphic and coloured phrases.

Stephen Crane places his Young Soldier in an untried regiment. And this is well contrived—if any contrivance there be in a spontaneous piece of work which seems to spurt and flow like a tapped stream from the depths of the writer's being. In order that the revelation should be complete, the Young Soldier has to be deprived of the moral support which he would have found in a tried body of men matured in achievement to the consciousness of its worth. His regiment had been tried by nothing but days of waiting for the order to move; so many days that it and the Youth within it have come to think of themselves as merely "a part of a vast blue demonstration." The army had been lying camped near a river, idle and fretting, till the moment when Stephen Crane lays hold of it at dawn with masterly simplicity: "The cold passed reluctantly from the earth. . . ." These are the first words of the war book which was to give him his crumb of fame.

The whole of that opening paragraph is wonderful in the homely dignity of the indicated lines of the landscape, and the shivering awakening of the army at the break of the day before the battle. In the next, with a most effective change to racy colloquialism of narrative, the action which motivates, sustains and feeds the inner drama forming the subject of the book, begins with the Tall Soldier going down to the river to wash his shirt. He returns waving his garment above his head. He had heard at fifth-hand from somebody that the army is going to move to-morrow. The only immediate effect of this piece of news is that a Negro teamster, who had been dancing a jig on a wooden box in a ring of laughing soldiers, finds himself suddenly deserted. He sits down mournfully. For the rest, the Tall Soldier's excitement is met by blank disbelief, profane grumbling, an invincible incredulity. But the regiment is somehow sobered. One feels it, though no symptoms can be noticed. It does not know what a battle is, neither does the Young Soldier. He retires from the babbling throng into what seems a rather comfortable dugout and lies down with his hands over his eyes to think. Thus the drama begins.

He perceives suddenly that he had looked upon wars as historical phenomenons of the past. He had never believed in war in his own country. It had been a sort of play affair. He had been drilled, inspected, marched for months, till he has despaired "of ever seeing a Greek-like struggle. Such were no more. Men were better or more timid. Secular and religious education had effaced the throat-grappling instinct, or else firm finance held in check the passions."

Very modern this touch. We can remember thoughts like these round about the year 1914. That Young Soldier is representative of mankind in more ways than one, and first of all in his ignorance. His regiment had listened to the tales of veterans, "tales of gray bewhiskered hordes chewing tobacco with unspeakable valour and sweeping along like the Huns." Still, he cannot put his faith in veterans' tales. Recruits were their prey. They talked of blood, fire, and sudden death, but much of it might have been lies. They were in no wise to be trusted. And the question arises before him whether he will or will not "run from a battle"? He does not know. He cannot know. A little panic fear enters his mind. He jumps up and asks himself aloud, "Good Lord, what's the matter with me?" This is the first time his words are quoted, on this day before the battle. He dreads not danger, but fear itself. He stands before the unknown. He would like to prove to himself by some reasoning process that he will not "run from the battle." And in his unblooded regiment he can find no help. He is alone with the problem of courage.

In this he stands for the symbol of all untried men.

Some critics have estimated him a morbid case. I cannot agree to that. The abnormal cases are of the extremes; of those who crumple up at the first sight of danger, and of those of whom their fellows say "He doesn't know what fear is." Neither will I forget the rare favourites of the gods whose fiery spirit is only soothed by the fury and clamour of a battle. Of such was General Picton of Peninsular fame. But the lot of the mass of mankind is to know fear, the decent fear of disgrace. Of such is the Young Soldier of "The Red Badge of Courage." He only seems exceptional because he has got inside of him Stephen Crane's imagination, and is presented to us with the insight and the power of expression of an artist whom a just and severe critic, on a review of all his work, has called the foremost impressionist of his time; as Sterne was the greatest impressionist, but in a different way, of his age.

This is a generalized, fundamental judgment. More superficially both Zola's "La Débâcle" and Tolstoi's "War and Peace" were mentioned by critics in connection with Crane's war book. But Zola's main concern was with the downfall of the imperial régime he fancied he was portraying; and in Tolstoi's book the subtle presentation of Rostov's squadron under fire for the first time is a mere episode lost in a mass of other matter, like a handful of pebbles in a heap of sand. I could not see the relevancy. Crane was concerned with elemental truth only; and in any case I think that as an artist he is non-comparable. He dealt with what is enduring, and was the most detached of men.

That is why his book is short. Not quite two hundred pages. Gems are small. This monodrama, which happy inspiration or unerring instinct has led him to put before us in narrative form, is contained between the opening words I have already quoted and a phrase on page 194 of the English edition, which runs: "He had been to touch the great death, and found that, after all, it was but the great death. He was a man."

On these words the action ends. We are only given one glimpse of the victorious army at dusk, under the falling rain, "a procession of weary soldiers became a bedraggled train, despondent and muttering, marching with churning effort in a trough of liquid brown mud under a low wretched sky . . . ," while the last ray of the sun falls on the river through a break in the leaden clouds.

This war book, so virile and so full of gentle sympathy, in which not a single declamatory sentiment defaces the genuine verbal felicity, welding analysis and description in a continuous fascination of individual style, had been hailed by the critics as the herald of a brilliant career. Crane himself very seldom alluded to it, and always with a wistful smile. Perhaps he was conscious that, like the mortally wounded Tall Soldier of his book, who, snatching at the air, staggers out into a field to meet his appointed death on the first day of battle—while the terrified Youth and the kind Tattered Soldier stand by silent, watching with awe "these ceremonies at the place of meeting"—it was his fate, too, to fall early in the fray.

2007–2003

FRANCISCO GOLDMAN

The first Roberto Bolaño novel I read was *Estrella distante*. It was Aura's copy and we were at the beach in Mazunte, and I read it pretty much in one sitting, with a few breaks to go in the water. She was a huge Bolaño fan. Bolaño had died about six months before. We'd started going out shortly after, and I remember that she'd told me that the day he died, all the bars of the Condesa had been filled with people crying, but what she really meant was that she'd been crying with her friend Senén, who'd studied literature with her at the Universidad Nacional Autónoma de México (UNAM) and who was now a bartender. He tended bar in the same place, come to think of it, that Bolaño's friend and somewhat kindred spirit, Horacio Castellanos Moya, always drank at. Senén, like Aura, always wanted to talk about literature, novels especially. I drank there too and was friends with both young Senén and not-so-young Horacio, who'd also become good friends with each other long before I met Aura. Horacio, especially when he was drunk, used to stand at the bar telling the most scarifying stories about the war in Salvador; I remember one about a very gross but darkly hilarious game that guerrillas played with a corpse. Senén and Horacio often spoke about Bolaño and his books too.

But apart from a few short stories, I didn't get around to reading him until that day at Mazunte. That's the same beach where, four years later, Aura broke her neck in the waves; she died twenty-four hours later in Mexico City. It's already harder for me to write these words than I'd thought it was going to be. During our honeymoon, in the summer of 2005, at another Mexican beach, I read *2666*. Now Bolaño and his writing are all mixed up in my mind and emotions with death, and with Aura, her death, and I guess they always will be.

Bolaño was more than this to us, but also this: he wrote about the worlds we'd lived in. For Aura, that was the UNAM (especially, of course, the opening section of *Los Detectives Salvajes* and all of *Amuleto*) and the splendid-ludicrous, inexhaustible, gritty Mexico City of youth; it was the romance of literature, of the middle-class intelligentsia, especially of Aura's parents' generation, who were young during the long era of Latin American revolutionary fervour, violence, and disillusionment. "[V]iolence, real violence, is unavoidable, at least for those of us who were born in Latin America during the fifties and were about twenty years old at the time of Salvador Allende's death," says the narrator of Bolaño's story "Mauricio ('The Eye') Silva." For me, twenty years older than Aura, a little younger than her parents, that violence and disillusionment was my experience too; not the fervour of Chile and Argentina in the 1960s and 1970s, but the revolutionary era's depressing second act, the even more brutal and often psychotic wars of Central America in the 1980s, which pretty much consumed my own twenties and early thirties.

Bolaño drew from reality in his fiction, and on his own life, yet his fiction is not really realist. His fiction pointed away from reality, and certainly away from mundane political or moral interpretations of reality, toward something else—poetry, open-endedness, a kind of philosophical and tragi-comic shock; his fiction always opens "new paths," as Bolaño said of Borges's writing. And it is partly this mysterious radical quality, sometimes even a quality of epic parable (someone in *2666*, Amalfitano maybe, says something along the lines that if you could solve the mystery of the murders of the women in Santa Teresa, you'd decipher the meaning of evil in our time) that makes his writing seem more kin to the spirit of Borges and even Kafka than to other Latin American writers he also admired, such as Lezama, Onetti, Cortázar, or Bioy.

Aura wrote an essay about Bolaño and Borges that she published in *Words Without Borders*, and it opened like this:

During their lifetimes, Jorge Luis Borges and Roberto Bolaño struggled against vanity and all things pretentious, aspirational, ordinary, and obliging. They are peculiar cases in literature, ones that the literary machine itself seems to reject. They were not bestsellers. During a substantial part of their lives, they existed either under the shadow of public rejection, or in the clandestinity of aesthetic infringement. The relationship they sustained with "their time" and the writers of their time was complex and peppered with barbs. Certainly, what they understood as literature had little to do with the desire to appease any aesthetics (social, moral, political, philosophical) other than their own. Their relationship with literature was almost sacred. They believed in little else and were consecrated to her alone, as if literature were (perhaps because it is) a matter of life and death.

Aura and her UNAM friends, especially, were possessive about Bolaño: he was *their* writer. Her friend Jorge Volpi got to know Bolaño, and he told him once, thinking especially of Aura, about his passionate young readers in Mexico City, and Bolaño laughed ruefully and said, "That's all I need, to become a cult writer at the UNAM." When Bolaño began to become the whole world's writer; when he was becoming—let's accept it, he did, regardless of how wonderful that was—New York literary fashion's writer of the moment, it was as if something was being torn away from Aura. It was sort of cute, watching her bewilderment. She even tried to pretend, for a while, that she no longer really liked Bolaño, but of course that wasn't true, and one of the last things she published was a review of *Amuleto*, along with Aira's *How I Became a Nun*, for the *Boston Review*.

For several months after Aura's death I couldn't read fiction, but then, when finally I could, pretty much the first thing I really yearned to read were the passages about Archimboldi's lover Ingeborg's death in the last book of *2666*, "The Part about Archimboldi." Like I've said, I read the novel on our week-long honeymoon on the Pacific. I nearly finished it; I tore through it, astounded and enthralled, and I am usually a slow reader (by comparison, *Los Detectives Salvajes* took me about a month). Aura had brought two novels with her, *Humboldt's Gift*, and

Madame Bovary in French. I suppose this makes it sound as if all we did on our honeymoon is read, which isn't really true, though so what if it was. It was a kind of eco-resort, there was lots of time . . . to visit the baby turtle hatchery and paddle canoes in the lagoon, and there was no electricity, so you really had to read by day. At night in the lamp-lit restaurant we drank margaritas and played Scrabble, and she always won. She finished her two novels pretty quickly and after that, every time I put *2666* down to go in the water or to the bathroom, I'd come back and find her reading it, and I'd say, "Give that back to me," and she'd plead, "Oh please, just let me finish this chapter!"

During the months I wasn't reading fiction—eventually I plunged into the canon of grief books, and read poetry—I kept thinking back to the scene of Ingeborg's death in *2666*, and though my memory of the scene wasn't really inaccurate, I imagined it taking up many more pages than it actually does, and imagined its imagery as more explicitly mystical, much less casually revealed, than it is. I recalled it as if it were a Rilke poem. Of course *2666* is one of the most Thanatos-haunted novels of all time (and also, I really think, one of the greatest, period). The Spanish novelist and critic Eduardo Lago described it in a review as a book written in a race against death, in which you can feel death cheering the writer on. It's a great book of grief, of multiple griefs, at times encyclopedic, and one of the lives the writer is grieving—the one life that contains all the book's blazing lives—is his own, because he knew he was dying, and that this was his last book, and apparently he knew that it was going to kill him, and on nearly every page of the book we see him taking death-defying narrative risks.

The psychoanalyst Darien Leader asks, of literature, theatre, cinema, and other arts, "Could their very existence be linked to the human necessity to mourn? . . . they have created something 'out of chaos and destruction' . . . and help bring out the universal nature of what the mourner feels, but not in the sense that they will all feel the same thing."

Ingeborg knows she is going to die. This is the scene that expanded so vividly in my memory, and that when I was finally ready to read fiction again, I knew I had to reread, over and over again. On a wintry night, coughing blood, Ingeborg vanishes from their cabin in the mountains, headed into the ravines where she and their rustic host once successfully hid his wife's murdered corpse. Finally Archimboldi finds her:

> Ingeborg's face was cold as ice. He kissed her cheeks until she slipped from his embrace . . . The sky was full of stars, many more than could be seen at night in Kempten, and many, many more than it was possible to see on the clearest night in Cologne. "It's a very pretty sky, darling," said Archimboldi, then he tried to take her hand and drag her back to the village but Ingeborg clung to a tree branch, as if they were playing, and wouldn't go. "Do you realize where we are, Hans?" she asked, laughing with a laugh that seemed to Archimboldi like a cascade of ice.

She tells him, "We're in a place surrounded by the past. All these stars . . ." and she draws his attention to the stars.

> "All this light is dead," said Ingeborg. "All this light was emitted thousands and millions of years ago. It's the past, do you see? When these stars cast their light, we didn't exist, life on Earth didn't exist, even Earth didn't exist. This light was cast a long time ago. It's the past, we're surrounded by the past, everything that no longer exists or exists only in memory or guesswork is there now, above us, shining on the mountains and the snow and we can't do anything to stop it."

After Ingeborg dies, Archimboldi drops from sight for a very long time.

Bolaño liked to say, and write, that the novel could contain every kind of poem. The scene of Ingeborg and the stars is—along with Henry King's "Exequy on his Wife"—the grief poem I reread the most. I think I'll just leave it at that.

Reflections on Willa Cather

KATHERINE ANNE PORTER

I never knew her at all, nor anyone who did know her; do not to this day. When I was a young writer in New York I knew she was there, and sometimes wished that by some charming chance I might meet up with her; but I never did, and it did not occur to me to seek her out. I had never felt that my condition of beginning authorship gave me a natural claim on the attention of writers I admired, such as Henry James and W. B. Yeats. Some proper instinct told me that all of any importance they had to say to me was in their printed pages, mine to use as I could. Still it would have been nice to have seen them, just to remember how they looked. There are three or four great ones, gone now, that I feel, too late, I should not have missed. Willa Cather was one of them.

There exist large numbers of critical estimates of her work, appreciations; perhaps even a memoir or two, giving glimpses of her personal history—I have never read one. She was not, in the popular crutch-word to describe almost any kind of sensation, "exciting"; so far as I know, nobody, not even one of the Freudian school of critics, ever sat up nights with a textbook in one hand and her works in the other, reading between the lines to discover how much sexual autobiography could be mined out of her stories. I remember only one photograph—Steichen's—made in middle life, showing a plain smiling woman, her arms crossed easily over a girl scout sort of white blouse, with a ragged part in her hair. She seemed, as the French say, "well seated" and not very outgoing. Even the earnestly amiable, finely shaped eyes, the left one faintly askew, were in some mysterious way not expressive, lacking as they did altogether that look of strangeness which a strange vision is supposed to give to the eye of any real artist, and very often does. One doesn't have to be a genius absolutely to get this look, it is often quite enough merely to believe one is a genius; and to have had the wild vision only once is enough—the afterlight stays, even if, in such case, it is phosphorescence instead of living fire.

Well, Miss Cather looks awfully like somebody's big sister, or maiden aunt, both of which she was. No genius ever looked less like one, according to the romantic popular view, unless it was her idol, Flaubert, whose photographs could pass easily for those of any paunchy country squire indifferent to his appearance. Like him, none of her genius was in her looks, only in her works. Flaubert was a good son, adoring uncle of a niece, devoted to his friends, contemptuous of the mediocre, obstinate in his preferences, fiercely jealous of his privacy, unyielding to the death in his literary principles and not in the slightest concerned with what was fashionable. No wonder she loved him. She had been rebuffed a little at first, not by his astronomical standards in art—none could be too high for her—but by a certain coldness of heart in him. She soon got over that; it became for her only another facet of his nobility of mind.

Very early she had learned to reverence that indispensable faculty of aspiration of the human mind toward perfection called, in morals and the arts, nobility. She was born to the idea and brought up in it: first in a comfortable farmhouse in Virginia, and later, the eldest of seven children, in a little crowded ranch house in Nebraska. She had, as many American country people did have in those times and places, literate parents and grandparents, soundly educated and deeply read, educated, if not always at schools, always at their own firesides. Two such, her grandmothers, taught her from her infancy. Her sister, Mrs. Auld, in Palo Alto, California, told it like this:

"She mothered us all, took care of us, and there was a lot to do in such a big family. She learned Greek and Latin from our grandmothers before she ever got to go to school. She used to go, after we lived in Red Cloud, to read Latin and Greek with a little old man who kept a general store down the road. In the evenings for entertainment—there was nowhere to go, you know, almost nothing to see or hear—she enter- tained us, it was good as a theater for us! She told us long stories, some she made up herself, and some were her versions of legends and fairy tales she had read; she taught us Greek mythology this way, Homer, and tales from the Old Testament. We were all story tellers," said her sister, "all of us wanted to be the one to tell the stories, but she was the one who told them. And we loved to listen all of us to her, when maybe we would not have listened to each other."

She was not the first nor the last American writer to be formed in this system of home education; at one time it was the customary educa- tion for daughters, many of them never got to school at all or expected to; but they were capable of educating their grandchildren, as this little history shows. To her last day Willa Cather was the true child of her plain-living, provincial farming people, with their aristocratic ways of feeling and thinking; poor, but not poverty-stricken for a moment; rock-based in character, a character shaped in an old school of good manners, good morals, and the unchallenged assumption that classic culture was their birthright; the belief that knowledge of great art and great thought was a good in itself not to be missed for anything; she subscribed to it all with her whole heart, and in herself there was the vein of iron she had inherited from a long line of people who had helped to break wildernesses and to found a new nation in such faiths. When you think of the whole unbelievable history, how did anything like this survive? Yet it did, and this life is one of the proofs.

I have not much interest in anyone's personal history after the tenth year, not even my own. Whatever one was going to be was all prepared for before that. The rest is merely confirmation, extension, develop- ment. Childhood is the fiery furnace in which we are melted down to essentials and that essential shaped for good. While I have been reading again Willa Cather's essays and occasional papers, and thinking about her, I remembered a sentence from the diaries of Anne Frank, who died in the concentration camp in Bergen-Belsen just before she was sixteen years old. At less than fifteen, she wrote: "I have had a lot of sorrow, but who hasn't, at my age?"

In Miss Cather's superb little essay on Katherine Mansfield, she speaks of childhood and family life: "I doubt whether any contemporary

writer has made one feel more keenly the many kinds of personal relations which exist in an everyday 'happy family' who are merely going
on with their daily lives, with no crises or shocks or bewildering complications. . . . Yet every individual in that household (even the children)
is clinging passionately to his individual soul, is in terror of losing it
in the general family flavor . . . the mere struggle to have anything of
one's own, to be oneself at all, creates an element of strain which keeps
everybody almost at breaking point.

" . . . Even in harmonious families there is this double life . . . the
one we can observe in our neighbor's household, and, underneath,
another—secret and passionate and intense—which is the real life that
stamps the faces and gives character to the voices of our friends. Always
in his mind each member is escaping, running away, trying to break
the net which circumstances and his own affections have woven about
him. One realizes that human relationships are the tragic necessity of
human life; that they can never be wholly satisfactory, that every ego
is half the time greedily seeking them, and half the time pulling away
from them."

This is masterly and water-clear and autobiography enough for me:
my mind goes with tenderness to the lonely slow-moving girl who happened to be an artist coming back from reading Latin and Greek with the
old storekeeper, helping with the housework, then sitting by the fireplace
to talk down an assertive brood of brothers and sisters, practicing her art
on them, refusing to be lost among them—the longest-winged one who
would fly free at last.

I am not much given to reading about authors, or not until I have read
what they have to say for themselves. I found Willa Cather's books
for myself, early, and felt no need for intermediaries between me and
them. My reading went on for a good many years, one by one as they
appeared: *O Pioneers!*; *The Song of the Lark*; *My Ántonia*; *Youth and the
Bright Medusa*; *Death Comes for the Archbishop*; *Obscure Destinies*; just
these, and no others, I do not know why, and never anything since, until
I read her notebooks about two years ago. Those early readings began in
Texas, just before World War I, before ever I left home; they ended in
Paris, twenty years later, after the longest kind of journey.

With her first book I was reading also Henry James, W. B. Yeats, Joseph Conrad, my introduction to "modern" literature, for I was brought up on solid reading, too, well aged. About the same time I read Gertrude Stein's *Tender Buttons*, for sale at a little bookshop with a shoe-shine stand outside; inside you could find magazines, books, newspapers in half-a-dozen languages, avant-garde and radical and experimental; this in a Texas coast town of less than ten thousand population but very polyglot and full of world travelers. I could make little headway with Miss Stein beyond the title. It was plain that she meant "tender buds" and I wondered why she did not say so. It was the beginning of my quarrel with a certain school of "modern" writing in which poverty of feeling and idea were disguised, but not well enough, in tricky techniques and disordered syntax. A year or two after *Tender Buttons* I was reading Joyce's *Dubliners*, and maybe only a young beginning writer of that time, with some preparation of mind by the great literature of the past, could know what a revelation that small collection of matchless stories could be. It was not a shock, but a revelation, a further unfolding of the deep world of the imagination. I had never heard of Joyce. By the pure chance of my roving curiosity, I picked up a copy of the book at that little shoeshine bookstore. It was a great day.

By the time I reached Paris, I had done my long apprenticeship, published a small book of my own, and had gone like a house afire through everything "new" that word meant something peculiar to the times—absolutely everything "new"—that was being published; also in music; also painting. I considered almost any painting with the varnish still wet, the artist standing by, so to speak, as more interesting than anything done even the year before. But some of the painters were Klee, Juan Gris, Modigliani. . . . I couldn't listen to music happily if it wasn't hot from the composer's brain, preferably conducted or played by himself. Still, some of the music was Stravinsky's and Béla Bartók's and Poulenc's. I was converted to the harpsichord by the first New York recital of Wanda Landowska. In the theater I preferred dress rehearsals, or even just rehearsals, to the finished performance; I was mad about the ballet and took lessons off and on with a Russian for two years; I even wrote a ballet libretto way back in 1920 for a young Mexican painter and scene designer who gave the whole thing to Pavlova, who danced it in many countries but not in New York, because the scenery was done on paper, was inflammable and she was not allowed to use it in New York. I saw photographs, however, and I must say they did not look in the least like anything I had provided for in the libretto. It was most unsatisfactory.

What has this to do with Willa Cather? A great deal. I had had time to grow up, to consider, to look again, to begin finding my way a little through the inordinate clutter and noise of my immediate day, in which very literally everything in the world was being pulled apart, torn up, turned wrong side out and upside down; almost no frontiers left unattacked, governments and currencies falling; even the very sexes seemed to be changing back and forth and multiplying weird, unclassifiable genders. And every day, in the arts, as in schemes of government and organized crime, there was, there had to be, something New.

Alas, or thank God, depending on the way you feel about it, there comes that day when today's New begins to look a little like yesterday's New, and then more and more so; you begin to suffer slightly from a sense of sameness or repetition: that painting, that statue, that music, that kind of writing, that way of thinking and feeling, that revolution, that political doctrine—is it really New? The answer is simply no, and if you are really in a perverse belligerent mood, you may add a half-truth—no, and it never was. Looking around at the debris, you ask has newness merely for its own sake any virtue? And you find that all along you had held and wound in your hand through the maze an unbreakable cord on which one by one, hardly knowing it, you had strung your life's treasures; it was as if they had come of themselves, while you were seeking and choosing and picking up and tossing away again, down all sorts of by-paths and up strange stairs and into queer corners; and there they were, things old and new, the things you loved first and those you loved last, all together and yours, and no longer old or new, but outside of time and beyond the reach of change, even your own; for that part of your life they belong to was in some sense made by them; if they went, all that part of your life would be mutilated, unrecognizable. While you hold and wind that cord with its slowly accumulating, weightless, unaccountable riches, the maze seems a straight road; you look back through all the fury you have come through, when it seemed so much, and so dismayingly, destruction, and so much just the pervasively trivial, stupid, or malignant-dwarfish tricks: fur-lined cups as sculpture, symphonies written for kitchen batteries, experiments on language very similar to the later Nazi surgical experiments of cutting and uniting human nerve ends never meant to touch each other: so many perversities crowding in so close you could hardly see beyond them. Yet look, you shared it, you were part of it, you even added to the confusion, so busy being new yourself. The fury and waste and clamor was, after all, just what you had thought it was in the first place, even if you had lost sight of it later—life, in a word, and great glory came of it, and splendid things that will go on living cleared of all the rubbish thrown up around their creation. Things you would have once thought incompatible to eternity take their right places in peace, in proper scale and order, in your mind—in your blood. They become that marrow in your bones where the blood is renewed.

I had liked best of all Willa Cather's two collections of short stories. They live still with morning freshness in my memory, their clearness, warmth of feeling, calmness of intelligence, an ample human view of things; in short the sense of an artist at work in whom one could have complete confidence: not even the prose attracted my attention from what the writer was saying—really saying, and not just in the words. Also I remember well my deeper impression of reserve—a reserve that was personal because it was a matter of temperament, the grain of the mind; yet conscious too, and practiced deliberately: almost a method, a technique, but not assumed. It was instead a manifesting, proceeding from the moral nature of the artist, morality extended to aesthetics—not aesthetics as morality but simply a development of both faculties along with all the others until the whole being was indivisibly one, the imagination and its expression fused and fixed.

A magnificent state, no doubt, at which to arrive; but it should be the final one, and Miss Cather seemed to be there almost from the first. What was it? For I began to have an image of her as a kind of lighthouse, or even a promontory, some changeless phenomenon of art or nature or both. I have a peculiar antipathy to thinking of anyone I know in symbols or mythical characters and this finally quietly alienated me from her, from her very fine books, from any feeling that she was a living, working artist in our time. It is hard to explain, for it was a question of tone, of implication, and what else? Finally, after a great while, I decided that Miss Cather's reserve amounted to a deliberate withholding of some vital part of herself as artist; not as if she had hidden herself at the center of her mystery but was still there to be disclosed at last; no, she had absented herself willfully.

I was quite wrong of course. She is exactly at the center of her own mystery, where she belongs. My immoderate reading of our two or three invaluably afflicted giants of contemporary literature, and their abject army of camp followers and imitators, had blurred temporarily my perception of that thin line separating self-revealment from self-exhibition. Miss Cather had never any intention of using fiction or any other form of writing as a device for showing herself off. She was not Paul in travesty, nor the opera singer in "The Diamond Mine," nor that girl with the clear eyes who became an actress: above all, not the Lost Lady. Of course she was all of them. How not? She made all of them out of herself, where else could they have taken on life?

Her natural lack of picturesqueness was also a good protective coloring: it saved her from the invasive prying of hangers-on: and no "school" formed in her name. The young writers did not swarm over her with flattery, manuscripts in hand, meaning to use her for all she was worth; publishers did not waylay her with seductions the instant her first little book appeared; all S. S. McClure could think of to do for her, after he published *The Troll Garden*, was to offer her a job as one of his editors on *McClure's Magazine*, where she worked hard for six mortal years before it seems to have occurred to her that she was not being a writer, after all, which was what she had started out for. So she quit her job, and the next year, more or less, published *Alexander's Bridge*, of which she afterward repented, for reasons that were to last her a lifetime. The scene, London, was strange and delightful to her; she was trying to make a novel out of some interesting people in what seemed to her exotic situations, instead of out of something she really knew about with more than the top of her mind. "London is supposed to be more engaging than, let us say, Gopher Prairie," she remarks, "even if the writer knows Gopher Prairie very well and London very casually."

She realized at once that *Alexander's Bridge* was a mistake, her wrong turning, which could not be retraced too instantly and entirely. It was a very pretty success, and could have been her finish, except that she happened to be Willa Cather. For years she still found people who liked that book, but they couldn't fool her. She knew what she had done. So she left New York and went to Arizona for six months, not for repentance but for refreshment, and found there a source that was to refresh her for years to come. Let her tell of her private apocalypse in her own words: "I did no writing down there, but I recovered from the conventional editorial point of view."

She then began to write a book for herself—*O Pioneers!*—and it was "a different process altogether. Here there was no arranging or 'inventing'; everything was spontaneous and took its own place, right or wrong. This was like taking a ride through a familiar country on a horse that knew the way, on a fine morning when you felt like riding. The other was like riding in a park, with someone not altogether congenial, to whom you had to be talking all the time."

What are we to think? For certainly here is a genius who simply will not cater to our tastes for drama, who refuses to play the role in any way we have been accustomed to seeing it played. She wrote with immense sympathy about Stephen Crane: "There is every evidence that he was a reticent and unhelpful man, with no warmhearted love of giving out opinions." If she had said "personal confidences" she could as well have been writing about herself. But she was really writing about Stephen Crane and stuck to her subject. Herself, she gave out quite a lot of opinions, not all of them warmhearted, in the course of two short little books, the second a partial reprint of the first. You hardly realize how many and how firm and how cogent while reading her fine pure direct prose, hearing through it a level, well-tempered voice saying very good, sensible right things with complete authority—things not in fashion but close to here and now and always, not like a teacher or a mother— like an artist—until, after you have closed the book, her point of view begins to accumulate and take shape in your mind.

Freud had happened: but Miss Cather continued to cite the old Hebrew prophets, the Greek dramatists, Goethe, Shakespeare, Dante, Tolstoy, Flaubert, and such for the deeper truths of human nature, both good and evil. She loved Shelley, Wordsworth, Walter Pater, without any reference to their public standing at the time. In her essay, "The Novel Demeublé," she had the inspired notion to bring together for purpose of comparison Balzac and Prosper Merimée; she preferred Merimée on the ground quite simply that he was the better artist: you have to sort out Balzac's meanings from a great dusty warehouse of misplaced vain matter—furniture, in a word. Once got at, they are as vital as ever. But Merimée is as vital, and you cannot cut one sentence without loss from his stories. The perfect answer to the gross power of the one, the too-finished delicacy of the other was, of course, Flaubert.

Stravinsky had happened; but she went on being dead in love with Wagner, Beethoven, Schubert, Gluck, especially *Orpheus*, and almost any opera. She was music-mad, and even Ravel's *La Valse* enchanted her; perhaps also even certain later music, but she has not mentioned it in these papers.

The Nude had Descended the Staircase with an epoch-shaking tread but she remained faithful to Puvis de Chavannes, whose wall paintings in the Panthéon of the legend of St. Genevieve inspired the form and tone of *Death Comes for the Archbishop.* She longed to tell old stories as simply as that, as deeply centered in the core of experience without extraneous detail as in the lives of the saints in *The Golden Legend.* She loved Courbet, Rembrandt, Millet and the sixteenth-century Dutch and Flemish painters, with their "warmly furnished interiors" but always with a square window open to the wide gray sea, where the masts of the great Dutch fleets were setting out to "ply quietly on all the waters of the globe. . . ."

Joyce had happened: or perhaps we should say, *Ulysses*, for the work has now fairly absorbed the man we knew. I believe that this is true of all artists of the first order. They are not magnified in their work, they disappear in it, consumed by it. That subterranean upheaval of language caused not even the barest tremor in Miss Cather's firm, lucid sentences. There is good internal evidence that she read a great deal of contemporary literature, contemporary over a stretch of fifty years, and think what contemporaries they were—from Tolstoy and Hardy and James and Chekhov to Gide and Proust and Joyce and Lawrence and Virginia Woolf, to Sherwood Anderson and Theodore Dreiser: the

first names that come to mind. There was a regiment of them; it was
as rich and fruitfully disturbing a period as literature has to show for
several centuries. And it did make an enormous change. Miss Cather
held firmly to what she had found for herself, did her own work in her
own way as all the others were doing each in his unique way, and did
help greatly to save and reassert and illustrate the validity of certain
great and dangerously threatened principles of art. Without too much
fuss, too—and is quietly disappearing into her work altogether, as we
might expect.

Mr. Maxwell Geismar wrote a book about her and some others, called
The Last of the Provincials. Not having read it I do not know his argument; but he has a case: she is a provincial; and I hope not the last. She
was a good artist, and all true art is provincial in the most realistic sense:
of the very time and place of its making, out of human beings who are
so particularly limited by their situation, whose faces and names are real
and whose lives begin each one at an individual unique center. Indeed,
Willa Cather was as provincial as Hawthorne or Flaubert or Turgenev,
as little concerned with aesthetics and as much with morals as Tolstoy,
as obstinately reserved as Melville. In fact she always reminds me of
very good literary company, of the particularly admirable masters who
formed her youthful tastes, her thinking and feeling.

She is a curiously immovable shape, monumental, virtue itself in
her art and a symbol of virtue—like certain churches, in fact, or exemplary women, revered and neglected. Yet like these again, she has her
faithful friends and true believers, even so to speak her lovers, and they
last a lifetime, and after: the only kind of bond she would recognize or
require or respect.

Trust the Tale, Not the Teller:
Hans Christian Andersen

HAROLD BLOOM

I

Andersen's prime precursors included Shakespeare and Sir Walter Scott, and his best work can be thought of as an amalgam of *A Midsummer Night's Dream* and the almost as magnificent "Wandering Willie's Tale" from Scott's *Redgauntlet*, with a certain admixture of Goethe and of the "Universal Romanticism" of Novalis and E. T. A. Hoffmann. Goethean "renunciation" was central to Andersen's art, which truly worships only one god, who can be called Fate. Though Andersen was a grand original in his fairy tales, he eagerly accepted from folklore its stoic acceptance of fate. Nietzsche argued that, for the sake of life, origin and aim had to be kept apart. In Andersen, there was no desire to separate origin and aim. It cost his life much fulfillment: he never had a home of his own or a lasting love, but he achieved an extraordinary literary art.

Like Walt Whitman's, Andersen's authentic sexual orientation was homoerotic. Pragmatically, both great writers were autoerotic, though Andersen's longings for women were more poignant than Whitman's largely literary gestures towards heterosexuality. But Whitman was a poet-prophet, who offered salvation, hardly Christian. Andersen professed a rather sentimental devotion to the Christ child, but his art is pagan in nature. His Danish contemporary, Kierkegaard, shrewdly sensed this early on. From the perspective of the twenty-first century, Andersen and Kierkegaard strangely divide between them the aesthetic eminence of Danish literature. I want to define precisely the qualities of Andersen's stories that go on making them imperishable. Kierkegaard himself rightly analyzed his own project as the illumination of how impossible it is to become a Christian in an ostensibly Christian society. Andersen covertly had a rather different project: how to remain a child in an ostensibly adult world.

I myself see no distinction between children's literature and good or great writing for extremely intelligent children of all ages. J. K. Rowling and Stephen King are equally bad writers, appropriate titans of our new Dark Age of the Screens: computer, motion pictures, television. One goes on urging children of all ages to read and reread Andersen and Dickens, Lewis Carroll and Edward Lear, rather than Rowling and King. Sometimes when I say that in public I am asked afterwards: is it not better to read Rowling and King, and then go on to Andersen, Dickens, Carroll and Lear? The answer is pragmatic: our time here is limited. You necessarily read and reread at the expense of other books. If we lived for several centuries, there might be world enough and time, but the reality principle forces us to choose.

Andersen called one of his memoirs *The Fairy Tale of My Life*. It makes clear how painful his emergence was from the working class of Denmark in the early nineteenth century. The driving purpose of his career was to win fame and honor while not forgetting how hard the way up had been. His memories of being read to from *The Arabian Nights* by his father seem stronger than those of the actual circumstances of his upbringing. Absorbing the biographies of Andersen is a curious process: when I stand back from what I have learned I have the impression of a remarkable directness in the teenage Andersen, who marched into Copenhagen and collapsed himself upon the kindness of strangers. This peculiar directness lasted all his life: he went throughout Europe introducing himself to Heine, Victor Hugo, Lamartine, Vigny, Mendelssohn, Schumann, Dickens, the Brownings, and many others. A hunter of big names, he hungered above all to become one himself, and won through by the invention of his fairy tales.

Andersen was an outrageously prolific author in every genre—novels, travelogues, poetry, stage plays—but he mattered and always will entirely because of his unique fairy tales, which he transmuted into a creation of his own, fusing the supernatural and the common life in ways that continue to surprise me, more even than do the tales of Hoffmann, Gogol, and Kleist, and setting aside those of the sublimely dreadful but inescapable Poe.

Sexual frustration is Andersen's pervasive though hidden obsession, embodied in his witches and icy temptresses, and in his androgynous princes. The progress of his fairy stories marches through more than forty years of visions and revisions, and even now has not been fully studied. Here I will begin with brief critical impressions and appreciations of six tales: "The Little Mermaid" (1837), "The Wild Swans" (1838), "The Snow Queen" (1845), "The Red Shoes"(1845), "The Shadow" (1847), and "Auntie Toothache" (1872).

On its vivid surfaces "The Little Mermaid" suggests a parable of renunciation, and yet in my own literary sense of the tale, it is a horror story, centering upon the very scary figure of the sea witch:

> She came to a large slimy clearing in the forest, where big fat water snakes gamboled and showed off their disgusting yellow-white undersides. In the middle of the clearing was a house built out of the white skeletons of shipwrecked humans; that was where the sea witch sat with a toad that she let eat out of her mouth the same way that people let a little canary eat sugar. She called the fat ugly water snakes her little chickens, and let them frolic on her huge spongy chest.
>
> "I think I know what you want," the sea witch said. "You are being very unwise. You can have it your way, but it's going to bring you grief, my lovely princess. You want to get rid of your fish tail and replace it with two stumps to walk on, like a human, so the young prince will fall in love with you, and you will have him and an immortal soul."

At that, the sea witch laughed so loudly and nastily that the toad and snakes fell to the ground and rolled around. "You came just in time," the witch said. "After sunrise tomorrow I wouldn't have been able to help you for another year. I'll make you a drink, but before the sun comes up, you must swim to land, sit on the shore, and drink it. Then your tail will split in two and shrink into what humans call 'pretty legs.' But it hurts—it's like a sharp sword going through you. Everyone who sees you will say that you're the loveliest girl that they have ever seen. You will keep your gliding walk; no dancer will soar like you. But every step you take will feel like you are stepping on a sharp knife that makes you bleed. If you're willing to suffer all this, I'll help you."

"Yes!" the little mermaid said in a quivering voice, and she thought about the prince and about winning an immortal soul.

"But remember," the sea witch continued, "as soon as you get a human form, you can't ever be a mermaid again. You can never swim down through the water to your sisters and your father's castle. And unless you win the prince's love so that he forgets his father and mother for your sake and thinks only about you and lets the pastor put your hands together so that you become man and wife, you won't get an immortal soul. The first morning after he has married someone else, your heart will break, and you'll turn into foam on the sea."

"I still want to do it," the little mermaid said. She was pale as a corpse.

"But you have to pay me too," the sea witch went on, "and I ask for quite a bit. You have the prettiest voice of anyone on the bottom of the sea, and I'm sure you imagine that you'll charm him. But you have to give me that voice. I want the most precious thing you own for my precious drink. As you know, I have to add my own blood to make the drink as sharp as a double-edged sword."

"But if you take my voice," the little mermaid said, "what will I have left?"

"Your beautiful figure," the witch said, "your soaring walk, and your eloquent eyes—with all that you can certainly enchant

302 | The Story About the Story II

a human heart. Well, well—have you lost heart? Stick out your little tongue. Then I'll cut it off as payment, and you'll get my powerful drink." (Translated by Diana Crone Frank and Jeffrey Frank)

There is a peculiar ghastliness about this, virtually unmatched in literary fantasy. It has the aesthetic dignity of great art, yet a shudder goes with it. Andersen's imagination is as cruel as it is powerful, and "The Little Mermaid" is least persuasive (to me) in its benign conclusion. The story should end when the mermaid leaps from ship to sea and feels her body dissolve into foam. Something in Andersen could not abide in this nihilistic sacrifice, and so he allows an ascension in which his heroine joins the daughters of the air, thus recovering her voice. The aesthetic difficulty is not sentimentality but sublimation, a defense against the erotic drive that may work for the rare saint but almost never convinces us in imaginative literature.

There is no consistent allegory in "The Little Mermaid," and whoever finds a moral in it should be shot, a remark I intend in the spirit of Mark Twain rather than in the mode of Flannery O'Connor. I prefer Andersen's revision of a Danish folktale, "The Wild Swans," which culminates in utter ambivalence when another mute maiden, the beautiful Elisa, undergoes a second marriage with a king so doltish he nearly burns her alive as a witch, at the prompting of an evil archbishop. The weird remarriage is appropriate in a tale where Elisa's eleven brothers experience a radical daily metamorphosis into eleven wild swans:

"We brothers," the oldest said, "are wild swans as long as the sun is up. When it sets, we get our human shape back. That's why we always have to make sure that we have solid ground underfoot when the sun sets. If we were flying among the clouds, we would, as human beings, plunge into the deep. We can't stay here, but there's a country as beautiful as this one on the other side of the ocean. It's a long distance. We have to cross the big ocean, and there are no islands on the way where we can stay for the night—only a solitary little rock juts up in the middle of the sea. It's just big enough for us to rest on side by side, and when the sea is rough, the water sprays high above us." (Translated by Diana Crone Frank and Jeffrey Frank)

That vision has the strangeness of lasting myth. There are disturbing overtones here. Are we, in our youth, wild swans by day, and human again only at night, resting on a solitary spot in the midst of an abyss? Meditating upon the self of half-a-century ago, at seventy-four I am moved to a Shakespearean sense of wonder by Andersen's marvelous extended metaphor.

In two famous stories of 1845, as he reaches meridian, Andersen achieved a fresh power of imagination. "The Snow Queen" is called by Andersen a tale in seven stories, or an "ice puzzle of the mind," a marvelous phrase taken from and alluding to the unfinished visionary novel of Novalis, *Heinrich von Ofterdingen*. Its evil troll, the Devil himself, makes a mirror, eventually fragmented, that is the essence of reductiveness; that is, what any person or thing is *really* like is simply the worst way it can be viewed. At the center of Andersen's tale are two children who at first defy all reductiveness: Gerda and Kai. They are poor, but while not sister and brother, they share fraternal love. The beautiful but icy Snow Queen abducts Kai, and Gerda goes in quest of him. An old witch, benign but possessive, appropriates Gerda, who departs for the wide world to continue her search for Kai. But my summary is a hopeless parody of Andersen's blithe irony of a narrative, where even the most menacing entities pass by in a phantasmagoric rush: talking reindeer, a bandit girl who offers friendship even as she waves a knife, the Northern Lights, living snowflakes. When Gerda finds Kai in the Snow Queen's castle, she warms him with kisses until he thaws. Redeemed, they journey home together to a perpetual summer of happiness, ambiguously sexual.

The fascination of "The Snow Queen" is Gerda's continuous resourcefulness and strength, which derives from her freedom or refusal of all reductiveness. She is an implicit defense of Andersen's power as a storyteller, his endless self-reliance. Perhaps Gerda is Andersen's answer to Kierkegaard, hardly Andersen's admirer. Gerda can be set against Kierkegaard at his uncanniest: *The Concept of Dread, The Sickness Unto*

304 | The Story About the Story II

Death, *Fear and Trembling*, *Repetition*. The titles themselves belong to the Snow Queen's realm, and not to Gerda's and Andersen's.

The alarming and famous story "The Red Shoes" always has frightened me. The beautiful red dancing shoes whirl Karen into a cursed existence of perpetual motion, that cannot be solved even when her feet (with her consent) are cut off. Only her sanctified death accomplishes liberation. Darkly enigmatic, Andersen's tale hints at what Freud called over-determination, and renders Karen into the antithesis of Gerda.

"The Shadow," composed during a hot summer in Naples in 1847, may be Andersen's most evasive masterpiece. The author and his shadow disengage from each other, in the tradition of tales by Chamisso and Hoffmann, and Andersen's shadow is malign and Iago-like. He comes back to Andersen, and persuades him to be a travel-companion, but as the shadow of his own shadow, as it were. The reader begins to suffer a metaphysical bewilderment, augmented by the involvement of a princess who sees too clearly, yet takes the original shadow as her consort. Andersen threatens exposure of identity, is imprisoned by his former shadow, and soon enough executed. This crazy and embittered parable prophesies Kafka, Borges, and Calvino, but more interestingly, it returns us to everything problematic and ambivalent about Andersen's relation both to himself and to his art.

My ultimate favorite story by Andersen is his chillingly hilarious "Auntie Toothache," composed less than three years before his death. He may have intended it as his *logos* or defining Word, and it is spoken by Andersen himself in the first person. As an inventor of a laughter that hurts, Andersen follows Shakespeare and prophesies Philip Roth. There is no figure in Andersen more menacing than Auntie Toothache:

> A figure sat on the floor; it was thin and long, like those that a child draws with a pencil on a slate. It was supposed to look like a person: its body was a single thin line; another two lines made the arms, the legs were single lines too, and the head was all angles.
>
> The figure soon became clearer. It wore a kind of dress— very thin, very fine—that showed that the figure belonged to the female sex.

I heard a humming. Was it her or was it the wind that buzzed like a horsefly in the crack of the windowpane?

No, it was Madame Toothache herself—Her Frightfulness, *Satania infernal is,* God save us from her visit.

"This is a nice place to live," she hummed. "It's a good neighborhood swampy, boggy ground. Mosquitoes used to buzz by here with poison in their sting. Now I'm the one with the stinger. It has to be sharpened on human teeth, and that fellow on the bed has such shiny white ones. They've held their own against sweet and sour, hot and cold, nutshells and plum pits. But I'm going to wiggle them, jiggle them, feed them with a draft, and chill them at their roots." (Translated by Diana Crone Frank and Jeffrey Frank)

As Her Frightfulness says: "Great poets must have great toothaches; small poets, small toothaches." There is a vertigo in the story: we cannot know whether Auntie Toothache and the amiable Aunt Millie (who encourages Andersen's poetry) are one person or two. The penultimate sentence is: "Everything goes into the trash."

The accent is of Koheleth (Ecclesiastes): all is vanity. Andersen was a visionary tale-teller, but his fairy-realm was malign. Of his aesthetic eminence, I entertain no doubts, but I believe that we still have not learned how to read him.

II

D. H. Lawrence, one of the major writers of shorter fictions in the twentieth century, bequeathed us a superb critical motto: "Trust the tale, not the teller." Andersen told us that his stories were the history of his life, and his critics and biographers largely follow him, yet I am skeptical. Like his major American contemporary, Whitman, Andersen's work seems easy but proves difficult. That both Whitman and Andersen were essentially homoerotic is scarcely a link between them. What does ally Whitman and Andersen are their mutual evasions of their own apparent projects. Whitman proclaimed himself the poet of democracy, yet his poetry is hermetic and elitist. Andersen invented what the last two

centuries have called "children's literature," but after some early stories he is no more available just to children than are Kafka and Gogol.
Rather, Andersen wrote for extraordinarily intelligent children of all
ages, from nine to ninety.

Sometimes I find that, for a moment anyway, my favorite Andersen
story is "The Collar," an apparent trifle of just two pages, but these are
as rammed with life and meaning as a fragment of parable of Kafka's
like "The Bucket Rider" or "The Hunter Gracchus." Composed in 1848
after a visit to England, "The Collar" ironizes both Andersen himself, an obsessive self-promoter, and the Danish newspapers, intensely
annoyed by the playing abroad of his one-man band.

One of Andersen's weirdest and greatest gifts is that his stories live
in an animistic cosmos, in which there are no mere objects whatsoever.
Every tree, bush, animal, artifact, item of clothing, lump of clay has
an anxious soul, a voice, sexual desires, a need for status, and a terror at the prospect of annihilation. Andersen's hysterical episodes of
alternating grandiosity and depression are very much at variance with
this created world where mermaids and ice maidens, swans and storks,
ducklings and fir trees, shoes and houses, collars and garters, bells and
winds, snowmen and wood nymphs, witches and toothaches, all possess
consciousness as capacious, cruel, and desperate for survival as our own.

Ostensibly a Christian, from the start Andersen was a narcissistic
pagan who worshipped Fate, she being for him a sadistic goddess we could
accurately name as Nemesis. Andersen's genius is deeply founded upon
an ancient animism, older than *The Arabian Nights*. Shakespeare, most
universal of geniuses, doubtless influenced Andersen with *A Midsummer
Night's Dream*, where charming little fairies become Bottom's retainers,
the wonderful fourfold of Mustardseed, Moth, Cobweb, and Peaseblossom.
So Andersenian are these little fellows that we might think that, revers-
ing time, Shakespeare took them from the Dane, except that they would
be darker beings in the work of the Odense storyteller. Andersen's universe is vitalistic, but more malign than not.

There have been visionary speculators like Jakob Boehme and
Swedenborg, William Blake and Whitman, who lived in realities that had
no inanimate objects, only sensibilities in every pebble and weed, every
scab on a stone fence. But these were prophets of apocalypse, urging all

things to reassume the forms of the human. Andersen, like his fellow-Dane, Prince Hamlet, is a prophet of annihiliation. A tiny story like "The Collar" is as much a self-study as is Hamlet a soliloquy. Like Andersen, the collar keeps proposing marriage, and is turned down by a garter, a hot iron, a scissors, and a comb. They ought not to be regarded as allegories of Riborg Voigt, Louise Collin, and Jenny Lind, but alone of Henrik Stampe and Harald Scharff. All goes merrily along until the collar ends up in the rag-bin of a paper mill, resignedly saying: "It's about time I was turned into white paper." By then, I have become fond of the collar, and so am rather shocked by the story's final paragraph:

> And that's what happened. All the rags were turned into white paper but the collar turned into this very piece of white paper that we're looking at now, the one on which this story is printed. That's because he boasted so terribly afterward about things that had never happened. That's something we should remember, so we don't behave the same way, because we never can tell whether we too might one day end up in the rag bin and be turned into white paper and have our whole story printed on it, even our innermost secrets, and then have to run around talking about them, just like the collar. (Translated by Tiina Nunnally)

This jocular nihilism is difficult to match, even in the insane Gogol or the mordant Calvino. If there is an aesthetic wholly equipped to analyze Andersen's peculiar power, I have not encountered it.

III

Andersen's novels, travelogues, poetry, and stage plays are now forgotten, except by specialists. Only in May 1835 did he find his own genre, the visionary stories that have been as widely translated and circulated as the Bible, Shakespeare, and *Don Quixote*. They are, for the most part, unique works that transcend their sources: the folk tales, *The Arabian Nights*, and the varied efforts of Goethe, Novalis, Tieck, Hoffmann, and several other German narrative writers. Andersen's first little booklet contained "The Tinderbox," "The Princess on the Pea," "Little Claus

and Big Claus," and "Little Ida's Flowers." Though the princess is pro-
verbial in her unease, it is "The Tinderbox" that opens out to what
will become Andersen's art. Kierkegaard, demolishing Andersen's novel
Only a Fiddler in a review, blamed the narrator for his lack of vision,
a re-ordering of the world that would get beyond Hegelian categories. Hegel, a remarkable reader of Shakespeare, said that the greatest
Shakespearean characters were "free artists of themselves." Perhaps
the Andersen of the fairy tales can be considered as having been himself a Shakespearean character, a Bottom or Feste or even a Malvolio
who was a free artist of himself. "The Tinderbox" lives not because of
its soldier or its witch, but the three uncanny dogs, whom I would not
wish to encounter, even if I did not fear dogs anyway, as I do.

Andersen's dogs, like all his other creatures and entities, have a
particular defining feature; in their case big eyes, which express their
exuberance even as the gusto of Andersen's language defines his
extravagance. Wandering beyond limits, or extravagance, is Andersen's
peculiar gift in his stories. Kierkegaard had chastised Andersen for lacking an irony of vision; the response of Andersen preceded the 1838
indictment, by three years, in those canine eyes. *Indirect communication*
is the mark of both Danish masters, as it is of Shakespeare's Prince
of Denmark. Had Kierkegaard reviewed the 1835 booklet, and not the
novel *Only a Fiddler*, we might have a different conception of the parallels between these two extraordinarily original writers.

IV

Kierkegaard and Andersen both developed into major erotic ironists,
though of very different kinds. Repetition is Kierkegaard's metaphor
for being willing to take up again any possibility believed to have transcendental potentialities, including the perpetual self-deception called
"falling in love." In Andersen, everything falls in love, with an emphasis upon "falling." Kierkegaard was post-Hegelian even as Andersen
was post-Goethean. Goethe's poetics of renunciation are at work in
all the fairy stories, many of which go back to the hidden model of
Aladdin in *The Arabian Nights*, probably mediated by Oehlenschläger's
Shakespearean drama *Aladdin*.

Irony of a very odd sort necessarily attends my attempt to contrast Andersen and Kierkegaard, totally diverse as personalities and as authors. And yet they have a shared greatness that goes beyond that of the other principal writers of Denmark's Golden Age. The startling originality that they possess in common can be exposed by my substituting the phrase "Andersen's stories" for the phrase "Kierkegaard's philosophy" in a famous formulation made in 1909 by the Marxist critic Georg Lukács: ". . . the deep meaning of Andersen's stories is that he places fixed points beneath the incessantly changing nuances of life, and draws absolute distinctions within the melting chaos of nuances."

Yet Kierkegaard indeed had three fixed points or stages: the aesthetic, the ethical, the religious. Transferred to Andersen, Lukács's observation exposes a mystery: is there any stage beyond the aesthetic feeling in Andersen's melting chaos of nuances? I think not, but is that the true link between Andersen and Shakespeare? Kierkegaard abandoned his ironies in favor of indirect communication of the ethical and the religious. Only at the very end does Hamlet transcend his own ironies, but in favor of nihilism and annihilation. Goethe, Ibsen, and Tolstoy allowed themselves to dally with the false surmise that nature would make a special exemption for genius, and release it from the necessity of dying. Andersen, like Hamlet, entertained no religious illusions, and we can set aside his sentimental effusiveness about the Christ *child*. Kierkegaard, emphasizing that a Christian society itself was an oxymoron, went down still proclaiming the impossibility of becoming a Christian, yet yearning for the category of the religious. Andersen was one of us, whoever we now are; Kierkegaard, who was re-created as twentieth century Existentialism, was not.

V

Post-modernity is as dead as Modernity now. Andersen and Kierkegaard are as High Romantic as Goethe and Novalis, Victor Hugo and Dickens, Manzoni and Whitman, or even as Hegel himself. Where Andersen differs is that instead of dreaming universal nightmares, like Poe, he entertained universal daydreams, the immemorial human mode of imaginary wish-fulfillment. "The Tinderbox" clearly contains the full range of the crucial daydream: king, queen, and government are shattered to pieces by the dogs, and the Aladdin-like soldier goes in a moment from the imminence of being hanged for having abducted the lovely princess to instead becoming king and marrying her, in a week-long celebration. Beyond his audacity, the soldier possesses no virtues, and the story is pure narrative, untouched by the ethical and the religious. As in *The Arabian Nights*, the story exists to postpone death, not to transcend it.

Among his contemporaries, the storyteller Andersen can be situated between Dickens, who dropped the Dane after he overstayed his welcome on what became a five-week visit, and Tolstoy, who loved the simplicity and directness of Andersen's narrative mode. To be located between Dickens and Tolstoy ought to destroy any composer of short fictions, but Andersen survives, as blithely insouciant as the indestructible soldier of "The Tinderbox." And yet neither Dickens nor Tolstoy is cruel, except insofar as nature and history are cruel. Andersenian daydreams, being largely free of history and of nature, frequently are cruel, even sadistic, perhaps because of androgynous drives. In Freud's project, the labor is to liberate thinking of its sexual past, or the sexual curiosity of children. Andersen, whose project was to remain child-like, tapped into the energies of the sexual past and derived from them the verve and pace of his art.

He was a long time learning that this was his only aesthetic resource and achievement: works in other genres kept tumbling out of him on into his fifties. By then, the world had taught him what only he could give it. Kierkegaard, in his astonishing attack upon *Only a Fiddler*, was a considerable agent in that teaching. The underground relationship between Kierkegaard and Andersen is charted in the biography of Andersen by Jens Andersen and might best be characterized as a mutual, lasting wound. Here, I want to compare Kierkegaard's "indirect communication" with its only apparent contrary in Andersen's direct communication, which frequently turns out to be indirect indeed at its deepest channels.

All of Kierkegaard is indirect communication, since his purpose is not to instruct us but to make it more difficult for us to read him. *Authorial* meaning is mocked by Kierkegaard's heteronyms, through which he indulges in hidden parodies both of Socratic and of Romantic irony, until we no longer know which is which. In Kierkegaard's *Concluding*

Unscientific Postscript, Johannes Climacus assures us that: "Inwardness cannot be directly communicated, for its direct expression is precisely externality . . . direct expression of feeling does not prove its possession, but the tension of the contrasting form is the measure of the intensity of inwardness . . ."

To Kierkegaard and Andersen one adds an even greater Danish melancholic, Prince Hamlet, the grandest representation we have of indirect communication. Hamlet rarely says what he means or means what he says. He stations himself beyond irony, as does Kierkegaard. On the surface Andersen seems the opposite of Hamlet and Kierkegaard, both of whom find in the direct expression of emotion an indication that what can be said is already dead in the heart. Yet how can we tell in the fairy tales what is alive or immolated in Andersen's heart? Trust the tale, not the teller, and so what do we hear in the stories? Clearly, for Andersen, there is never a kind of contempt in the act of speaking. He is all but desperate to cry out endlessly, to project himself into his own tales. Like Dickens, his former friend, Andersen was renowned for his mesmerizing performances when reading his own stories to audiences. Both writers were throwbacks to ancient rhapsodes, and each had shamanistic attributes, particularly the androgynous Andersen.

All his biographers stress that there were two of him, the Dane in Denmark, vulnerable and obsessed by supposed under-appreciation, and the showman abroad, the *Wunderkind* of Weimar and of London, the endlessly wandering Dane sailing to Byzantium. Childlike in Denmark, Andersen was childish abroad, living his daydreams. He was as much an international celebrity as Lord Byron before him and Hemingway later. Byron and Hemingway, we know, were as androgynous as Andersen, though much more sexually active than the reluctant Dane, who visited bordellos only to gaze upon the whores, never to touch them. Andersen's real analogue was Whitman, whose sexual career, bar an homoerotic encounter or two, was altogether with himself.

Andersen was an international and domestic flirt—with both genders—and, like Kierkegaard, a theorist of seduction yet actually a monument to narcissism. Denmark's two major writers of its Golden Age were self-obsessed monomaniacs, Captains Ahab pursuing a White Whale, but unlike the American protagonist of *Moby-Dick,* both Danes were too shrewd to attempt harpooning what each rightly understood was his own solipsistic vision. This is to commend the twin Danes: Kierkegaard's subtle intellect rivals the insights of Schópenhauer, Nietzsche, and Freud, while an ancient wisdom out of the folk abides in Andersen, who will say and imagine anything, while evading or obliterating the pragmatic consequences of his own narrations.

VI

Franz Kafka of Prague may seem an odd parallel to Hans Christian Andersen of Odense, but reading Kafka's stories, fragments, and parables side-by-side with Andersen's fairy tales is for me an illuminating process, which I recommend to others. A lifelong preoccupation with Kafka, the greatest of all post-Biblical Jewish writers, not excluding Freud, has persuaded me that the seer of Prague deliberately made his own work uninterpretable. But that merely shifts the stance of the interpretation, since the critic's enterprise then becomes the question of just *why* Kafka invented his own uninterpretability. With deference to Andersen's many skilled scholars, I have yet to learn more than the rudiments of how to read Andersen, even as American criticism still does little to appreciate the nuances of Whitman. To approach Andersen or Whitman with the "Open, Sesame!" of Homoerotic Poetics seems to me useless. Bisexuality is prevalent in imaginative literature: Shakespeare himself is all his women and his men. To read Andersen as an allegorist of androgyny is to smother his tales in a grimy blanket of ideology, one that has already asphyxiated academic and journalistic considerations of literature throughout the English-speaking world.

I start again by asking what it is that is uninterpretable in a superb work like "The Marsh King's Daughter." A first answer is, to muse upon Andersen's storks and swans, who tend to be ambiguous representations of what Andersen is uneasiest with in himself. All functionaries and messengers in Kafka parody angels in Hebraic tradition, since Kafka composed a New Kabbalah. The bird-like Andersen created a new kingdom of animation, of which Walt Disney became the parodist. Objects in Andersen are livelier than most of us, while birds and beasts ascend to uncanny realms we cannot touch.

Kierkegaardian "repetition" is akin to Andersen's animism, because both identify transcendental possibilities with the self-sacrificing generosity of womankind. Dead at forty-two, Kierkegaard had broken off his one-year betrothal when he was twenty-eight, realizing he was unfit to become a hero-of-repetition, that is, a married man. Andersen made marriage proposals to three different women, all of whom refused, as he certainly must have expected. A married Hans Christian Andersen is an even weirder oxymoron than a married Kierkegaard, or indeed a married Nietzsche or a married Kafka.

Storks and swans are masters of Kierkegaardian repetition, as are elephants, all of whom marry for love and forever. I know that I verge upon madness here, but derangement is another term for the genius of Andersen, Kierkegaard, Nietzsche and Kafka. Ibsen, as much a troll as his own Hedda Gabler, married miserably, and Strindberg fared still worse. All six writers were doomed to identify God with women, which does not (and should not) endear them to feminists. Romanticism, still exalting women in William Butler Yeats and, more benevolently, in D. H. Lawrence, destructively utilized the female as image of transcendence, which ought to remind us that Kierkegaard and Andersen join Shelley and Novalis as the highest of High Romantics.

VII

"The Marsh King's Daughter" is a superb High Romantic prose poem, akin to Shelley's *Alastor* and Novalis's *Hymns to the Night*. Bizarre and ambitious, this fantasy is wildly eclectic and baroque, elaborately absorbing everything that Andersen could garner. Its motto might be: "I have made a heap of all that I could find." The tale is a delightfully absurd fusion of Egypt and Vikings, ostriches and storks, swans' skins and inner swans, quagmire monarchs and what you will. *A Midsummer Night's Dream* may be the repressed model, with its "sweet thunder" that gives us a "musical discord" of antithetical realms colliding, mixing up fairies, Warwickshire artisans, universally mixed-up young lovers, and mythological personages.

Is a coherent interpretation of "The Marsh King's Daughter" possible, that is to say, persuasive? I would reply that the story's meaning, like its crucial setting, is a bog. We never meet the Bog-King, though we know him well enough through the initial personality of his daughter Helga, the split heroine of the story. By day she is a marvelous beauty with a sadistic soul, but each night she turns into a large frog with a sweetly sad disposition, gazing at her Viking foster-mother with the lovely eyes of an infant swan. Her night-soul is inherited from her angelic Egyptian princess-mother, who was dragged down into the marshy depths and raped by the doubtless hideous king.

The plot of this story is absurdly sinuous and scarcely tolerates retelling. Uneven as the strange tale is, it touches sublimity at several points, and seems to me Andersen's boldest experiment in storytelling. The Christian element in the story seems to me an aesthetic blemish, and centers on a handsome young muscular priest captured by the Vikings. Eventually, though dead, he wins the restored marsh-maiden, who is gathered up to heaven in a ray of light. As a Christian allegorist, Andersen is always half-hearted, and Kierkegaard shrewdly anticipated his rival's pragmatic apostasy. Insofar as Andersen is a theist, thus gilding his authentic shamanism and animism, he seems to me rather more Judaic than Christian, and he certainly considered the Trinity to be concepts but not persons. It was fitting that his last decade was spent largely as the household guest of two wealthy Danish Jewish families who understood his anxieties and took superb care of the aging and then dying writer.

Female suffering, in "The Marsh King's Daughter" as elsewhere in Andersen's stories, is powerfully but unhealthily conveyed, since I cannot see how the strong elements of sadomasochism are to be evaded by readers of any age. Feminist critics would be off-target in protesting this, since the androgynous Andersen identifies with his victimized maidens. Kierkegaard nastily but accurately diagnosed this androgyny in his early attack upon *Only a Fiddler*, but Andersen converted his bisexuality into an aesthetic resource.

VIII

Memorability in a story has many mothers and fathers, because a story we cannot forget is a perpetual success. Andersen, escaping his own childhood, adopted his way into families, from the Collins to the

Melchiors. He sought love as desperately as Kierkegaard fled it. On some level, Kierkegaard's formidable polemic on the impossibility of becoming a Christian in a formally Protestant Denmark was also a lament on the impossibility of loving and being loved. Andersen is a greater fantasist than he is a wisdom writer, but to master phantasmagoria *and survive it* is an exercise in wisdom.

What truly is going on in the superbly baroque "Daughter of the Marsh King"? The story's strength is the impossibly mixed nature of Helga, a vicious beauty by day and an ugly, sweet-souled frog by night. And yet the brutal and lovely Helga is high-spirited and boisterously happy, while the virtuous frog is miserable. Children and adults alike are not going to learn any Christian lessons from that, and the aesthetic glory of the tale departs with the advent of the captive young Christian priest. We have two colliding stories served together by an Andersen who knows better than to invest in unhappiness. When I recall the story, I recall the best marriage in Andersen's work, that of the noble Mr. Stork and the pragmatic Mrs. Stork, who sensibly insists her husband deserves to be both appreciated and rewarded.

Kierkegaard and Andersen won very different victories over each other during the twentieth century. The Western world's intelligentsia—literary, philosophical, and theological—became obsessed with Kierkegaard, while children of all nations went on reading Andersen. Kierkegaard, a great ironist, abandoned irony for subjectivity, a truth not necessarily Christian. Andersen, wounded by his origins into the embrace of irony, shrouded his savagery with neo-Christian sentimentalism, but his essential cruelty and pragmatic misogyny break through anyway. I learn from Kierkegaard and am fascinated by Andersen, but personally they were as uncanny as Ibsen, Strindberg, Dickens, and Tolstoy. All of them were trolls, unlike Chekhov, Samuel Beckett, and Calvino, who were wholly human. "Nothing is got for nothing" was Emerson's iron New England Law of Compensation. Andersen gave the world a wealth of stories, at a high cost.

Contributors

The most recent of **MARTIN AMIS**'s more than two dozen books of fiction and nonfiction is *Lionel Asbo: State of England*. "Philip Larkin 1922–1985" was first published in *Vanity Fair* and appears in Amis's *Visiting Mrs. Nabokov and Other Excursions*.

MARGARET ATWOOD has published many novels, story collections, non-fiction works, children's books, and books of poems. Her most recent novel is *MaddAddam*. "Ten Ways of Looking at *The Island of Doctor Moreau* by H. G. Wells" was first published as an introduction to a reprint of Wells's book and appears in Atwood's *Writing with Intent: Essays, Reviews, Personal Prose, 1983–2005*.

NICHOLSON BAKER is the author of more than a dozen books. His third book, *U and I*, about John Updike, is a common frame of reference for many who write creative criticism today. "Defoe, Truthteller" was first published in *Columbia Journalism Review* and appears in Baker's most recent book, *The Way the World Works: Essays*.

Tackling a dizzying range of subjects, **JACQUES BARZUN** produced more than forty books over the course of his lifetime. "Lincoln the Writer" was first published in the *Saturday Evening Post* and was then reprinted as a stand-alone volume, *Lincoln the Literary Genius*. It appears in *Jacques Barzun on Writing, Editing, and Publishing*.

CHARLES BAXTER is the author of ten books of fiction, three collections of poems, and two collections of essays. His most recent book is *Gryphon:*

Gryphon: New and Selected Stories. "Sonya's Last Speech, or, Double-Voicing: An Essay in Sixteen Sections" was first published in *Colorado Review* and appears in Baxter's *Burning Down the House: Essays on Fiction.*

WALTER BENJAMIN's significant impact on literature, art, criticism, and philosophy is perhaps better measured by the influence of a small set of unclassifiable essays. "The Storyteller: Reflections on the Works of Nikolai Leskov" appears in a common English translation of his essays, *Illuminations.*

In addition to his many books of poems, JOHN BERRYMAN produced a steady stream of creative criticism on a broad range of subjects. "The Development of Anne Frank" appears in *The Freedom of the Poet.*

Widely regarded as the preeminent critic of his generation, HAROLD BLOOM has published more than twenty books of literary criticism, and edited many more. His most recent book is *The Shadow of a Great Rock: A Literary Appreciation of the King James Bible.* "Trust the Tale, Not the Teller: Hans Christian Andersen" first appeared in *Subtropics* and *Orbis Litterarum*, and a truncated version of the essay serves as the introduction to *Bloom's Modern Critical Views: Hans Christian Andersen.*

SUSAN CHEEVER has published a number of works of literary biography, five novels, and four memoirs. Her most recent book is *Louisa May Alcott: A Personal Biography.* "*Little Women*" is excerpted from *American Bloomsbury: Louisa May Alcott, Ralph Waldo Emerson, Margaret Fuller, Nathaniel Hawthorne, and Henry David Thoreau: Their Lives, Their Loves, Their Work.*

MICHAEL DIRDA won a Pulitzer Prize for his decades of creative criticism in the *Washington Post.* His most recent book is *On Conan Doyle: Or, the Whole Art of Storytelling.* "*Sir Gawain and the Green Knight*" appears in *Classics for Pleasure.*

In addition to *Invisible Man*, RALPH ELLISON published a significant number of creative criticisms in several collections of essays. "Stephen Crane and the Mainstream of American Fiction" was first published as an introduction to a reprint of *The Red Badge of Courage* and appears in *The Collected Essays of Ralph Ellison*.

FRANCISCO GOLDMAN is the author of a half-dozen works of fiction, journalism, memoir, and criticism. His most recent novel is *Say Her Name*. "2007–2003" was first published in *Brick*.

Long an advocate and practitioner of innovative writing about reading, VIVIAN GORNICK is the author of more than ten books, the most recent of which is *Emma Goldman: Revolution as a Way of Life*. "Grace Paley" was first published in *Women's Review of Books* and appears in Gornick's *The End of the Novel of Love*.

J. C. HALLMAN is the author of a number of books, including *The Chess Artist*, *In Utopia*, and *The Hospital for Bad Poets*. His book-length creative criticism about Nicholson Baker, *B & Me: A True Story of Literary Arousal*, is forthcoming from Simon & Schuster. He lives in New York City.

ELIZABETH HARDWICK published three novels and four books of creative criticism. "Billy Budd" is an excerpt from *Herman Melville*, the last book she published during her lifetime.

HENRY JAMES's tempestuous feelings about criticism and critics are made clear again and again in the famous prefaces to the 24-volume "New York Edition" of his collected novels and stories, which stand as testament to his inimitable career. In addition to fiction, James produced an untold number of reviews, literary obituaries, critical treatments, and platonic dialogues on literature that, collectively, may be the most oft-consulted and cited body of work by those who practice creative criticism today.

Of **WENDY LESSER**'s many books, the most recent is *Music for Silenced Voices: Shostakovich and His Fifteen Quartets*. She is the founding editor of the *Threepenny Review*, which over three decades has published creative criticism by a great many writers. "The First Novel" was most recently published in Lesser's *Nothing Remains the Same: Rereading and Remembering*.

PHILLIP LOPATE has written or edited more than twenty books, the most recent of which is *To Show and to Tell: The Craft of Literary Nonfiction*. A longtime theorist and teacher of nonfiction, he is now the director of the nonfiction graduate program at Columbia University. "Worldliness and Regret: *The Charterhouse of Parma*" was first published in the *American Scholar* and appears in Lopate's *Portrait Inside My Head: Essays*.

Over the course of his lifetime, **THOMAS MANN** produced several dozen books, including *The Magic Mountain* and *Doctor Faustus*, along with many essays of creative criticism. "*Anna Karenina*" appears in *Essays of Three Decades*.

H. L. MENCKEN chronicled the evolution of his prickly aesthetic in more than thirty-five books. He had a long-standing contentious relationship with Theodore Dreiser. "Theodore Dreiser" appeared in *A Book of Prefaces*.

JOYCE CAROL OATES is the author of more than fifty books, including, most recently, *The Accursed*, as well as a significant number of essay collections and book-length creative criticisms. "Frankenstein's Fallen Angel" was first published as an introduction to a reprint of Shelley's novel and appears in Oates's *(Woman) Writer: Occasions and Opportunities*.

In addition to the short stories upon which her reputation rests, **KATHERINE ANNE PORTER** published a great number of creative criticisms. "Reflections on Willa Cather" was first published in *Mademoiselle* and appears in Porter's *The Days Before*.

DAVID SHIELDS is the author of more than a dozen books, most recently *How Literature Saved My Life*. "The Only Solution to the Soul Is the Senses: A Meditation on Bill Murray and Myself" was first published in *Tin House* and reappeared in substantially different form in *Enough about You: Notes toward the New Autobiography*.

ZADIE SMITH's most recent novel is *NW*. "*Their Eyes Were Watching God*: What Does *Soulful* Mean?" was first published as an introduction to a reprint of Hurston's novel and appeared in the *Guardian*. It was published most recently in Smith's *Changing My Mind: Occasional Essays*.

Author of more than two dozen books, JAMES THURBER is best known for his short stories and humor writing. He produced many creative criticisms as well. "The Wings of Henry James" first appeared in *The New Yorker* and was reprinted in the last of Thurber's books published during his lifetime, *Lanterns and Lances*.

JANE TOMPKINS is the author of a number of books, most recently *A Life in School: What the Teacher Learned*. "*The Last of the Breed*: Homage to Louis L'Amour" is excerpted from *West of Everything: The Inner Life of Westerns*.

DAVID FOSTER WALLACE published more than a dozen works of fiction and nonfiction. "Certainly the End of *Something* or Other, One Would Sort of Have to Think (Re John Updike's *Toward the End of Time*)" was first published as a review in the *New York Observer* and appears in Wallace's *Consider the Lobster*.

Copyright Notes and Permissions